MW00445360

Coding Surgical Procedures
Beyond the Basics

Coding Surgical Procedures
Beyond the Basics

Gail I. Smith
MA, RHIA, CCS-P

DELMAR
CENGAGE Learning™

Australia • Brazil • Japan • Korea • Mexico • Singapore • Spain • United Kingdom • United States

DELMAR
CENGAGE Learning

Coding Surgical Procedures: Beyond the Basics

Smith, Gail I.

Vice President, Career and Professional Editorial: Dave Garza

Director of Learning Solutions: Matthew Kane

Senior Acquisitions Editor: Rhonda Dearborn

Managing Editor: Marah Bellegarde

Product Manager: Jadin Babin-Kavanaugh

Editorial Assistant: Chiara Astriab

Vice President, Career and Professional Marketing: Jennifer Baker

Executive Marketing Manager: Wendy Mapstone

Senior Marketing Manager: Nancy Bradshaw

Marketing Coordinator: Erica Ropitzky

Production Director: Carolyn Miller

Production Manager: Andrew Crouth

Senior Content Project Manager: James Zayicek

Senior Art Director: Jack Pendleton

Technology Product Manager: Mary Colleen Liburdi

Technology Project Manager: Christopher Catalina

© 2011 Delmar, Cengage Learning

ALL RIGHTS RESERVED. No part of this work covered by the copyright herein may be reproduced, transmitted, stored, or used in any form or by any means graphic, electronic, or mechanical, including but not limited to photocopying, recording, scanning, digitizing, taping, Web distribution, information networks, or information storage and retrieval systems, except as permitted under Section 107 or 108 of the 1976 United States Copyright Act, without the prior written permission of the publisher.

For product information and technology assistance, contact us at **Cengage Learning Customer & Sales Support, 1-800-354-9706**

For permission to use material from this text or product, submit all requests online at **www.cengage.com/permissions**. Further permissions questions can be e-mailed to **permissionrequest@cengage.com**.

2010 Current Procedural Terminology (CPT) © 2009 American Medical Association. All Rights Reserved.

Library of Congress Control Number: 2009938606

ISBN-13: 978-1-4354-2778-5
ISBN-10: 1-4354-2778-5

Delmar
5 Maxwell Drive
Clifton Park, NY 12065-2919
USA

Cengage Learning is a leading provider of customized learning solutions with office locations around the globe, including Singapore, the United Kingdom, Australia, Mexico, Brazil and Japan. Locate your local office at: **international.cengage.com/region**

Cengage Learning products are represented in Canada by Nelson Education, Ltd.

To learn more about Delmar, visit **www.cengage.com/delmar**
Purchase any of our products at your local college store or at our preferred online store **www.ichapters.com**

Notice to the Reader

Publisher does not warrant or guarantee any of the products described herein or perform any independent analysis in connection with any of the product information contained herein. Publisher does not assume, and expressly disclaims, any obligation to obtain and include information other than that provided to it by the manufacturer. The reader is expressly warned to consider and adopt all safety precautions that might be indicated by the activities described herein and to avoid all potential hazards. By following the instructions contained herein, the reader willingly assumes all risks in connection with such instructions. The publisher makes no representations or warranties of any kind, including but not limited to, the warranties of fitness for particular purpose or merchantability, nor are any such representations implied with respect to the material set forth herein, and the publisher takes no responsibility with respect to such material. The publisher shall not be liable for any special, consequential, or exemplary damages resulting, in whole or part, from the readers' use of, or reliance upon, this material.

Printed in Canada
1 2 3 4 5 6 7 12 11 10

Table of Contents

Preface

Introduction

Many coding professional find it difficult to refine their coding skills after obtaining basic education in the use of Current Procedural Terminology (CPT). How does a coding professional move beyond entry level? This book addresses the need for coders to continue their learning process with a focus on the surgery section. The contents and application exercises of this working text will help to bridge the gap between a new coder and experienced professional coder. The surgery section of CPT is the largest chapter and spans all body systems. For this reason, some consider this the most challenging area of coding. Surgical coding requires knowledge and skill in all body systems from the integumentary system to auditory system. The coding professional must apply knowledge about surgical procedures, anatomy of the human body, and official coding guidelines while interpreting a surgeon's documentation. The successful integration of all of these skills leads to the correct coding assignment. Accurate coding is vital for reimbursement as well as supporting data sources from which health care professionals make important decisions.

This book follows the organization of Current Procedural Terminology (CPT) for the surgery section. Every chapter includes the following:

- Explanation of common surgical procedures
- Diagrams for visual illustration of key surgical techniques
- Coding Tips
- References to official coding guidelines
- Exercises
- Self-assessment tools
- Coding references/web resources

The content of this book will apply to coders in all health care settings. Most of the surgical procedures highlighted in this text are frequently performed, but the skills acquired from applying a systematic approach to coding can be transferred to other less commonly performed procedures. Due to the nature of the medical specialty and CPT coding guidelines, some chapters are more complex than others.

Although this is not a billing textbook, it is impossible to concentrate on accurate assignment of CPT codes without discussing the role of the Centers for Medicare and Medicaid Services (CMS) in coding decisions. This textbook cannot address all of the nuances of coding advice by third-party payers. Many references will be made to the official coding guidelines provided by the publisher of CPT: American Medical Association.

Expectations for Use of this Textbook

It is expected that a student has a background in CPT and has completed at least one basic CPT coding course. This textbook is intended to broaden the scope of understanding and increase the skill level for coding surgical procedures. The variety of case studies (e.g., operative reports) included in this text can be classified as basic, intermediate, or advanced, depending on the coder's level of expertise.

Organization of the Textbook

This textbook is organized into 11 chapters and 1 appendix.

- Chapter 1, "Introduction to Surgical Coding," provides the foundation for the textbook. The content includes a systematic method of abstracting information from operative reports to support coding selections. As an overview, the chapter highlights the use of CPT and HCPCS Level II modifiers and official coding references.

- Chapters 2–11 are organized by the main body systems located in the surgical section of CPT.

- Appendix A provides answers to selected self-assessment exercises.

Features of the Textbook

Each chapter in the textbook includes the following features:

- **Chapter outline** organizes chapter topics at a glance.

- **Key terms** list presents new vocabulary for each chapter.

- **Objectives** list the expected learning outcomes after completion of the chapter.

- **Explanations** of common surgical procedures are given.

- **Coding tips** provide recommendations and hints for selecting codes.

- **Exercises and case studies** allow for immediate application of concepts covered in the chapters.

- **Internet links** encourage you to expand your field knowledge.

- **Chapter reviews** feature additional activities such as medical terminology assessments, fill-in-the-blank diagrams, matching exercises, and coding assessments that use patient records and operative notes.

- An **answer key** to selected exercises is provided with rationales and key documentation.

Supplements

The following supplements are available with this textbook.

- **Instructor's Manual** (ISBN 1435427793) features full answer keys with rationales and supporting documentation for each textbook exercise, case study, and review question.

- **Instructor Resources CD-ROM** (ISBN 1435427807) includes a **Computerized Test Bank** with more than 400 questions and Internet testing capability, **presentations written in PowerPoint®** to accompany each chapter, and an electronic version of the **Instructor's Manual**.

About the Author

Gail I. Smith, MA, RHIA, CCS-P is an associate professor and director of the health information management (HIM) program at the University of Cincinnati in Cincinnati, Ohio. She has been an HIM professional and educator for more than 30 years. Prior to joining the faculty at the University of Cincinnati, she was director of a health information technology associate degree program and was health information manager in a multihospital health care system.

Smith has served as a coding consultant for many years and authored *Basic CPT/HCPCS Coding* for the American Health Information Management Association (AHIMA). In addition, Smith served as a coding consultant and educator for the American Medical Association (AMA) for several years. As a member of the AMA consultant team, she was responsible for physician education. Smith is an active member of the American Health Information Management Association and previously served on the Board of Directors. Smith received her bachelor's degree from the Ohio State University and her master's degree in education from the College of Mt. St. Joseph in Cincinnati, Ohio.

Reviewers

Diane Roche Benson, CMA (AAMA), MSA, BS, CPC
University Professor of Health Sciences
Wake Technical Community College, University of Phoenix
Raleigh, NC

Sheryl S. Chambers, CBCS
Medical Instructor
Harrison College
Terre Haute, IN

Michelle Cranney, MBA, RHIT, CCS-P, CPC
Program Director
Virginia College Online
Birmingham, AL

Carline Dalgleish, M.A., B.S., CMA-A
Curriculum Development Specialist; Professor/Faculty
University of Phoenix Online
Arlington, TX

Melissa H. Edenburn, RHIA
Part-Time Faculty
McLennan Community College
Waco, TX

Virginia Escobedo, CPC, NCICS
Virginia College at Austin
Austin, TX

Deborah Fazio, CMAS, RMA
MBC Program Director
Sanford Brown College
Middleburg Heights, OH

Sharon M. Goucher-Norris, BS, CCS-P, NCICS, HIA, ALHC
Lead Instructor
Everest College
Vancouver, WA

Judy Hurtt
Instructor
East Central Community College
Decatur, MS

Mary F. Koloski, CBCS, CHI
Health Insurance Billing & Coding, Program Coordinator
Florida Career College
Clearwater, FL

Lynn G. Slack, BS, CMA
Kaplan Career Institute—ICM Campus
Pittsburgh, PA

Robyn Stambaugh, RHIT
Program Manager, Medical Coding
Central Carolina Technical College
Sumter, SC

Georgia Turner, BBA, CHI, CBCS
Program Director
Virginia College at Birmingham
Birmingham, AL

Sheryl Whipple, BBA, AAS, RHIT
HIT Program Coordinator, Instructor
American Commercial College

Acknowledgments

I wish to acknowledge my husband, Mark, and daughter, Kristin, for their constant support and for making my life a series of "ups." I feel blessed that you are in my life.

To my HIM support team—June Bronnert, Martha Fowler, and Lynn Kuehn —for always being there in times of stress and my hour of need.

A special thanks is given to Kim Zapf, RHIT, CCS, for her contributions.

Gail I. Smith

Introduction to Surgical Coding

Chapter Outline

Introduction

Advancing Your Skills as a Professional Coder

Operative Section of the Health Record

How to Read an Operative Report

Definition of Surgical Package

Coding Guidelines

National Correct Coding Initiative (NCCI)

Separate Procedure

Review of Surgical Modifiers

Coding and Reimbursement

Use of Coding References

Key Terms

Centers for Medicare and Medicaid Services (CMS)

CPT Assistant

HCPCS Level II

Healthcare Common Procedure Coding System (HCPCS)

Medicare Claims Processing Manual

Mutually Exclusive

National Correct Coding Initiative (NCCI)

operative section

Outpatient Code Editor (OCE)

separate procedure

unbundling

Objectives

At the conclusion of this chapter, the student should be able to:

- Identify the skills and knowledge necessary for advancing in the area of surgical CPT coding.
- Describe the components of an operative section of a health record.
- Explain the elements of an operative report.
- Abstract key documentation to contribute to an accurate CPT code assignment.
- Define a surgical package.
- Define the National Correct Coding Initiative (NCCI).
- Review the types of NCCI edits.
- Explain the use of CPT and HCPCS Level II modifiers.
- Identify the uses of coded data.
- List and describe official CPT coding references.

2010 Current Procedural Terminology © 2009 American Medical Association. All Rights Reserved.

Introduction

This chapter provides a foundation for the study of surgical Current Procedural Terminology (CPT) coding. Before moving ahead into the surgical sections (e.g., integumentary), the building blocks must be in place. These building blocks include skill in reading an operative report, recognizing the impact of reimbursement guidelines on coding assignments, and applying official CPT guidelines. This first chapter should serve as a self-assessment for the coding professional. Your study of CPT coding will not be complete after reading this textbook; it will be a lifelong journey.

Advancing Your Skills as a Professional Coder

Many coders face the dilemma of improving their coding skills beyond the basic level. This predicament addresses the age-old conflict of not being hired because you lack experience, yet you cannot get experience unless you have a coding position. Some coding managers state that it can take six months to a year to train a new coder. Advancing to the next level in coding requires a combination of knowledge and skill in the following:

- Reading and interpreting key documentation that contributes to an accurate coding assignment
- Applying knowledge of medical terminology and anatomy of the human body
- Applying official CPT coding guidelines
- Applying Medicare guidelines (if applicable)
- Interpreting operative reports
- Successfully using references and resources

This book will provide examples, tips, practice exercises, reputable references, and self-assessment tools to help you progress beyond the basic level. The end of every chapter will contain important references for researching surgical procedures, coding guidelines, and anatomy illustrations.

Operative Section of the Health Record

The operative report is just one document that is included in the **operative section** of the health record. Although various titles are used, a typical operative section includes the anesthesia record, intraoperative record (sometimes called operative record), and recovery room record. If any specimens are removed during surgery, the pathology report will become part of this section.

Components of an Operative Report

Most operative reports (see Operative Report 1-1 as an example) contain the following key items:

- Preoperative diagnosis—tentative diagnosis before surgery
- Postoperative diagnosis—diagnosis after the surgery has been performed
- Surgical procedure—concise statement of the procedure(s) performed
- Indications for procedure—facts leading up to the decision for the surgery
- Details of procedure—narrative detailed description of the surgical procedures
- Signature of surgeon

> **Note:**
>
> *Coders should reference the entire health record to synthesize operative care for the patient (e.g., pathology report). Documentation guidelines require that the surgeon write or dictate an operative report immediately after surgery.*

In addition, the surgeon will also include type of anesthesia, date of surgery, any complications, estimated blood loss, specimens removed, and the names of the surgical assistants (if applicable).

How to Read an Operative Report

Reading an operative report for the first time can be a daunting task. How does a coder approach a three-page operative report? How do you know what is important? How can you translate technical surgical jargon into an accurate code assignment? There are several quick answers to these questions, such as finding the "action" surgical terms and understanding the components of a surgical procedure, but this skill must be practiced with a systematic approach. This approach will be demonstrated throughout the textbook. Coding professionals typically refer to the surgical procedure section (concise statement) of the operative report first to determine the main surgical procedure. Common procedural terms include:

- Incision
- Excision
- Destruction
- Amputation
- Introduction
- Endoscopy
- Repair
- Suturing
- Manipulation

The patient's diagnosis will tell the coder "why" the procedure is being performed. Next, reading the operative report will help to establish the technique, reveal a complication, or uncover other extenuating circumstances that may affect the coding decision. The details are hidden within the operative report.

EXAMPLE: If the surgeon documents that a colonoscopy was performed, reading the operative report will reveal if any polyps were removed, the technique used to remove them, or perhaps if the procedure was discontinued due to a poor prep.

Operative Report 1-1 and the corresponding Pathology Report 1-1 will serve as examples in an exercise for abstracting documentation needed for coding purposes. As a rule, do not attempt to assign a code for a surgical procedure you do not understand. An experienced coder will review the documentation and seek answers to the type of questions in Exercise 1-1.

Exercise 1-1: Abstracting Documentation

1. Why was the patient being treated surgically?

2. What is the main surgical procedure?   Biopsy

3. Review the coding options in the CPT Index (and subsequently the Tabular section). What documentation is needed to accurately select a code?

4. Refer to the operative report to abstract the detailed information to accurately assign a code.

2010 Current Procedural Terminology © 2009 American Medical Association. All Rights Reserved.

OPERATIVE REPORT 1-1

PREOPERATIVE DIAGNOSIS: Elevated prostate-specific antigen

POSTOPERATIVE DIAGNOSIS: Elevated prostate-specific antigen

PROCEDURE PERFORMED: Prostate needle biopsy

ANESTHESIA: None

COMPLICATIONS: None

BLOOD LOSS: Less than 10 cc

INDICATIONS FOR OPERATION: The patient is a 65-year-old gentleman who was found to have a PSA of 8.1. He was therefore consented for a prostate needle biopsy.

DETAILS OF PROCEDURE: Patient walked to the operating room and climbed on the table. He moved into the lateral decubitus position. A digital rectal exam was performed. The prostate was smooth and firm with no palpable nodules. The ultrasound probe was then inserted into the rectum, and the prostate was visualized using the ultrasound. There were no suspicious lesions seen on the ultrasound. We then proceeded to check 10 prostate needle biopsy specimens. Two specimens were taken from the right base, two from the right mid, two from the right apex, followed by two from the left base, one from the left mid, and one from the left apex. We only took one specimen on the left mid and apex because of the patient's discomfort. The patient was able to walk back to the postanesthesia care unit in stable condition. We will follow up on the pathology results and call the patient.

PATHOLOGY REPORT 1-1

GROSS DESCRIPTION:

Specimen A, labeled "right base PNBX," consists of two fragments of soft white core biopsies, which measure in aggregate 1.5 cm in length and 0.1 cm in diameter. The specimen is entirely submitted in one Cassette A.

Specimen B, labeled "right mid PNBX" consists of two fragments of soft white core biopsies, which measure in aggregate 1.3 cm in length and 0.1 cm in diameter. The specimen is entirely submitted in one Cassette B.

Specimen C, labeled "right apex PNBX," consists of two fragments of soft white core biopsies, which measure in aggregate 1.9 cm in length and 0.1 cm in diameter. The specimen is entirely submitted in one Cassette C.

Specimen D, labeled "right base PNBX," consists of two fragments of soft white core biopsies, which measure in aggregate 1.1 cm in length and 0.1 cm in diameter. The specimen is entirely submitted in one Cassette D.

Specimen E, labeled "left mid PNBX," consists of one fragment of soft white core biopsies, which measures 0.4 cm in length and 0.1 cm in diameter. The specimen is entirely submitted in one Cassette E.

Specimen F, labeled "left apex PNBX," consists of one fragment of soft white core biopsies, which measures in aggregate 0.3 cm in length and 0.1 cm in diameter. The specimen is entirely submitted in one Cassette F.

MICROSCOPIC EXAM/DIAGNOSIS:

Specimen A: Benign prostatic tissue

Specimen B and C: Prostatic tissue with acute and chronic inflammation and focal high-grade prostatic intraepithelial neoplasia (PIN)

Specimens D, E, and F: Benign prostatic tissue

2010 Current Procedural Terminology © 2009 American Medical Association. All Rights Reserved.

Abstracting Documentation from Operative Section

Exercise 1-2: Abstracting Documentation

Read Operative Report 1-2 and corresponding Pathology Report 1-2 to answer the questions following the reports.

OPERATIVE REPORT 1-2

PREOPERATIVE DIAGNOSIS: Lesion, skin of nose (left side)

POSTOPERATIVE DIAGNOSIS: Lesion, skin of nose

PROCEDURE: Nasal cyst removal with primary closure

ANESTHESIA: Local

BRIEF HISTORY: Patient is an 84-year-old male who presented to the clinic complaining of a 10-month history of a nasal cyst. Patient states that it has slowly increased in size and has been stable for the past couple of months. He presented to the clinic with the hopes of having it removed. After full explanation of the risks and benefits of that procedure, the patient consented for the operation.

DETAILS OF PROCEDURE: After consent, the patient was brought to the OR. Local anesthetic including 1% lidocaine was used subcutaneously to the nose. An elliptical marker outlined the nasal area. Sterilely prepped with Betadine. Head wrapped and covered throughout the procedure. Using a #15 blade scalpel, an incision was made around the 1 cm cyst-like lesion. Using the #15 blade, the cyst was undermined and removed in whole. Total excised diameter was 2.0 cm. Hemostasis maintained using Bovie electrocautery. The wound was closed with #5-0 PDS, then used for subcutaneous approximation of the transverse incision. #5-0 nylon was used to approximate the superficial epidermis edges. Bacitracin ointment was applied. Hemostasis was maintained successfully. The patient tolerated the procedure well.

PATHOLOGY REPORT 1-2

GROSS DESCRIPTION:

One specimen received in formalin labeled with demographics and "nasal cyst." It consists of an ellipse of skin measuring 1.7 × 0.8 × 0.5 cm. The specimen is serially sectioned revealing a cyst 0.3 cm in diameter containing white mucous-like material. Representative sections to include the entire cyst are submitted in three cassettes.

MICROSCOPIC DIAGNOSIS:

Skin nose, consistent with sebaceous adenoma

Integral Surgical Services

Exercise 1-2: Abstracting Documentation

1. What technique was used to remove the lesion?
Excision

2. What key elements are needed to assign a code?
technique location size

3. Was the lesion benign or malignant?

4. What was the excised diameter?

5. Why is the specimen size in the pathology report different from the operative report?

6. What coding guidelines are applicable to this procedure?

7. What is the correct code assignment?

Another skill for abstracting documentation for coding purposes is to be able to separate the main procedure(s) from minor services that are integral to the procedure. The following are examples of typical services that are integral:

- Local, topical, or regional anesthesia administered by the physician performing the procedure
- Prepping, positioning, and prepping the patient
- Insertion of intravenous (IV) access to administer medication
- Evaluation of surgical field

Refer to Operative Report 1-1 (biopsy of prostate). Note that the following services are integral to the biopsy procedure:

- Positioning: He moved into the lateral decubitus position.
- Examination: A digital rectal exam was performed. The prostate was smooth and firm with no palpable nodules (*evaluation of surgical field*).
- Approach: The ultrasound probe was then inserted into the rectum, and the prostate was visualized using the ultrasound.
- Obtaining specimens: Two specimens were taken.

With the exception of the ultrasound guidance (radiology section CPT), all of the above services would be considered integral to the biopsy procedure.

Additional Surgical Services (Integral)

In additional to the services listed above, there are many minor services that are included as part of the surgery and do not warrant an additional CPT code. The following is a sample of these services:

- Wound irrigation
- Insertion and removal of drains

- Use of suction devices
- Isolation of structures that are limiting access to the surgical field (e.g., muscles)
- Application of surgical dressings

Definition of Surgical Package

The CPT Surgery Guidelines provide a definition for services that are included in a given CPT code. This surgical package includes the operation per se; the following services are always included in the surgical CPT code:

- Local infiltration, metacarpal/metatarsal/digital block or topical anesthesia
- Subsequent to the decision for surgery, one related E/M encounter on the date immediately prior to or on the date of procedure (including history and physical)
- Immediate postoperative care, including dictating operative notes and talking with the family and other physicians
- Writing orders
- Evaluating the patient in the postoperative recovery area
- Typical postoperative follow-up care

The services included in a surgical package may vary depending on the third-party payer guidelines. For example, the Centers for Medicare and Medicaid Services (CMS) policies for a surgical package are based on major and minor surgeries. For up-to-date policies for Medicare or Medicaid claims, it is best to reference the **Medicare Claims Processing Manual** on CMS's website.

Coding Guidelines

In addition to reading and interpreting the documentation in the health record, a coder must be familiar with the official coding guidelines. Although there are many newsletters, websites, and Listservs that are dedicated to coding issues, there are only three official references for coding guidance:

- *Current Procedural Terminology, Fourth Edition (CPT-4)*
- *CPT Assistant*, published monthly by the American Medical Association (AMA)
- Centers for Medicare and Medicaid Services (CMS)

Role of the American Medical Association

The American Medical Association (AMA) is the primary, authoritative reference for CPT guidelines and changes. The AMA publishes *CPT Assistant*, a monthly newsletter that provides information on the correct application of CPT codes.

In addition, AMA publishes a yearly book titled *CPT Changes: An Insider's View*, which highlights new and revised codes. There is not a separate AMA book of CPT coding guidelines. Interspersed in CPT-4 are notes and coding guidance, which is the basis for accurate code assignments.

Role of Centers for Medicare and Medicaid Services

Centers for Medicare and Medicaid Services (CMS) is the federal agency that administers Medicare and Medicaid. To ensure that claims are processed consistently, CMS developed **HCPCS Level II** codes that are used to identify products, services, and supplies that are not included in CPT. CPT is Level I of CMS's **Healthcare Common Procedure Coding System (HCPCS)**, supplementing alphanumeric codes and modifiers applicable to identifying services for federally funded (and other insurance) patients.

2010 Current Procedural Terminology © 2009 American Medical Association. All Rights Reserved.

In addition, CMS publishes regulations for payment of services that may supersede AMA's coding principles.

> **EXAMPLE:** CPT provides a code for a diagnostic screening colonoscopy (45378). CMS advises providers (of Medicare or Medicaid services) to identify this procedure with one of two HCPCS Level II codes:
>
> G0121   Colorectal cancer screening on individual not meeting the criteria for high risk
>
> G0105   Colorectal cancer screening colonoscopy on individual at high risk
>
> The federal interpretation of use of CPT codes and modifiers are published in the form of transmittals, manuals, and other documents or electronic files (e.g., National Correct Coding Initiative). These files can be found on CMS's website (all website links are provided at the end of each chapter).

National Correct Coding Initiative (NCCI)

In January 1996, the Centers for Medicare and Medicaid Services (CMS) developed a system of edits to promote correct coding of health care services and support appropriate payment of claims. The **National Correct Coding Initiative (NCCI)** provides a guide for health care providers (and carriers) to correct coding practices. On CMS's website, there are two separate files for NCCI edits: one for physicians and another for hospital outpatient services. The edits are incorporated within the **Outpatient Code Editor (OCE)**, which determines payment for hospital Outpatient Prospective Payment System (OPPS) services. Bypass modifiers and coding pairs in the OCE may differ from those in the NCCI because of differences between facility and professional services.

Types of NCCI Edits

One type of NCCI edit file provides code pairs that should not be reported together (see Table 1-1). Column 1 codes should not be billed with Column 2 codes. Table 1-1 reinforces the coding guideline that excision of lesions includes a simple wound repair. These types of edits prevent unbundling. **Unbundling** is a term that describes a coding practice where multiple procedures are billed for a group of procedures that are covered by a single comprehensive code. These two codes should not appear on the bill for the same encounter. It is important to note that modifiers may override some of the NCCI edits (if applicable).

> **EXAMPLE:** A patient is seen in the physician's office for removal of a lesion of the leg (code 11406), and he asks the physician to suture his lacerated arm (unrelated to the lesion). Then it would be appropriate to append modifier 59 with code 12001 to indicate that a distinct procedural service was provided.

CODE DESCRIPTIONS:

11406   Excision, benign lesion including margins, except skin tag (unless listed elsewhere), trunk, arms, or legs; excised diameter over 4.0 cm

12001   Simple repair of superficial wounds of scalp, neck, axillae, external genitalia, trunk, and/or extremities (including feet); 2.5 cm or less

Another type of NCCI edit is called **Mutually Exclusive**. The CMS tables display Column 1 and Column 2, indicating that they should not be billed together. Table 1-2 identifies two codes describing breast

Table 1-1

Column 1	Column 2
11406	12001

2010 Current Procedural Terminology © 2009 American Medical Association. All Rights Reserved.

Table 1-2 Mutually Exclusive Edits

Column 1	Column 2
19102	19103

Table 1-3 Mutually Exclusive Edits

Column 1	Column 2
58543	58552

biopsies. Code 19102 identifies the percutaneous needle core technique, and code 19103 represents the automated vacuum-assisted (or rotating) biopsy device. For this edit, the assumption is that the surgeon performs one or the other. If circumstances dictated that the surgeon performed *each* of these procedures, one on each breast, then the anatomic modifiers of LT (left) and RT (right) would bypass the edit and permit use of the codes together on the claim form. Use of modifiers to override NCCI edits must be justified.

CODE DESCRIPTIONS:

19102   Biopsy of breast; percutaneous, needle core, using imaging guidance

19103   Biopsy of breast; automated vacuum-assisted or rotating biopsy device, using imaging guidance

Another example of an NCCI edit in Table 1-3 reveals a circumstance when there is no logical rationale for these two codes to be billed together. The surgeon performed either one or the other. It is an important responsibility of the coder to understand the use of these edits. Coding software products will query the coder to ask if a modifier should be applied. The modifiers should not be automatically appended with a modifier to override an edit. As a general guideline, procedures should be reported with the HCPCS/CPT codes that most comprehensively describe the services performed.

CODE DESCRIPTIONS:

58543   Laparoscopy, surgical, supracervical hysterectomies, for uterus greater than 250 g

58552   Laparoscopy, surgical, with vaginal hysterectomy, for uterus 250 g or less; with removal of tube(s) and ovary(s)

Separate Procedure

In the Surgery Guidelines section of CPT-4, there is a description of the phrase "separate procedure." Some CPT codes include the term "separate procedure" within the descriptor. This phrase means that the designated **"separate procedure"** code should not be reported separately with a related procedure.

EXAMPLE: The surgeon documents that a diagnostic anoscopy was performed, during which a biopsy of the rectal tissue was taken. Note the following CPT codes and descriptors.

46600   Anoscopy; diagnostic, with or without collection of specimen(s) by brushing or washing (separate procedure)

46606   Anoscopy; with biopsy, single or multiple

CPT code 46600 has the designation of a "separate procedure"; therefore, it would not be assigned with the 46606 code. The correct coding assignment for this procedure would only be 46606. The (diagnostic) anoscopy becomes the approach; therefore, it would not warrant a separate code assignment. Note that anoscopy is included in the description for 46606. If the surgeon stated that a diagnostic anoscopy was performed with excision of a benign lesion of the buttocks, then CPT code 46600 would be assigned along with the excision of lesion code (114xx). The anoscopy procedure is not related to the excision of lesion, and the surgeon's work would justify assigning both codes.

2010 Current Procedural Terminology © 2009 American Medical Association. All Rights Reserved.

CMS interprets the "separate procedure" designation by explaining that it should not be reported when performed with another procedure in an anatomically related region through the same skin incision, orifice, or surgical approach. The rationale for this interpretation surrounds the amount of "work" related to performing a procedure.

Review of Surgical Modifiers

Appendix A of CPT contains a complete list of CPT modifiers and selected HCPCS Level II (National) modifiers approved for ambulatory surgery center (ASC) hospital outpatient use. These modifiers provide a means to report or indicate that a procedure has been altered by some specific circumstance but not changed in its definition. Modifiers serve as a method of communication between the health care provider and third-party payers. Modifiers are an integral part of the coding system, and their use may affect payment or prevent claim denials. Table 1-4 is appropriate for use with surgical CPT codes:

Table 1-4: Use of CPT Modifiers for Surgical Procedures

Modifier	Short Description	Approved for Physician and/or Hospital Use (ASC)
22	Increased Procedural Services—work required is substantially greater than typically required.	Physician only
47	Anesthesia by Surgeon—report circumstance when surgeon administers anesthesia (regional or general).	Physician only
50	Bilateral Procedure—procedure performed in duplicate (e.g., both legs) when code descriptor does not differentiate.	Physician and hospital
51	Multiple Procedures—procedures performed at the same session by same provider. Primary procedure reported as listed, secondary procedure(s) appended with modifier 51.	Physician only
52	Reduced Services—this modifier has several uses and is interpreted differently by AMA and CMS (see examples following this table). AMA definition: Procedure partially reduced in scope or eliminated at the discretion of the physician. *(NOTE: Refer to individual payer guidelines for use of modifier 52.)*	Physician and hospital *(for hospital outpatients or ambulatory surgery centers, see modifiers 73 and 74)*
53	Discontinued Procedure—physician elects to discontinue a procedure.	Physician only (see modifiers 73 and 74 for hospital use)
54	Surgical Care Only—physician performs surgery but does not provide pre- and postoperative care.	Physician only
55	Postoperative Management Only—physician provides only postoperative care.	Physician only
56	Preoperative Management Only—physician provides only preoperative management.	Physician only
58	Staged or Related Procedure or Service by the Same Physician During the Postoperative Period.	Physician and hospital
59	Distinct Procedural Service—communicates that the procedures that are not normally reported together should be reported (e.g., different session, different site).	Physician and hospital
62	Two Surgeons—procedure warrants that two physicians work together as primary surgeons.	Physician only
63	Procedure Performed on Infants Less than 4 kg	Physician only
66	Surgical Team—complex procedure required a team.	Physician only
73	Discontinued Outpatient Procedure Prior to Anesthesia Administration—surgery cancelled after patient is taken to operating room and prepared for surgery but before anesthesia is administered.	Hospital only
74	Discontinued Outpatient Procedure after Anesthesia Administration—surgery cancelled after anesthesia is administered or after procedure was begun.	Hospital only
76	Repeat Procedure or Service by Same Physician (note that this modifier is not restricted for use by physicians)—indicates that a procedure was repeated subsequent to the original procedure.	Physician and hospital
77	Repeat Procedure by Another Physician—procedure performed by another physician had to be repeated.	Physician and hospital

78	Unplanned Return to Operating/Procedure Room by the Same Physician Following Initial Procedure for a Related Procedure During the Postoperative Period—unplanned, *related* procedure following initial procedure during the postoperative period.	Physician and hospital
79	Unrelated Procedure or Service by the Same Physician During the Postoperative Period—procedure was *unrelated* to the original procedure.	Physician and hospital
80	Assistant Surgeon—primary surgeon requested an assistant surgeon; the assistant surgeon would bill the same procedure CPT code.	Physician only
81	Minimum Assistant Surgeon—services of an assistant are needed for a portion of the procedure.	Physician only
82	Assistant Surgeon (when qualified resident surgeon not available)—use in teaching facilities if there is no approved training program related to the medical specialty required for the surgical procedure or no qualified resident is available.	Physician only

CMS Definitions of Modifiers

CMS provides its own interpretation for modifiers that are communicated via Transmittals and in the Medicare Claims Processing Manual.

EXAMPLE 1: CPT modifier 52 must not be used with an E/M service code (Medicare Transmittal 1776, October 25, 2002).

EXAMPLE 2: Modifier 52 is used to indicate partial reduction or discontinuation of services that do not require anesthesia (Chapter 4 of Medicare Claims Processing Manual—Part B Hospital).

Use of modifiers will be reinforced throughout this textbook

HCPCS Level II Modifiers

CMS developed a list of modifiers that are also used by many carriers. Some of the codes can be found in Appendix A of CPT, but the complete list can be found in the HCPCS electronic files on the CMS website. HCPCS codes and modifiers are updated yearly.

EXAMPLE: EXAMPLES OF HCPCS MODIFIERS

LT   Left side (used to identify procedures performed on the left side of the body)

GH   Diagnostic mammogram converted from screening mammogram on same day

G6   ESRD patient for whom less than 6 dialysis sessions have been provided in a month

Exercise 1-3: Use of Modifiers

Assign the appropriate CPT code(s) and CPT/HCPCS Level II modifiers for the following scenarios.

1. Physician performs a flexible sigmoidoscopy, but the scope cannot be passed due to poor prep. IV sedation was given.

a. What is the correct coding assignment for physician services?

_____

b. What is the correct coding assignment for hospital outpatient services?

_____

2010 Current Procedural Terminology © 2009 American Medical Association. All Rights Reserved.

2. Patient is scheduled for a laparoscopic cholecystectomy, taken to the OR, is prepped, and anesthesia is given. Hyperthermia develops, and the procedure is cancelled.

   a. What is the correct coding assignment for physician services?

   _____

   b. What is the correct coding assignment for hospital outpatient services?

   _____

3. The surgeon performs a colonoscopy. During the procedure, a biopsy is taken from edematous tissue in the ascending colon, and a polyp was removed by hot biopsy forceps in the descending colon. Give the correct coding assignment for physician and hospital:

   _____

4. The surgeon performed a total abdominal hysterectomy with bilateral salpingo-oophorectomy. During the procedure, the physician encountered dense intestinal adhesions requiring enterolysis. Documentation in the operative report stated that it took one hour to free the adhesions so the procedure could progress. What is the correct coding assignment for the physician and the hospital?

   _____

5. A patient was seen in the physician's office for severe pain in the left knee. The surgeon performed an arthrocentesis to remove the excess fluid. What is the correct coding assignment for the physician's services?

   _____

Coding and Reimbursement

As mentioned previously, modifiers may affect reimbursement or prevent claim denials. It is important to note that use of an HCPCS code or modifier does not guarantee reimbursement. An insurance carrier may ask for documentation (e.g., operative report) to support the services identified on the claim. If documentation does not support the procedure code or modifier, then the claim may be denied. For example, if a patient has a surgical procedure that is determined to be cosmetic and the insurance carrier does not cover these types of services, then the claim will be denied. If a coder consistently appends modifier 59 to override edits (unbundling), then it may lead to penalties. The ultimate goal of a coder is to assign codes that reflect the documentation in the health record.

Although most of the attention on coding surrounds reimbursement, it should be noted that coded data is used for a variety of purposes beyond reimbursement (e.g., population-based registries). Coded diagnoses and procedures are analyzed to help make important decisions on health care services in our country. Trending data leads to policies that affect all health care consumers.

Use of Coding References

Having access to coding references is vital for the success of a coder. Most coding software packages contain NCCI edits and modifier reminders. Billing software packages provide another layer of edits that help to create a "clean claim." All of these support services allow the coder to concentrate his or her efforts on interpreting the documentation and applying the coding guidelines. At the end of each chapter in this text is a list of websites and references that will assist a coder with becoming more proficient and confident with coding. Many of the exercises and examples will reference *CPT Assistant*, the official source for CPT coding advice. At a minimum, every coder should have the following references in his or her library (electronic or hard copy):

- Medical dictionary
- Anatomy illustrations
- List of websites that describe surgical procedures
- *CPT Assistant*

Summary

- Coding professionals must successfully integrate a variety of skills and knowledge: application of guidelines, abstracting documentation, comprehending surgical procedures, and proficiency at researching.
- The entire medical record should be reviewed before assigning CPT codes.
- Third-party payers often publish their own coding policies.
- CMS and other third-party payers institute edits to support consistent and accurate code assignments.
- Official CPT coding guidelines appear in the CPT book itself with clarification and insight provided in *CPT Assistant.*
- Coded data is used for a variety of purposes.

Internet Links

American Medical Association: *http://www.ama-assn.org*
Links to coding products and services; purchase subscription to *CPT Assistant*; conducts yearly symposium.

American Health Information Management Association: *http://www.ahima.org*
Coding products and education; online community for members.

Centers for Medicare and Medicaid Services (CMS): *http://www.cms.hhs.gov*
Home page for links to all references.

CMS National Correct Coding Initiative: *http://www.cms.hhs.gov/NationalCorrectCodInitEd/*
Links for physicians and hospitals.

CMS Outpatient Code Editor: *http://www.cms.hhs.gov/OutpatientCodeEdit/*

CMS Manuals and Transmittals: *http://www.cms.hhs.gov/manuals/*
Provides coding advice.

Review

I. Medical Terminology Assessment

To move beyond the basic level in coding, a professional coder must commit to a plan of lifelong learning. In addition to researching coding guidelines, coders must continue to expand their knowledge of medical terminology, surgical procedures, and anatomic descriptions. The following is a self-assessment to evaluate your level of expertise with medical terms and surgical procedures.

2010 Current Procedural Terminology © 2009 American Medical Association. All Rights Reserved.

Multiple Choice

Choose the best answer to the following.

1. Which of the following is removal of the gallbladder?
   - a. cholecystotomy
   - b. cystectomy
   - c. cholecystectomy
   - d. cholecystostomy

2. Which of the following procedures would ONLY be performed on a female patient?
   - a. colporrhaphy
   - b. EGD
   - c. cysturethroscopy
   - d. nephrolithotomy

3. Which of the following can be identified as a malignant skin lesion?
   - a. lipoma
   - b. epidermoid cyst
   - c. condyloma
   - d. basal cell carcinoma

4. The surgeon performed an exploration of the patient's voice box. Which of the following procedures was performed?
   - a. tracheostomy
   - b. laryngoscopy
   - c. pharyngoscopy
   - d. mediastinotomy

5. The patient was diagnosed as having a stone in the tube leading from the kidney to the bladder. Which of the following correctly describes this condition?
   - a. calculus of the urethra
   - b. ureterolithiasis
   - c. salpingolithiasis
   - d. urethratresia

6. The surgeon repairs a fracture of the upper arm bone. This bone is called:
   - a. humerus
   - b. ulna
   - c. radius
   - d. femur

7. With the use of a needle, the surgeon removes excess fluid from the patient's lung. Which of the following best describes this procedure?
   - a. auscultation
   - b. percussion
   - c. aspiration
   - d. thoracolysis

8. The surgeon removes the patient's fallopian tubes and ovaries. What is this procedure called?
   - a. hysterectomy
   - b. salpingo-oophorectomy
   - c. salpingectomy
   - d. tubal ligation

9. The physician documents the use of an instrument that emits electrical sparks to destroy a skin lesion. The technique of using "electrical sparks" is referred to as:
   - a. fulguration
   - b. cryosurgery
   - c. ectropion
   - d. curetment

10. Which of the following structures can be found in the ear?
    - a. atrium
    - b. alveolus
    - c. mandible
    - d. incus

2010 Current Procedural Terminology © 2009 American Medical Association. All Rights Reserved.

II. Coding Assessment

Apply CPT guidelines to assign CPT surgical codes to the following procedures. Append modifiers if applicable. Do not attempt to assign modifier 51 (multiple procedures) since its use is often subject to payer guidelines.

1. Wound repair of the following lacerations: 2.0 cm of left elbow (simple), 1.5 cm of right elbow (simple), 3.0 cm of chin (closed in layers), and 2.5 cm of right knee (simple).

   Code(s) _____

2. Excision of benign right breast mass, located by radiological marker. (Code for surgical services and assume that the radiologist placed the marker.)

   Code(s) _____

3. Removal of squamous cell carcinoma of the cheek (excisional diameter of 0.5 cm).

   Code(s) _____

4. Arthrodesis of interphalangeal joint of left great toe.

   Code(s) _____

5. Open reduction of fracture of right proximal tibia with application of short leg cast.

   Code(s) _____

6. Bronchoscopy with transbronchial lung biopsy.

   Code(s) _____ 31628 _____

7. Repair of malfunctioning electrodes in a dual-chamber cardiac pacemaker.

   Code(s) _____ 33220 _____

8. Initial repair of strangulated incisional hernia with Marlex mesh graft.

   Code(s) _____

9. Cystourethroscopy with resection of 3.3 cm bladder tumor.

   Code(s) _____

10. Vaginal hysterectomy (270 g uterus) with bilateral salpingo-oophorectomy.

    Code(s) _____ 58291 _____

2010 Current Procedural Terminology © 2009 American Medical Association. All Rights Reserved.

2 Integumentary System

Chapter Outline

Key Terms

acellular dermal
replacement

adjacent tissue transfer

allograft

autograft

complex wound repair

debridement

deep fascia

dermal autograft

dermis

epidermal autograft

epidermis

excisional biopsy

fascia

fine needle aspiration

full thickness

incisional biopsy

integumentary system

intermediate wound
repair

lesion

lipoma

Mohs micrographic
surgery

needle core biopsy

partial mastectomy

pedicle skin graft

primary defect

puncture aspiration

radical mastectomy

secondary defect

simple complete
mastectomy

simple wound repair

skin biopsy

skin replacement

skin substitute

split thickness

subcutaneous fascia

subcutaneous layer

subcutaneous
mastectomy

tissue-cultured autograft

xenograft

Objectives

At the conclusion of this chapter, the student should be able to:

- Define key terms.
- Distinguish between the different methods for removing lesions.

2010 Current Procedural Terminology © 2009 American Medical Association. All Rights Reserved.

- Differentiate among simple, intermediate, and complex wound repairs.
- Describe techniques for performing skin grafts.
- Explain Mohs micrographic surgery.
- Differentiate among nonsurgical breast biopsies, surgical breast biopsies, and mastectomy procedures.
- Apply coding guidelines for integumentary system procedures.
- Given a case study, correctly assign CPT codes for surgical cases.

Introduction

The skin is the largest organ of the body. Included in the **integumentary system** are hair, nails, sweat, and oil glands. The main purpose of the skin is to protect the body from external elements such as chemicals and temperature.

The **epidermis** has four separate layers of epithelial tissue. As its name suggests, it is the outermost layer of the skin. Beneath the epidermis is the **dermis,** which is composed of dense connective tissue with collagen fibers, which gives the skin elasticity. In addition, the dermis includes nerves, blood vessels, and hair follicles. Beneath the dermis is the subcutaneous layer (see Figure 2-1). The **subcutaneous layer** is not actually considered part of the skin, but it helps to anchor the skin to the underlying structures. Within the subcutaneous fatty layer is a superficial **fascia** layer, which binds the skin to the parts beneath.

The **subcutaneous fascia** is located directly beneath the dermis and stores fat and water and provides passageways for nerves and blood vessels. Beneath that lies the **deep fascia,** the strong

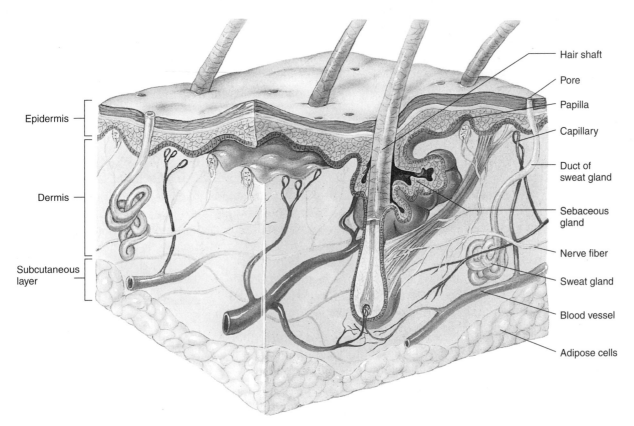

Figure 2-1 The layers of the skin and some of its appendages

2010 Current Procedural Terminology © 2009 American Medical Association. All Rights Reserved.

connective tissue layer that is considered part of the musculoskeletal system. It aids muscle movement and also provides a passageway for nerves and blood vessels. In some areas of the body, it provides an attachment site for muscles and acts as a cushioning layer between muscles.

Note:

There are two layers of fascia: superficial layer (integumentary system) and deeper layer, which is in the musculoskeletal system.

Incision and Drainage (I&D) of Abscess

Although several integumentary system codes are available to identify incision and drainage (I&D) of an abscess, it should be noted that codes also appear in other sections of CPT.

> **EXAMPLE:**
>
> 42725   Incision and drainage abscess, retropharyngeal or parapharyngeal, external approach
>
> 46050   Incision and drainage, perianal abscess, superficial

The "Skin and Subcutaneous" section of CPT lists codes for superficial abscesses and hematomas. The description for code 10060 provides examples of these types of abscesses (e.g., carbuncle, suppurative hidradenitis, cutaneous or subcutaneous abscess, cyst, furuncle, or paronychia). More extensive procedures involving incision and drainage of a deeper or larger hematoma/abscess are reported with codes specific to anatomic regions.

> **EXAMPLE:**
>
> **Case #1:**   Patient is seen in the physician's office for an infected inclusion cyst of the arm that is incised and drained. (CPT code 10060)
>
> **Case #2:**   Patient presents with a post-traumatic hematoma of the left thigh. The large hematoma extended into the subcutaneous tissues and underlying fascia. (CPT code 27301)

How does a coder distinguish between a simple and complicated I&D? The coding of complicated I&D should be based on the level of difficulty involved with the treatment. What makes it a difficult procedure (e.g., use of drains and extensive packing)? Did it take longer? These are examples of indications that it could be complicated. Many coding policies suggest that the physician should be queried for a definitive answer.

Biopsy vs. Excision of Lesion

Coders are sometimes misled by the term "skin biopsy." A **skin biopsy** involves removing a small amount of skin tissue for microscopic evaluation. This tissue sample is examined pathologically and assists the physician with making a diagnosis. This is sometimes called an **incisional biopsy**. There are three common methods for skin biopsies: shave, punch, and excisional. As it implies, shaving is scraping the outermost layers of skin. For deeper skin lesions, a punch biopsy is performed. The physician removes a small round piece of tissue with a hollow instrument. During this procedure, the entire lesion may be excised, so review documentation carefully.

If the physician states that an **excisional biopsy** was performed, the coder must carefully review the documentation. A piece of tissue may be excised (cut out) and submitted for a pathological diagnosis. However, if the procedure involves removing the *entire lesion*, then the procedure is no longer considered a biopsy. This procedure would be coded as an excision of lesion. The CPT code selection for skin biopsies is based on the number of lesions (11100, 11101).

Coding Tip:

If a skin biopsy is performed on a lesion and the lesion is subsequently removed (in the same operative session), then only the excision of lesion code is assigned.

2010 Current Procedural Terminology © 2009 American Medical Association. All Rights Reserved.

Several Biopsies Performed on Different Lesions or Sites

If a physician elects to remove several lesions from different areas of the body (during the same operative episode), then code 11100 is reported for the first lesion, and code 11101 is reported for each additional separate lesion that is biopsied (*CPT Assistant,* October 2004).

Debridement

The term **debridement** refers to the removal of dead, damaged, or infected tissues. The coding ranges differentiate among debridement down to or through the skin full thickness (dermis), down through the subcutaneous tissue (fascia), or muscle or bone. There are several guidelines for coding debridement of wounds. For example, in many situations debridement becomes part of the routine cleansing process.

> **EXAMPLE:** A child falls down the steps and requires stitches for a superficial wound. The physician cleans the wound (removing dirt and gravel) to prepare the skin for the wound closure. In this case, the debridement would be considered part of the normal wound closure and would not require an additional debridement code.

> Wound closures of the skin require documentation of the depth (partial thickness, full thickness, or deep into the subcutaneous tissue, muscle, or bone): codes 11040–11044.

> > **Partial thickness:** epidermis and part of the dermis

> > **Full thickness:** both layers (epidermis and dermis)

> **EXAMPLE:** A patient is seen in the emergency department (ED) after a bicycle accident. An examination of the wounds revealed multiple superficial abrasions, contaminated by gravel, dirt, and glass. The ED physician cleans the wound and removes the superficial skin layer along with the contaminated tissue. An ointment and bandages were applied. (CPT code 11040)

- Several codes are provided for debridement associated with open fractures (11010–11012).

- A series of debridement codes can be found in the "Medicine" section of CPT for services performed by non-physician professionals. The Active Wound Care Management codes (97597–97606) are typically performed by physical therapists or wound care nurses.

Removal of Lesions

The definition of **lesion** is very broad. In general terms, a lesion is any abnormal tissue. Skin lesions range from moles to basal cell carcinoma. See Figure 2-2 for examples of skin lesions. It is important to note that some removals of skin lesions are identified by codes from other sections of CPT, not just the integumentary system. Excision of integumentary lesions are defined as full thickness (through the dermis) while excision of tumors of musculoskeletal systems include removal of growth from soft tissue, superficial or deep subcutaneous tissue, and subfascial or intramuscular tissue.

> **EXAMPLE:**
>
> 27618   Excision, tumor, soft tissue of leg or ankle area, subcutaneous; less than 3 cm
>
> 27619   Excision, tumor, soft tissue of leg or ankle area (subfascial eg. intramuscular); less than 5 cm

There are a variety of CPT codes to represent the work of the physician. Coders must analyze documentation to abstract key elements, such as:

- Was the lesion benign or malignant?

- What technique was used to remove the lesion (laser, excision, or shaving)?

2010 Current Procedural Terminology © 2009 American Medical Association. All Rights Reserved.

- Where was the location of the lesion?
- Were there any additional procedures performed, such as intermediate wound closure?
- What was the excised diameter (greatest clinical diameter) of the lesion?

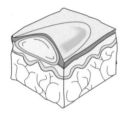

Bulla (large blister):
Same as a vesicle only greater than 10 mm
Example:
Contact dermatitis, large second-degree burns, bulbous impetigo, pemphigus

Macule:
Localized changes in skin color of less than 1 cm in diameter
Example:
Freckle

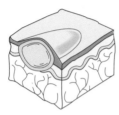

Nodule:
Solid and elevated; however, they extend deeper than papules into the dermis or subcutaneous tissues, greater than 10 mm
Example:
Lipoma, erythema, cyst, wart

Papule:
Solid, elevated lesion less than 1 cm in diameter
Example:
Elevated nevi

Pustule:
Vesicles or bullae that become filled with pus, usually described as less than 0.5 cm in diameter
Example:
Acne, impetigo, furuncles, carbuncles

Ulcer:
A depressed lesion of the epidermis and upper papillary layer of the dermis
Example:
Stage 2 pressure ulcer

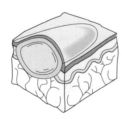

Tumor:
The same as a nodule only greater than 2 cm

Example:
Benign epidermal tumor basal cell carcinoma

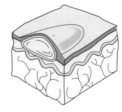

Vesicle (small blister):
Accumulation of fluid between the upper layers of the skin; elevated mass containing serous fluid; less than 10 mm
Example:
Herpes simplex, herpes zoster, chickenpox

Urticaria, Hives:
Localized edema in the epidermis causing irregular elevation that may be red or pale, may be itchy
Example:
Insect bite, wheal

Figure 2-2 Skin lesions

2010 Current Procedural Terminology © 2009 American Medical Association. All Rights Reserved.

Benign vs. Malignant

Many of the code selections require documentation about the morphology of the lesion. Best practices dictate that the coder examines the pathology report for a definitive diagnosis. Note that, if lesions are destroyed during the procedure, there will be no pathology report; therefore, the physician's diagnosis will be referenced for coding purposes.

Exercise 2-1: Malignant vs. Benign

Read the following lesion descriptions, and identify each as "M" for malignant or "B" for benign.

B ___ **1.** Seborrheic keratosis

___ **2.** Molluscum contagiosum

B ___ **3.** Sebaceous adenoma

___ **4.** Trichoepithelioma

B ___ **5.** Pyogenic granuloma

___ **6.** Nevus

B ___ **7.** Squamous cell carcinoma

___ **8.** Keloid

B ___ **9.** Dermatofibroma

___ **10.** Lentigo maligna melanoma

Lesions of Uncertain Morphology

If a pathology report states that the lesion is of uncertain morphology, coding guidelines state that the code selection should reflect the knowledge, skill, time, and effort of the physician.

Removal of Skin Lesion

Table 2-1 provides a quick glance of the variety of codes available for removal of skin lesions. Note that the key determining factor for code selection is the *technique* used by the physician.

Excision of Lesions with Subsequent Wound Repairs

An excision of a skin lesion includes a simple repair of the wound created as a result of the procedure. If the defect requires a layered closure (dermal with suturing of at least one of the deeper layers of subcutaneous and nonmuscle fascial tissue), then an additional code would be assigned from the "Intermediate Repair" section (12031–12057)—the logic being that the physician's time and expertise would be extended past the normal routine closure of the wound.

Size of Lesions

In several code descriptions, the size of the lesion contributes to the correct assignment. The code requires documentation of the excised diameter.

Excised Diameter = greatest clinical diameter of lesion + skin margins

---

Table 2-1 Codes for Removal of Skin Lesions

Technique	Code Range	Brief Description	Documentation	Coding Comments
Paring/cutting	11055–11057	Paring with scalpel	Number of lesions removed	Often performed for corns and calluses.
Shaving of epidermal or dermal lesions	11300–11313	Slicing without full-thickness dermal excision	• Anatomic site • Size	Transverse incision or horizontal slice made through the skin and passes below depth of lesion. Wound does not require suture closure.
Excision—benign lesions	11400–11446	Excision of benign lesions (full thickness through the dermis)	• Morphology as benign • Anatomic site • Size	Includes simple closure. Important to report "excised diameter" of lesion(s).
Excision—malignant lesions	11600–11646	Excision of malignant lesions	• Morphology as malignant • Anatomic site • Size	Includes simple closure. Important to report "excised diameter" of lesion(s).
Destruction—benign or premalignant lesions	17000–17250	Removal by electrosurgery, cryosurgery, laser, or chemical treatment	• Morphology as benign or premalignant • Anatomic site • Number of lesions removed	Many destruction of lesion codes are classified in other chapters by anatomic site. If remnants of lesion are removed (curettement), it is included in the code.
Destruction—malignant lesions, any method	17260–17286	Removal by electrosurgery, cryosurgery, laser, or chemical treatment	• Morphology as malignant • Anatomic site • Number of lesions removed	Many destruction of lesion codes are classified in other chapters by anatomic site. If remnants of lesion are removed (curettement), it is included in the code.

For example, if the physician states that the 3.0 cm malignant lesion of the cheek was excised and there were 0.5 cm margins removed around the diameter of the lesion, coding selection would be based on:

3.0 cm + 0.5 cm + 0.5 cm = 4.0 cm excised diameter of cheek (malignant)

Code assignment: 11646 Excision, malignant lesion, face (4.0 cm)

Reference Chart:

1 mm =	0.1 cm
10 mm =	1.0 cm
0.3937 inch =	1.0 cm
1 inch =	2.54 cm

Each lesion that is excised separately is coded separately. If two lesions are removed with only one excision, then only one excision code is reported. Guidelines for excision of malignant lesions state that, when a frozen section is performed and an additional excision is required (during the same operative episode), only one code is reported. If a re-excision is performed at a subsequent operative episode, then the appropriate code with modifier 58 (staged procedure) is reported.

In some cases, the malignant lesion is removed, and the patient returns to the operating room (OR) at a later day for re-excision for positive margins for malignancy. The re-excision is reported as though it were the original malignant lesion. Report the lesion as malignant even though the pathology report may indicate benign (lack of residual malignant tumor).

Coding Tip:

A common error is for coders to add the sizes of the excised skin lesions and report as one code.

2010 Current Procedural Terminology © 2009 American Medical Association. All Rights Reserved.

Lipomas

A **lipoma** is a fatty benign tumor of the subcutaneous layer of the skin. Lipomas are the most common form of soft tissue tumor. Most lipomas are found on the trunk, thighs, and forearms, although they may be found elsewhere. Accurate code assignment will require review of the documentation to determine how far the physician incised to remove the lipoma. If the lipoma is located within the layers of skin, a code from the integumentary system will be selected. If the lipoma is located deep in the subfascial or submuscular tissues, the appropriate code will come from the musculoskeletal system (*CPT Assistant*, August 2004).

Exercise 2-2: Coding Lesions

Directions: Assign CPT codes to the following procedures. Append CPT/HCPCS Level II modifiers if applicable. Concentrate on application of coding guidelines, and do not focus on sequencing codes or assignment of modifier 51.

1. The physician excises a basal cell carcinoma of the nose (1.0 cm) with skin margins of 0.5 cm around the lesion.

   Code(s) _____

2. A 41-year-old patient has a history of a mole on her back that recently has changed shape and color. A biopsy was performed in the physician's office last week, and it was positive for malignant melanoma. She presents now for excision of the lesion.
   The patient was brought to OR and prepped and draped in sterile fashion. The area around the lesion was infused with 15 cc of 1% lidocaine. The skin was incised, and the incision was carried down in an elliptical fashion around the 1.5 cm melanoma. The margins around the lesion were 0.5 cm. The specimen was sent to the pathology department, and the wound was closed with staples.

   Code(s) _____

3. A patient is seen in the physician's office for a persistent irritation from a skin growth on her left hand. Examination revealed a small pedunculated skin growth (0.5 cm), a condyloma. Liquid nitrogen was applied to remove the lesion.

   Code(s) _____

4. The physician documents in the health record that the 2.0 cm papule of the foot required dermal shaving with electrosurgical feathering to smooth the wound edges.

   Code(s) _____

5. Operative Report

   Preoperative Diagnosis: Lipoma of the right shoulder

   Postoperative Diagnosis: Same

   Procedure: Removal of lipoma

   The patient was taken to OR and prepped and draped in the usual manner. A longitudinal incision was made, centered over the palpable and visible mass, carried down through the skin. The mass was dissected down through the deltoid muscle, down to the level of the subscapulares tendon of the shoulder joint. Mass was dissected free through the muscle-slitting incision. Bleeding was controlled with hemostats and Bovie cautery. Estimated blood loss was 30 cc. The wound was closed with 2-0 chromic gut, subcutaneous layer with 2-0 plain catgut, and skin with 2-0 Dermalon. The patient tolerated the procedure well.

   Code(s) _____

2010 Current Procedural Terminology © 2009 American Medical Association. All Rights Reserved.

Wound Repairs

Wound repairs are classified as simple, intermediate, and complex. To use codes from this section, the wounds would have been repaired utilizing sutures, staples, or tissue adhesives (singly or in combination with adhesive strips). It is important to read the CPT note that appears before code 12001 for coding guidelines.

Adding Repairs

If multiple wounds are repaired and those wounds are in the same classification (simple, intermediate, or complex) *and* from the same anatomical CPT description groupings, then the sum of the repairs are added and reported as one code.

> **EXAMPLE:** Patient required two simple wound repairs: 2.0 cm of chin and 3.0 cm of forehead. Correct code assignment: 12013.

Simple Repair

A **simple wound repair** is a single layer closure. The code selection is dependent on the anatomic site and size of the repair. Documentation should support that the wound was superficial without significant involvement of deeper structures. Some wounds will require only the use of adhesive strips (Steri-Strips) to close the wound. This type of repair is not coded separately and would be included in the Evaluation and Management code of the visit. When a physician removes a lesion, the simple repair is included.

Use of Tissue Adhesives

If the wound is closed with the use of tissue adhesives (only), then Medicare guidelines require use of HCPCS Level II code *G0168, Wound closure utilizing tissue adhesive(s)* instead of the CPT code.

Intermediate Repair

Intermediate wound repair requires a layered closure of one or more deeper layers of subcutaneous tissue and superficial (nonmuscle) fascia, in addition to the skin (epidermal and dermal) closure. If there were documentation that a single closure of a heavily contaminated wound was performed, then this also would be coded as an intermediate repair.

If a lesion is excised and an intermediate wound closure is required, then the wound repair would be coded in addition to the excision of the lesion.

Complex Repair

This type of wound repair requires documentation that supports the coding assignment. Documentation would include more than a layer closure with scar revision, debridement, extensive undermining, stents, or retention sutures.

If a lesion is excised and a **complex wound repair** is required, then the wound repair code would be coded in addition to the excision of the lesion.

Exercise 2-3: Wound Repairs

Directions: Assign CPT codes to the following procedures. Append CPT/HCPCS Level II modifiers if applicable. Concentrate on application of coding guidelines, and do not focus on sequencing codes or assignment of modifier 51.

2010 Current Procedural Terminology © 2009 American Medical Association. All Rights Reserved.

1. A patient is seen in the emergency department (ED) for a 1.0 cm laceration on the distal pad aspect of her right thumb. The wound was anesthetized by digital block with 1.5 cc of 2% lidocaine, as well as some local infiltration of 0.2 cc. The wound was irrigated with 500 cc of sterile and normal saline. It was sutured with two 5-0 simple interrupted Ethilon sutures and then three Steri-Strips with benzoin to approximate the wound edges. Sterile dressing was applied.

   Code(s) _____

2. The patient is presented with a 3.0 cm laceration on the left side of the cheek. The patient was prepped and draped in the usual manner, and local anesthesia of 1% lidocaine was administered. The wound was closed with multiple layers and required extensive cleansing and debridement.

   Code(s) _____

3. A 58-year-old female accidentally stuck her arm through a glass door and suffered several lacerations. The physician performed a 2.5 cm intermediate wound repair of the forearm, a 3.5 cm intermediate wound repair of the elbow, and a 2.5 cm superficial repair of the wrist.

   Code(s) _____

4. Operative Report

   Preoperative Diagnosis: Sebaceous cyst, wrist

   Postoperative Diagnosis: Sebaceous adenoma, dorsum of right palm

   Operation: Excision of lesion of hand, excised diameter (2.0 cm × 0.8 cm × 0.3 cm)

   Procedure: After the patient's right hand was prepped and draped in the usual manner, and after obtaining satisfactory analgesia with infiltration of local anesthesia, an elliptical skin incision was made surrounding the skin lesion. The skin lesion was completely excised with a normal rim of skin. Deep subcutaneous tissue was closed with interrupted 4-0 Dexon; skin approximated with subcuticular 4-0 Dexon. A bandage was applied after application of Neosporin ointment.

   Code(s) _____

5. Emergency Department Record

   A 34-year-old female is seen following an automobile accident. She sustained multiple facial contusions and lacerations, along with scalp lacerations. There were two scalp lacerations totaling 3 cm, which were anesthetized, cleansed, and closed with 4-0 Vicryl. The 15 cm of facial lacerations required an intermediate layered closure of subcutaneous wounds with removal of pieces of glass. The other 10 cm of facial lacerations were cleansed after minimal debridement and closed with 6-0 mild chromic.

   Code(s) _____

Skin Grafts

Skin grafts require transplantation of skin from one location to another. In most circumstances, the patient's own skin is used for the graft to reduce the risk of rejection. Grafts are commonly performed due to trauma (burns, lacerations), infection, and to repair a wide local excision as a result of surgical removal of cancer. Accurate coding assignment will depend on working knowledge of definitions, abstracting key documentation, and application of coding guidelines. Carefully review coding guidelines that appear before codes 14000, 15002, and 15570.

Kinds of Grafts

CPT code descriptions incorporate a variety of terms applicable to skin grafts. Grafts may be anatomically classified (split thickness) or by origin (autograft). The following are common terms associated with skin-grafting procedures:

2010 Current Procedural Terminology © 2009 American Medical Association. All Rights Reserved.

- **Autograft**—tissue transplanted from one site to another on the same individual
- **Allograft** (homograft)—tissue transplanted from one individual to another
- **Dermal autograft**—epidermis and subcutaneous fat have been removed, can be used in place of fascia
- **Epidermal autograft**—consisting primarily of epidermal tissue, including keratinocyte cells but with little dermal tissue
- **Full thickness**—consists of all layers of skin down to fat (see Figure 2-3)
- **Skin replacement**—tissue or graft that permanently replaces lost skin with healthy skin
- **Skin substitute**—biomaterial, engineered tissue or combinations of materials and cells/tissue that can be substituted for skin autograft or allograft
- **Split thickness**—removal of epidermis and very thin portion of the dermis
- **Xenograft** (heterograft)—tissue transplanted from one species to another (pig to human)

Coding for Skin Grafts

Reporting of CPT codes is based on size and location of the _recipient site_. In addition, documentation should support the type of graft (or skin substitute). Calculation of the size of the defect requires the coder to multiply the dimension of the original wound site.

> **EXAMPLE:** Wound measuring 4 cm × 6 cm = 24 sq cm

Adjacent Tissue Transfer or Rearrangement (14000–14061)

This grafting procedure involves transferring healthy sections of skin or tissue to an adjacent wound. The flaps of transferred skin remain connected at one or more of the borders and are moved to cover the nearby defect. Common types of local flaps include Z-plasty, W-plasty, and V-Y plasty. **Adjacent tissue transfer** involves a primary and secondary defect, both of which are repaired during the adjacent tissue transfer procedure. The **primary defect** is the original defect to be closed. The **secondary defect** is created by the movement of tissue necessary to close the primary defect. Both measurements are measured together to determine the code for this type of repair.

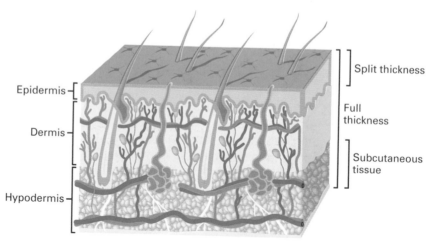

Figure 2-3 Depth of full-thickness and split-thickness cross sections.

2010 Current Procedural Terminology © 2009 American Medical Association. All Rights Reserved.

EXAMPLE: The patient required a skin graft of the hand. The physician used an adjacent tissue transfer from the arm to cover the defect of the hand. The primary defect measured 2.0 sq cm, and the secondary defect measured 4.8 sq cm for a total of 6.8 sq cm. Correct code assignment: 14040.

Excision of Lesion with Adjacent Tissue Transfer

It is important to note that, if the surgeon excises a lesion and subsequently covers the defect with an adjacent tissue transfer, the code of the tissue transfer is the only code assigned. The excision of lesion codes are not separately reportable with codes 14000–14302.

Skin Replacement Surgery and Skin Substitutes (15002–15431)

Preceding the graft codes are a series of surgical preparation codes (15002–15005), which apply to creation of recipient site by excision of open wounds, burn eschar, or scar. Skin grafts may be categorized as pinch, split thickness, full thickness, autograft, allograft, xenograft, or **tissue-cultured skin substitute.**

Epidermal autograft (15110–15116)

Epidermal autografts include the superficial epidermal layer, which is very thin. These grafts are harvested from the patient's own body (autograft).

Dermal autograft (15130–15136)

Dermal autograft procedures involve a deeper layer of skin and are harvested from the patient's own body. Dermal grafts may also be placed using tissue from another human donor (allograft) or in combination with skin replacement products. Reporting codes for this procedure should be selected from the following range: 15130–15136.

Tissue-Cultured Epidermal Autograft (15150–15157)

This range of codes identifies a process where a small piece of skin is harvested, and, from that piece, new skin cells are reproduced in the laboratory. Because the graft is generated from the patient's own skin, rejection is minimized, and doctors can "grow" as much skin as needed to cover the patient's defect. The harvesting process may be reported separately with code 15040. Grafting products that involve only the epidermal layer include CEA, Epicel®, and EpiDex® and are typically used in the treatment of skin ulcers.

Acellular Dermal Replacement (15170–15176)

Acellular dermal replacement grafts involve a synthetic replacement material of dermal-like tissue ("neodermis"). The formation of the neodermis typically takes 14 to 21 days. The outer layer eventually will be removed after the skin has regenerated. The product most commonly used for this type of graft is Integra®.

Full-Thickness Free Skin Grafts (15200–15261)

A free skin graft is distinct from adjacent tissue transfers in that the grafts are unattached from their blood supply (donor site) and reattached to the recipient area. As with most of the graft codes, the descriptions differentiate between size and location.

Allograft Skin for Temporary Wound Closure (15300–15321)

For this coding range, the procedure involves using skin from human cadavers to provide temporary coverage until the skin can be permanently placed over the defect. This procedure is often used to treat full-thickness burns. A common product name is Alloderm®.

2010 Current Procedural Terminology © 2009 American Medical Association. All Rights Reserved.

Allograft/Tissue-Cultured Allogeneic Skin Substitute (15340–15341)

Tissue-cultured allogeneic skin substitute products are produced in the laboratory and contain both a dermal and epidermal layer; the product Apligraf® is commonly used. Code 15340 is assigned for this procedure. This procedure is often used for treatment of noninfected partial- and full-thickness skin ulcers due to venous insufficiency and in the management of diabetic foot ulcers.

If a tissue-cultured allogeneic skin substitute product involves only the dermal layer, a code from 15360–15366 would be reported. This treatment is often used for diabetic foot ulcers, pressure ulcers, and for burn treatment. Common products include Transcyte® and Dermagraft® .

Xenografts (15400–15401)

This procedure applies a nonhuman skin graft or biologic wound dressing. Some common products include E-Z Derm, which is a biosynthetic wound dressing that is porcine derived, and Mediskin, which is a collagen material consisting of fresh, sterile porcine skin.

Acellular Xenogeneic Implant (15430–15431)

These manufactured implants are used to reinforce soft tissue. Common types include Oasis® and Surgisis® , which are decellularized, sterile, freeze-dried porcine small intestinal submucosal tissue.

Excision of Lesion with Reconstructive Repair

Unlike coding guidelines for excision of lesion with adjacent skin graft, if a removal of a lesion creates a defect that requires reconstructive closure (skin replacement or flaps), then both the excision and reconstructive closure codes are assigned.

Pedicle Grafts (15570–15738)

With a **pedicle skin graft,** a portion of the skin used from the donor site will remain attached to the donor area, and the remainder is attached to the recipient site. The blood supply remains intact at the donor location and is not cut loose until the new blood supply has completely developed. This procedure is more likely to be used for hands, face, or neck areas of the body.

Exercise 2-4: Skin Grafts

Directions: Assign CPT codes to the following procedures. Append CPT/HCPCS Level II modifiers if applicable. Concentrate on application of coding guidelines, and do not focus on sequencing codes or assignment of modifier 51.

1. The patient sustained third-degree burns of the legs from a home fire three weeks ago. A small skin graft was harvested during that encounter and submitted for tissue culturing. The patient is now admitted for grafting of the epidermal-cultured tissue (70 sq cm).
   Code(s) _____ 15150, 15155 _____

2. The patient presents with noninfected diabetic foot ulcer that is débrided and cleansed. A total of approximately 30 sq cm of Apligraf® was applied to the wound and sutured in place.
   Code(s) _____

3. Operative Report
   Preoperative Diagnosis: Basal cell carcinoma of right nasal tip
   Postoperative Diagnosis: Basal cell carcinoma, skin of right nasal tip; seborrheic keratosis of skin of right cheek

Procedures: Excision of lesion of the right nasal tip, full-thickness skin graft

This 70-year-old patient had a basal cell carcinoma excised from his nasal tip with bilobed flap closure several years ago. During the past six months, he developed an elevated intermittently ulcerated lesion on the right lower nasal tip in the region of the dome of the alar cartilage. This was separate from the previous area. There were two distinct elevations with increase capillaries present and slight pigmentation. This appears to be basal cell carcinoma. The whole lesion measured about 1.3 cm in diameter. It was felt that a skin graft was needed for coverage. He also had a 0.5 cm keratosis on his right cheek.

Description of Procedure: Under satisfactory premedication, the patient was brought to the OR, and, using a 4½ loupe magnification, the area of planned excision was mapped out. Then 1% Xylocaine with epinephrine was utilized to anesthetize the nasal tip and also the keratosis of the right cheek and right post auricular region. Level of excision was down to the alar cartilage. Specimen was sent for frozen section. The diagnosis of basal cell carcinoma was confirmed. The 0.5 cm excised diameter lesion of the cheek was also excised and sent to pathology. Full-thickness skin graft was then harvested from the right post auricular region. The area was then closed after some cauterization of small bleeder. Closure was with interrupted 4-0 Vicryl and then a running 4-0 Prolene horizontal mattress suture. Graft was defatted and then sewn into position. The length of the graft was 1.5 cm × 1.0 cm. 5-0 nylon was utilized, which was tied down over a Xeroform wet cotton stent. A Band-Aid was placed over the keratosis. The patient tolerated the procedure well and was sent to recovery.

Code(s) _____

Mohs Micrographic Surgery (17311–17315)

Mohs micrographic surgery is an advanced treatment procedure for removal of complex or ill-defined skin cancer. Physicians trained to perform this surgery serve as the surgeon, pathologist, and reconstructive surgeon. With the use of a microscope, the physician removes specimens (tissue blocks) to ensure precise removal of cancerous tissue while preserving healthy tissue. Mohs micrographic surgery codes are reported instead of excision codes (11600–11646 and 17260–17286) and surgical pathology codes.

Coding of Breast Procedures

Coding professionals are advised to review the health record documentation carefully before assigning procedure codes for breast procedures. Procedures include nonsurgical biopsies, surgical biopsies, and mastectomies. The following is a list of common procedures performed for a "suspicious area" in the breast:

Puncture aspiration (19000–19001): Physician inserts a syringe needle into the cyst, and the fluid is evacuated.

Fine needle aspiration (10021–10022): An extremely small needle is inserted through the skin of the breast to remove fluid to cells for analysis.

Needle core biopsy (percutaneous) (19100–19102): A needle removes one or more "cores" of breast tissue.

Biopsy using automated vacuum assisted or rotating device (19103): Biopsy is taken with the use of specialized equipment.

> **Note:**
>
> *Many code selections differentiate between the procedure performed "with imaging" and one that is not.*

Breast Biopsy—Incisional vs. Excisional

Note:

Remember to append modifiers for LT, RT, or 50 for breast procedures.

If the surgeon takes a piece of tissue from a suspicious mass, this procedure is called an incisional biopsy (19101). If the entire lesion is removed, then it is considered an "excision," and the mass is submitted for pathological diagnosis. Careful review of documentation is vital for selection of the correct code. It is not unusual for the surgeon to state that an excisional biopsy was performed when the entire lesion was removed. There are several codes to identify an excision of breast mass (lesion). One of the most common procedures performed for excision of breast tumor (mass, lesion, etc.) is 19120. Note that this code is used for both males and females and should be reported once, regardless of the number of lesions excised through the same incision. If a radiological marker (clip or needle) is inserted preoperatively to assist with the exact location of the "suspicious area," then code 19125 is reported. An add-on code is appropriate to identify each additional lesion (19126). Note that a separate code should be assigned for the actual placement of the radiologic marker (19290–19291).

Exercise 2-5: Breast Procedures

Directions: Assign CPT codes to the following procedures. Append CPT/HCPCS Level II modifiers if applicable. Concentrate on application of coding guidelines, and do not focus on sequencing codes or assignment of modifier 51.

1. Operative Report

Preoperative Diagnosis: Left breast nodule

Postoperative Diagnosis: Left breast nodule

Procedure: Left breast excisional biopsy

Anesthesia: Local anesthesia, 1% Xylocaine plus sedation

The patient was brought to the OR with the dominant nodule noted in the 9:00 o'clock position of the left breast. Because this was persistent and clearly a dominant nodule, the patient was brought to the OR for excisional biopsy.

Under adequate sedation, the left breast was prepped with DuraPrep and sterilely draped. Then 1% Xylocaine plain was infiltrated in the skin and subcutaneous tissues with layered anesthesia; a curvilinear incision was then made in the medial aspect of the left breast, about midway between the areola and border of the breast. This was carried down with dissection with a knife, then electrocautery and a generous portion of breast tissue was removed along with the nodule. Hemostasis was easily achieved with electrocautery, and the wound was closed with 3-0 Vicryl subcutaneous and subcuticular sutures. Benzoin and Steri-Strips were used for skin approximation. The specimen was sent fresh to pathology. The area was dressed with a light sterile dressing. The patient was transferred to recovery in satisfactory condition.

Code(s) _____

2. Operative Report

Preoperative Diagnosis: Right breast calcification on mammogram

Postoperative Diagnosis: Same

Procedure: Right needle localization excision breast calcifications

The patient is a 38-year-old female who presented with mammographic lesions that have increased in size over the six-month period. After discussing the options, benefits, and risks, she elected to proceed with the right needle localized breast biopsy.

Procedure: The patient was placed on the table in supine position. Under IV sedation, the right breast was prepped and draped in the usual fashion. Local was injected into the dermal and deep dermal tissues, and right circumareolar incision was made in the upper outer quadrant of the right breast. Sharp dissection was used dissecting around the tip of the wire. Once this was done, the lesion was sent to radiology, where it was confirmed the lesion was removed. All bleeding was controlled with the use of a Bovie and 3-0 Vicryl suture ligatures. Once the bleeding was controlled, the wound was in the skin. Benzoin and Steri-Strips were placed. Sterile dressing was applied. Frozen section evaluation showed this to be most consistent with fibrocystic tissue. The patient tolerated the procedure well.

Code(s) _____

3. A patient was seen in the physician's office with a lump in the left breast. The physician used a 22-gauge needle for a fine needle analysis of the breast mass. Fluid was aspirated and sent to lab for analysis.

Code(s) _____10021_____

Mastectomy Procedures

There are several codes to identify mastectomy procedures. Coders are encouraged to review the documentation to determine the extent of the excision. See Figure 2-4.

Note the following procedures and descriptions:

Partial Mastectomy (Lumpectomy) (19301–19302): If the surgeon removes a lesion or mass along with adequate surgical margins, this is referred to as a partial mastectomy or lumpectomy.

Simple Complete Mastectomy (19303): Procedure includes removal of all breast tissue, along with a portion of skin and nipple through an elliptical incision. The physician may document a "modified" simple mastectomy, which means the skin and nipple were left intact.

Subcutaneous Mastectomy (19304): This procedure is similar to the simple complete mastectomy except the breast is dissected from the pectoral fascia and from the skin.

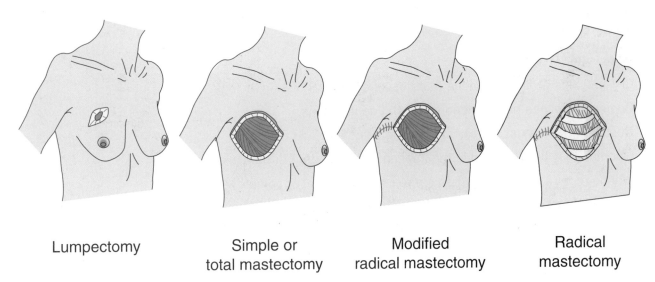

Lumpectomy   Simple or   Modified   Radical
                    total mastectomy   radical mastectomy   mastectomy

Figure 2-4 Types of mastectomy

2010 Current Procedural Terminology © 2009 American Medical Association. All Rights Reserved.

Radical and Modified Radical Mastectomy (19305–19307): Careful review of this coding range reveals variation of the mastectomy procedures. Review documentation in the operative report to determine the extent of the procedure. Note the differences between the code selections

19305 Mastectomy, radical: including pectoral muscles and axillary lymph nodes

19306 Mastectomy, radical: including pectoral muscles, axillary lymph nodes, *and internal mammary lymph nodes* (Urban type operation)

19307 Mastectomy, modified radical: including axillary lymph nodes, with or without pectoralis minor muscle, but *excluding pectoralis major muscle*

> **Note:**
>
> *Each of the mastectomy codes contain an instructional note to guide the coder to assign code 19340 if an implant was inserted at the same surgical session or 19342 if it was performed at a later date.*

Breast Reconstruction

Breast reconstruction is surgery to rebuild a breast's shape after a mastectomy. A variety of reconstructive procedures are performed on patients who have had a mastectomy. The surgeon forms a breast mound by using an implant or tissues from the abdomen, back, or buttocks. Implants are silicone sacs filled with salt water or silicone gel. The type of reconstruction depends on the patient's body type, age, and size of defect. Some of the most common reconstructive procedures are listed below:

Breast Reconstruction with Tissue Expander (19357): A balloon-like device is inserted under the skin near the area to be repaired and then gradually filled with salt water over time, causing the skin to stretch and grow. The time involved in tissue expansion depends on the individual case and the size of the area to be repaired.

Latissimus Dorsi Flap Breast Reconstruction (19361): Physician dissects a portion of the latissimus muscle from the patient's back; the muscle-skin flap remains attached to the main artery and is then rotated to the front of the chest through a tunnel under the patient's armpit so that it extends through to the mastectomy incision.

Transverse Rectus Abdominis Myocutaneous Flap (TRAM) (19367–19369): A muscle-skin flap transfer where the rectus abdominis muscle is divided but kept attached to its blood supply. It is passed through a connecting tunnel between the elevated chest skin and the inferiorly positioned flap. The muscle is contoured to make a breast mound.

Summary

- CPT provides a range of codes that describe removal of skin lesions.
- Coding guidelines are provided within the descriptions.
- Documentation must support the coding selection.
- Lipomas may be classified in the integumentary system or musculoskeletal.
- Wound repairs are described as simple, intermediate, or complex.
- A variety of terms and methods are used for skin grafts.
- Mohs micrographic surgery is a specialized procedure for removing skin cancer.
- Breast procedure codes identify various methods for biopsies, removal of lesions, and mastectomy procedures.

2010 Current Procedural Terminology © 2009 American Medical Association. All Rights Reserved.

Internet Links

American Academmy of Dermatology: *http://www.aad.org*
Click on "Public Center" for links to sites about diseases of the skin.

American Academy of Facial Plastic and Reconstructive Surgery: *http://www.aafprs.org*
Click on "Procedures" for links. Includes a glossary and page featuring common surgical procedures.

American Society of Plastic Surgeons: *http://www.plasticsurgery.org*
Click on "Procedures."

National Cancer Institute: *http://www.cancer.gov*
Follow links from home page for references about common cancer types.

Review

I. Crossword Puzzle

Integumentary System

Across
5. superficial wound repair
6. pig skin
7. partial removal of breast tissue
9. fatty tumor

Down
1. skin from patient's body
2. outer layer of skin
3. malignant skin lesion
4. layered closure
8. removal of breast tissue specimen

2010 Current Procedural Terminology © 2009 American Medical Association. All Rights Reserved.

II. Case Studies

Case Study 2-1: Physician Office Record

This 9-year-old boy fell off his bicycle and sustained three lacerations—one on his left knee, one on his right knee, and one on his left hand. Left knee: 5.5 cm laceration involving deep subcutaneous tissue and fascia, repaired with layered closure using 1% lidocaine local anesthetic Right knee: 7.0 cm laceration repaired under local anesthetic, with a single-layer closure. Left hand: 2.5 cm laceration of the dermis, repaired with simple closure using Dermabond tissue adhesive.

Assessment: Wounds of both knees and left hand requiring suture repair.

Plan: Follow up in 10 days for suture removal. Call office if there are any problems or complications.

Code(s) _____

Case Study 2-2: Operative Report

Diagnosis: Benign lesion, left ring finger (3 cm)

Operation: Excision of lesion of left ring finger and repair of defect

Findings: The patient is a 32-year-old male referred by his dermatologist for treatment of a recurrent lesion of his left ring finger. The patient states that the process began approximately six months ago with a rapidly enlarging lesion, which became tender. This was treated initially with cryotherapy and antibiotics, which resulted in gradual recurrence. This was followed by shave biopsy, which resulted in rapid recurrence and enlargement in size. The risks, benefits, and alternatives to definitive excisional biopsy were therefore discussed with the patient, who has consented to the procedure.

Procedure: The patient was taken to the OR, and the entire left hand was prepped and draped in the usual manner. Adequate anesthesia was achieved through a digital block by depositing approximately 2 cc's of 2% lidocaine near the neurovascular bundles. The lesion was identified and marked within a transverse ellipsoid for an excision. The specimen was excised at the subdermal level with the scalpel. The wound was then irrigated, and hemostasis was restored with electrocautery. The proximal skin flap was then elevated to allow approximation and repair. A dissection was performed over a distance of greater than 1 cm. This allowed advancement of this flap and approximation with minimal tension. The flap was held in position with sutures of 5-0 Vicryl. The wound was then dressed with Xeroform gauze and soft cotton sponges. The finger was immobilized in an aluminum splint secure with tube gauze.

Code(s) _____

Case Study 2-3: Operative Report

Preoperative Diagnosis: Right upper arm lipoma

Postoperative Diagnosis: Right upper arm lipoma

Procedure Performed: Excision of right upper arm lipoma

Indications for Procedure: The patient is a 49-year-old gentleman with a painful mass in the right upper arm, just lateral to the bicep muscle, and he desired removal.

Details: The patient was taken to the operating room and placed on the table in supine position. After monitored anesthesia care with sedation was begun, the patient was prepped and draped in the usual sterile manner. An incision was made in a longitudinal fashion along the upper arm over the 2.0 cm lipoma, which was deep in the subfascia. Bipolar electrocautery was used to obtain hemostasis; a two-layer closure was performed using 3-0 Vicryl for the deep layer and a running Monocryl on the skin. Dermabond was then applied. The patient tolerated the procedure well with no complications. He was discharged to the recovery room awake and in good condition.

Code(s) _____

Case Study 2-4: Operative Report

Preoperative Diagnosis: Neoplasm of left facial region/upper lip, 6 mm in length

Postoperative Diagnosis: Dermal lesion of upper lip

Procedure: Excision of lesion of upper lip with intermediate layered closure

Indications: This 62-year-old female has a history of a residual neoplasm that has been refractory to two prior surgical interventions. The procedure will be performed with frozen sections.

Procedure: Patient was taken to the OR and placed in supine position. After adequate anesthesia and analgesia, the site was marked. After adequate marking, the patient was prepped in normal fashion. Then 1% Xylocaine with 1:100,000 epinephrine was injected. A #15 blade was then used to make an elliptical incision that produced 0.3 cm margins around the lesion. The lesion was removed and sent to the laboratory for frozen section. After wide undermining was performed, the pathology report came back with no evidence of residual tumor. With this, hemostasis was gained with electrocautery. #4-0 Vicryl was used to close the subcutaneous tissues. #5-0 Vicryl was used to aid in closure of the superficial subcutaneous tissues. #6-0 Ethilon was then used to close the skin. Steri-Strips and tincture of benzoin was applied. All instruments and sponge counts were correct. The patient tolerated the procedure well.

Code(s) _____

Case Study 2-5: Operative Report

Preoperative Diagnosis: Left lower leg ulceration

Postoperative Diagnosis: Left lower leg ulceration

Operation: Debridement of ulcer of left leg

The patient was in the operating room under IV sedation and had the left leg prepped with a Betadine scrub. Then 1% Xylocaine was injected into the subcutaneous tissues and surrounding this ulceration, which was a full thickness of the skin with blackened eschar. There was some surrounding cellulitis. There was no obvious abscess. Full thickness of the necrotic skin was excised down to the fascial level. There was bleeding in the capillary level of the fascia. The area was dressed with some antibiotic ointment. Sterile Telfa and 4 × 4's and a Kerlix were placed. The leg was elevated, and she was returned to recovery in satisfactory condition.

Code(s) _____

Case Study 2-6: Emergency Department Record

A 32-year-old machinist is seen for evaluation and treatment of a laceration sustained at work this morning from a piece of sheet metal. The laceration is 5.5 cm long and extends down the ulnar side of the palm to the side of the hand proximally. It is full thickness, extending down through the subcutaneous tissue.

Procedure: The wound was cleansed with Betasept and sterile water. It was then anesthetized with 1% lidocaine and then again cleansed on the inside once anesthesia was achieved. All tissue is viable, and no major blood vessels or nerve injuries are apparent. He did have normal sensation and motion of all fingers prior to receiving the local anesthesia. There were a couple of small subcutaneous blood vessels that were ligated, with 3-0 Vicryl to achieve hemostasis. No tendon injuries were present. The deep layers of the subcutaneous tissue were reapproximated with interrupted 3-0 Vicryl. The skin was closed with 4-0 Prolene sutures and vertical mattress sutures. Antibiotic ointment was placed, and a bulky sterile dressing was applied.

The patient was instructed in wound care and on signs of infection. Discharge instructions were given along with prescription for antibiotic.

Code(s) _____

Case Study 2-7: Operative Report

Preoperative Diagnosis: Open right skin and foot ulcers

Postoperative Diagnosis: Same

Procedure: Split-thickness skin graft, right shin (10 cm × 4½ cm); split-thickness skin graft, right foot (1 cm × 1 cm)

History: The patient is a 95-year-old lady who has had a slow-healing ulcer of the right shin associated with an infection that required a large debridement. Following angioplasty and revascularization, the wound has granulated nicely and is ready for skin grafting. The patient agreed to proceed understanding the risks, benefits, and other options.

2010 Current Procedural Terminology © 2009 American Medical Association. All Rights Reserved.

Technique: The patient was brought to the operating room and placed on the operating table in the supine position. After adequate induction of anesthesia, the right thigh as well as the right shin was prepped and draped in a sterile fashion to include the foot. Debridement was performed to the right shin and foot wounds using a curette. The granulated base looked excellent. The Zimmer valvulotome was then used to harvest a 1 inch wide segment of vein from the right thigh. It was then meshed 1½ to 1. The skin graft was then cut to an approximate size and stapled onto the larger skin wound on the shin. A small piece of the remaining skin was used to cover the wound on the dorsum of the right foot, also stapling this in place. Reston and Adaptic were used for compression, and a clean, sterile, dry compressive dressing was applied. Tegaderm was applied to the right thigh after applying topical adrenaline. The patient was then transferred to the recovery room in stable condition, having tolerated the procedure well.

Code(s) _____

Case Study 2-8: Operative Report

Preoperative Diagnosis: Basal cell carcinoma of the right leg

Postoperative Diagnosis: Basal cell carcinoma of the right leg

Operation: Wide excision of the basal cell carcinoma with frozen section. Closure of the wound by local arrange of tissues. Steri-Strip and Xeroform gauze.

Anesthesia: 1% Xylocaine with 1:100,000 adrenaline local infiltration

Brief History: The patient stated that she developed a lesion over her right leg about a year back. It was very small and has been gradually getting larger. The lesion used to form a scab, and the scab would come off and reform. The lesion was not healing, so she consulted her doctor and was referred to a dermatologist, who did a biopsy. The report was a basal cell carcinoma. She was referred to me for a wide excision.

Examination: Upon examination, there is about a 1.5 cm ulcerated lesion over the right leg. It is soft, nontender, and mobile on the deeper structures. It has a pinkish surface.

Procedure: While the patient was lying supine on the operating table, the right leg and thigh were cleaned with pHisoHex, and sterile drapes were applied. The incision was marked with about 3 mm of margin using a marking pen, and local anesthetic was then infiltrated under the markings. An incision was made with the help of a #15 blade. The incision was deepened down to the subcutaneous level, and the lesion was excised from the subcutaneous level with the help of a #15 blade. The specimen was sent for frozen section, which revealed the margins were clear. Hemostasis was achieved by saline compresses. The wound edges were first aligned in position by advancing from the sites and held up in position using interrupted 5-0 nylon sutures. There were dog ears at each end, and these dog ears were marked with a marking pen and excised with the help of a #15 blade. The remaining wound was then sutured using interrupted 5-0 nylon sutures. The suture line was dressed with one-half inch Steri-Strips, Xeroform gauze, dry gauze, and a cling bandage; dressing was applied. The patient tolerated the procedure well and left the room in good condition.

Code(s) _____

Case Study 2-9: Operative Report

Preoperative Diagnosis: Biopsy-proven malignant melanoma. Clark Level I, right shoulder veoplasm, left heel

Postoperative Diagnosis: Same

Operation:

1. Wide excision of malignant melanoma, Clark Level I, right shoulder with wide undermining, rotation, and advancement flap reconstruction.

2. Excision of left heel pigmented neoplasm, rule out dysplasia verus melanoma with repair.

Procedure: The patient was placed on the operating table in the prone position with the back of the left heel prepped and draped in sterile fashion, utilizing 1% Xylocaine with epinephrine block of the two sites.

The right shoulder lesion was outlined with Brilliant Green in the lines of relaxation, excised in full-thickness fashion down to the fascial level. The excised diameter of the lesion was 6.0 cm × 2.0 cm, including margins. Undermining over the fascial level was then performed with rotation flaps elevated into position and sutured deeply at the fascial level with #5-0 PDS interrupted, #6-0 PDS superficial dermis, and #6-0 PDS running intracuticular on the skin.

My attention was then turned to the left heel, where the pigmented neoplasm was outlined in Brilliant Green; excised diameter 1.8 cm × 0.9 cm × 0.4 cm. Lesion was excised in full-thickness fashion and closed in layers at the non-muscle fascial level and #4-0 black nylon interrupted on the skin.

Code(s) _____

Case Study 2-10: Operative Report

Preoperative Diagnosis: Right breast mass

Postoperative Diagnosis: Same

Operation: Excisional biopsy

Indications: The patient on routine mammogram was noted to have a right mass of concern. The mass was not palpable. Therefore, the patient was scheduled for needle localization biopsy.

Procedure: The patient was brought to the surgery center and then taken to the main operating room. After general endotracheal anesthesia was obtained, the patient was prepped in the usual sterile fashion. Earlier in the morning, the patient had been sent to radiology, where needle localization of the mass in question was performed.

A circumareolar incision was made, and the tissue flap was then raised and carried down toward the wire's entrance through the skin. When the wire was identified, a small Kelly was placed on the wire, and another Kelly over this, and the wire was then pushed through the skin and grasped beneath the skin. Dissection was then carried around the specimen in a posterior fashion. This was done using Metzenbaum scissors. The specimen was then removed. It was noted that the wire was within the specimen that was removed.

The specimen was sent to pathology. Hemostasis was then carefully obtained using electrocautery. After packing the wound and irrigating the wound, electrocautery was once again used to obtain hemostasis. It was noted by radiology that the specimen that was excised contained the area in question. After hemostasis was once again carefully checked, the skin was closed with #4-0 Dexon in a running subcuticular fashion. The patient was extubated in the operating room and transferred to the recovery room in stable condition.

Code(s) _____

3 Musculoskeletal System

Chapter Outline

Key Terms

arthrodesis
bunions
closed reduction
closed treatment

external fixation
exostosis
hallux valgus
internal fixation

meniscectomy
open fracture treatment
open reduction

percutaneous skeletal fixation spinal instrumentation

Chapter Objectives

At the conclusion of this chapter, the student should be able to:

- Correctly identify the anatomical structures of the musculoskeletal system.
- Describe situations when excision of lesions (tumors) is classified to the musculoskeletal system.
- Identify components to the wound exploration codes.
- Differentiate between the various treatments for fractures.
- Distinguish between the codes for arthrodesis.
- Identify characteristics of the techniques for treatment of bunions.
- Differentiate between coding guidelines (CMS vs. AMA) for coding multiple procedures performed during arthroscopic knee surgeries.
- Apply coding guidelines for musculoskeletal system procedures.
- Given a case study, correctly assign CPT codes for surgical cases.

2010 Current Procedural Terminology © 2009 American Medical Association. All Rights Reserved.

General Rule for Referencing Notes

As a general rule, coding professionals need to review the coding guidelines that appear throughout the surgical sections. For example, a long explanatory note appears before code 20000, which provides definitions and references for accurately reporting CPT code assignments.

Introduction

The musculoskeletal system provides form, stability, and movement to the human body. In addition to bones, the system includes muscles, cartilage, tendons, ligaments, joints, and connective tissue. This chapter will focus on common surgical procedures related to incisions, wound exploration, treatment of fractures, bunions, and endoscopic techniques. See Figure 3-1.

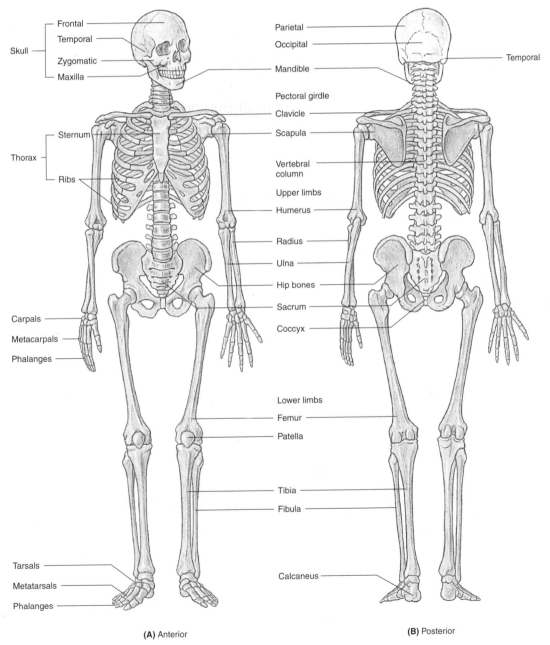

Figure 3-1   The human skeletal system. (A) Anterior view. (B) Posterior view.

2010 Current Procedural Terminology © 2009 American Medical Association. All Rights Reserved.

Incisions

As discussed in the integumentary system chapter, some neoplasms (e.g., lesions, tumors, etc.) may extend into the musculoskeletal system. Documentation in the health record may reveal that the growth was removed (or incised, in the case of an abscess) from the soft, superficial, or deep subcutaneous tissue or subfascial/intramuscular tissue. In this case, the CPT code would be selected from the musculoskeletal system section.

> **EXAMPLE:**
>
> 20000   Incision of soft tissue abscess (e.g., secondary to osteomyelitis); superficial.

Wound Exploration—Trauma (e.g., Penetrating Gunshot, Stab Wound)

Careful examination of the coding guidelines for this range (20100–20103) reveals that documentation should support the following:

- Surgical exploration and enlargement of the wound

- Extension of dissection (used to determine the penetration)

- Debridement

- Removal of foreign bodies (e.g., glass, gravel)

- Ligation or coagulation of minor subcutaneous and/or muscular blood vessels, of the subcutaneous tissue, muscle fascia, and/or muscle, not requiring thoracotomy or laparotomy

Treatment of Fractures

There are a variety of procedures associated with treatment of fractures (broken bones). An accurate code assignment depends on a thorough review of health record documentation to obtain key pieces of documentation, such as the exact location of the fracture and type of treatment. The treatment of a fracture depends upon the type and location of the fracture and if there are any other injuries. As an example, treatment of a fracture or dislocation of the forearm and wrist reveal a code selection of more than 30 codes. In this section, the coder would have to review the documentation to determine:

- What area of the bone was fractured (e.g., both radius and ulna, shaft, and distal radial)? See Figure 3-2.

- What was the treatment (e.g., open, closed, or percutaneous skeletal fixation)?

- Did the treatment include manipulation or not?

It is important to remember that the code assignment should reflect the work and technique performed by the physician. Fracture reduction may be performed by **open** (surgical) or closed (nonsurgical) techniques. The term "reduced" is the technical term that means realigning the bones. The following definitions will provide an overview of the common types of treatment:

Closed Treatment

Closed treatment involves traction, casts, splints, or braces. A **closed reduction** realigns the bone by manipulation (without a surgical incision). The physician pushes the broken bone into position. (See Figure 3-3.) Several CPT codes differentiate between with and without manipulation.

2010 Current Procedural Terminology © 2009 American Medical Association. All Rights Reserved.

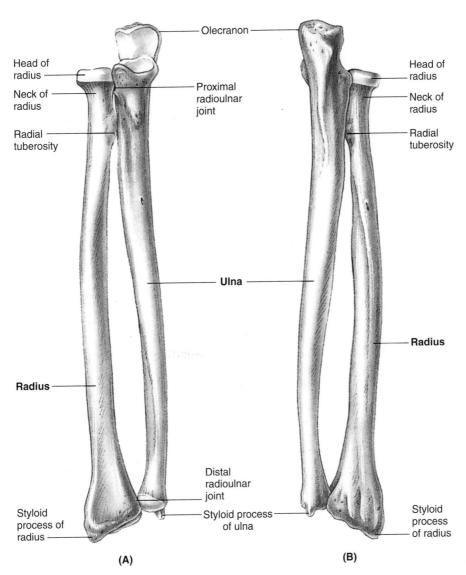

Figure 3-2 Right radius and ulna. (A) Anterior view. (B) Posterior view.

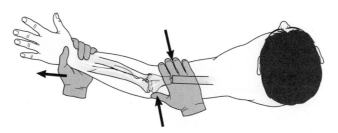

Figure 3-3 Closed manipulation (reduction) of fractured left humerus

Open Treatment with Internal Fixation

The surgical management of a fracture is described as an **open reduction.** The surgeon reduces the fracture into its normal alignment, and then it is held together with the use of internal fixation devices. **Internal fixation** stabilizes and joins the ends of the broken bones with mechanical devices such as metal plates, pins, rods, wires, or screws. (See Figure 3-4.)

2010 Current Procedural Terminology © 2009 American Medical Association. All Rights Reserved.

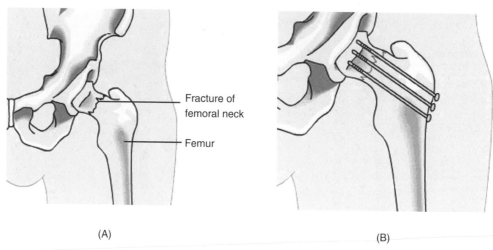

(A)   (B)

Figure 3-4 Internal fixation. (A) Fracture of femoral neck. (B) Internal fixation pins are placed to stabalize the bone; these are not removed.

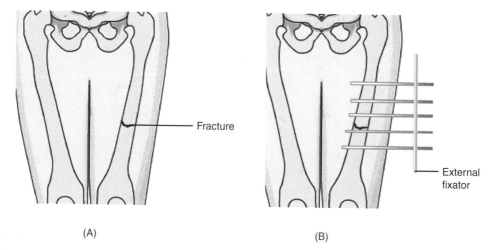

(A)   (B)

Figure 3-5 External fixation. (A) Fracture of femur epiphysis. (B) External fixation stabilizes the bone and is removed after the bone has healed.

External fixation

External fixation is a method of immobilizing bones to allow a fracture to heal. Pins or screws are put through the skin and bone above and below the fracture. These are connected to metal bars on the outside of the skin to form a frame around the fracture. (See Figure 3-5.)

Percutaneous Skeletal Fixation

Percutaneous skeletal fixation is not considered open or closed. With radiologic guidance, the surgeon places a fixation (e.g., pin) across the fracture site.

Bone Grafting

Several coding selections identify "with bone grafting (includes obtaining graft)." If examination of the fracture shows that a quantity of bone has been lost, especially if there is a gap between broken bone ends, the surgeon may elect that a bone graft be performed to avoid delayed healing.

2010 Current Procedural Terminology © 2009 American Medical Association. All Rights Reserved.

Coding for Splinting, Strapping, and Casting Procedures

For CPT coding, guidelines state that strapping and casting services is included in the surgical services and not reported separately. If the service is provided in the emergency department for comfort or stabilizing and the patient is to follow up with another physician for definitive fracture treatment, only the splinting, strapping, or casting code is reported. In this type of situation, do not assign a CPT code for fracture treatment without a reduction. The only time closed treatment is assigned is when the entire fracture treatment is performed during that episode of care, with no reduction planned.

Exercise 3-1: Treatment of Fractures and Wounds

Assign CPT codes to the following procedures. Append CPT/HCPCS Level II modifiers if applicable. Concentrate on application of coding guidelines, and do not focus on sequencing codes or assignment of modifier 51.

1. The patient is diagnosed with a displaced fracture of the proximal end of the right femoral neck. Percutaneously, the surgeon inserts pins to stabilize the fracture. A long leg cast was applied.
   Code(s) _____ 27235 - RT _____

2. The patient is admitted for a nonunion fracture of the left proximal tibia. The surgeon performs an open reduction with bone grafting from the iliac crest.
   Code(s) _____ 27724 - LT _____

3. The surgeon performs an open reduction internal fixation (ORIF) for a Monteggia fracture and application of a splint.
   Code(s) _____ 24635 _____

4. A 14-year-old male is seen in the emergency department (ED) after suffering a left arm injury in a football game. The X-ray reveals a radius shaft fracture. The ED physician applies a short arm splint (static) and instructs the patient to see the orthopedic surgeon tomorrow.
   Code(s) _____ 29125 - LT _____

5. Abstract of emergency department record: Patient seen in the ED following a fight that resulted in a stabbing of his left thigh. The 2" long laceration was deep, penetrating through the skin and fatty tissues. The area was prepped and draped in the usual sterile fashion. The area was anesthetized with 1% Xylocaine. The wound was extended posteriorly as it was opened. A small vessel was suture ligated with 3-0 silk sutures. The wound was explored down to the muscle fascia. The fascia was sutured with three simple sutures of 3-0 Prolene. The wound was then irrigated and subcutaneous simple sutures of 4-0 Vicryl were applied. The skin was closed with interrupted vertical mattress sutures of #5-0 nylon. The wound was treated with Neosporin ointment and bandages. He was referred to his primary care physician for follow-up.
   Code(s) _____ 20103 _____

Surgical Treatment of Spine (Vertebral Column)

The spine is divided into four regions: cervical, thoracic, lumbar, and sacrococcygeal (Figure 3-6).

Arthrodesis

Spine fusion (**arthrodesis**) is a surgical procedure that joins, or fuses, two or more vertebrae. The procedure is often performed to stabilize the spine after a traumatic injury, infection, or tumor. During the procedure, bone is taken from the pelvic bone or from a bone bank. The bone is used to make a bridge

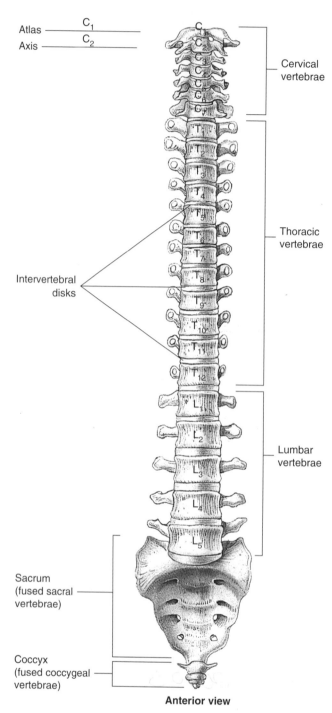

Atlas ——— C₁
Axis ——— C₂

Cervical vertebrae

Thoracic vertebrae

Intervertebral disks

Lumbar vertebrae

Sacrum
(fused sacral vertebrae)

Coccyx
(fused coccygeal vertebrae)

Anterior view

Figure 3-6 The vertebral column

between adjacent vertebrae. For coding purposes, bone-grafting procedures are reported separately and in addition to arthrodesis (20930–20938).

Arthrodesis codes are classified by the anatomical approach used and the technique used to accomplish the fusion.

Approach for Arthrodesis Procedures	Range of Codes
Anterior or anterolateral approach technique	22548–22585
Posterior, posterolateral, or lateral transverse process technique	22590–22632

2010 Current Procedural Terminology © 2009 American Medical Association. All Rights Reserved.

Spinal Instrumentation

Spinal instrumentation utilizes surgical procedures to implant devices into the spine to provide stability. Types of devices include rods, hooks, braided cable, plates, screws, and threaded interbody cages. Instrumentation codes are reported separately and in addition to arthrodesis (22840–22848 and 22851).

Exercise 3-2: Spinal Surgery

Assign CPT codes to the following procedures. Append CPT/HCPCS Level II modifiers if applicable. Concentrate on application of coding guidelines, and do not focus on sequencing codes or assignment of modifier 51.

1. The surgeon performs a posterior arthrodesis of L5-S1 for degenerative disc disease utilizing morselized autogenous iliac bone graft harvest through a separate fascial incision. Threaded cylindrical titanium intervertebral cage used for spinal instrumentation.

Code(s) _____

2. A two-level posterior lumbar interbody fusion with cages L4-L5 and L5-S1. During the procedure, bone was harvested from the iliac crest (morselized).

Code(s) _____

Treatment of Bunions

Bunions are a bony protuberance at the base of the big toe. (See Figure 3-7.) As a result of the bunion, the big toe angles toward the other toes and causes a condition called **hallux valgus.** Due to the new angulation of the toe, inflammatory changes cause pain. The deformity is worsened as the metatarsal bone grows a bony protrusion (**exostosis**), and the tendons may eventually become tight, adding to the pain.

For surgical intervention, a simple resection requires the bony protuberance on the side of the metatarsal bone to be shaved off. See Figure 3-8.

Further review of the range of surgical treatment of bunion codes (28290–28299) reveals progressively more complex procedures. All of the CPT codes include (as an integral part of the main procedure) capsulotomy, arthrotomy, synovial biopsy, synovectomy, tendon release, tenotomy, tenolysis,

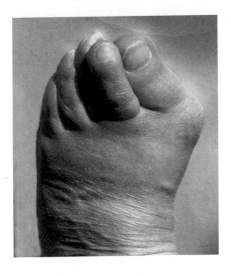

Figure 3-7 Bunion

2010 Current Procedural Terminology © 2009 American Medical Association. All Rights Reserved.

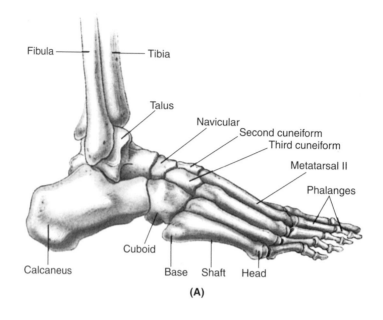

(A)

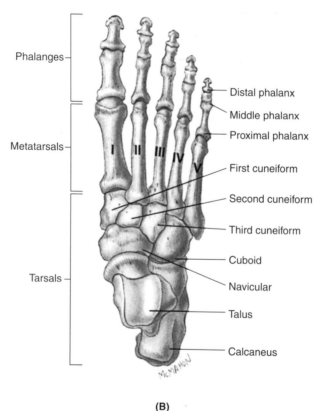

(B)

Figure 3-8 (A) Right ankle and foot, lateral view. (B) Right ankle and foot, superior view.

excision of medial eminence, excision of associated osteophytes, placement of internal fixation, scar revision, articular shaving, and removal of bursal tissue when performed at the first MTP joint. The following is a summary of key documentation to distinguish between the procedures:

- **Simple Exostectomy (28290):** Phalangeal osteotomy to correct deformity.

- **Keller (McBride or Mayo) Procedure (28292):** Keller is a simple resection of the base of the proximal phalanx with removal of the medial eminence. McBride includes a distal soft tissue release. A resection of metatarsal head (Mayo) is rarely performed for bunions.

2010 Current Procedural Terminology © 2009 American Medical Association. All Rights Reserved.

- **Keller-Mayo Procedure with Implant (28293):** Resection of all or half of metatarsophalangeal joint with insertion of double- or single-stemmed implant.

- **Joplin Procedure (29294):** Includes tendon transplants.

- **Metatarsal Osteotomy (Mitchell, Chevron, or Concentric Type Procedures) (29296):** Mitchell includes a distal metatarsal osteotomy performed through the neck of the first metatarsal. Distal chevron or concentric osteotomy combines the transverse osteotomy in the coronal plane of the metatarsal neck to lateralize the head. Documentation may also include insertion of bone graft and angle tendon lengthening. An Austin technique is also included in this code.

- **Lapidus-Type Procedure (28297):** This procedure includes a distal soft tissue rearrangement.

- **Phalanx Osteotomy (28298):** This procedure includes removal of a medially based bony wedge from the base of the proximal phalanx to reorient its axis. It is the preferred procedure for hallus valgus interphalangeus.

- **Double Osteotomy (28299):** Includes double osteotomy of first metatarsal or metatarsal and proximal phalanx. Procedure is performed for severe hallus valgus.

Arthroscopic Meniscectomy of Knee

The cartilage attached to (serving as connecting material) between the femur and the tibia/fibula is called meniscus. The lateral (outer) and medial (inner) menisci provide structural integrity to the knee. An abrupt turn or sudden blow can cause a tear (see Figure 3-9).

Arthroscopy permits the surgeon to either repair or remove the damaged meniscus. CPT codes differentiate between the excision (**meniscectomy**) and meniscus repair, in addition to the identification of medial and/or lateral. In certain circumstances, the surgeon may need to perform arthroscopic procedures in different compartments of the same knee during the same operative session. For example, if the surgeon performs an arthroscopic medial meniscectomy and debrides the area in the patella, a coding assignment of 29881 (arthroscopic meniscectomy) and 29877 (arthroscopic debridement) would be appropriate since the debridement occurred in a different compartment. However, CMS guidelines differ. CMS has created an HCPCS Level II add-on code:

```
G0289   Arthroscopy, knee, surgical, for removal of loose body, foreign body,
        debridement/shaving of articular cartilage (chondroplasty) at the time
        of other surgical knee arthroscopy in a different compartment of the
        same knee.
```

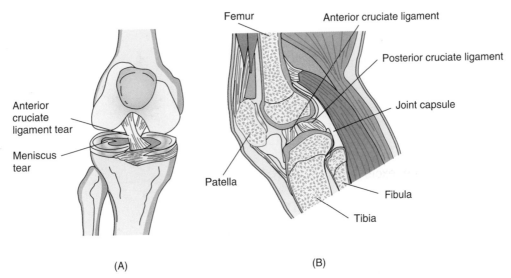

(A)   (B)

Figure 3-9 (A) Meniscus and anterior cruciate ligament tears. (B) Knee joint.

2010 Current Procedural Terminology © 2009 American Medical Association. All Rights Reserved.

CMS further defines use of this code by stating it can only be reported once per compartment (maximum of two), and it should only be reported when the physician spends at least 15 minutes in the additional compartment.

Exercise 3-3: Bunion Surgery and Arthroscopy Procedures

Assign CPT codes to the following procedures. Append CPT/HCPCS Level II modifiers if applicable. Concentrate on application of coding guidelines, and do not focus on sequencing codes or assignment of modifier 51.

1. Surgeon performs a bunionectomy procedure that resulted in resection of a portion of the medial eminence. The metatarsal neck was osteomized in a chevron fashion.
Code(s) _____

2. The surgeon performs an arthroscopy of the shoulder with partial synovectomy.
Code(s) _____

3. The patient (with Medicare insurance) undergoes an arthroscopic medial meniscectomy with extensive debridement of the lateral compartment, which takes 20 minutes.
Code(s) _____

Summary

- Some excision of skin lesions are classified to the musculoskeletal system section.

- A detailed criterion establishes the use of wound exploration codes.

- A variety of fracture treatment codes exists, and the selection is based on technique, anatomic site, and situation surrounding the treatment.

- Strapping, splinting, and casting is included in the surgical procedure codes.

- Arthrodesis codes are differentiated by surgical approach.

- Bunion procedures are differentiated by the surgical technique.

- Guidelines differ (AMA vs. CMS) for meniscectomy procedures of the knee when they are performed in addition to other surgical treatment in a different compartment of the same knee.

Internet Links

American Academy of Orthopaedic Surgeons: *http://www.aaos.org*
Click "Patient Information"

Medline Plus: *http://www.nlm.nih.gov/medlineplus/tutorials/kneearthroscopy/htm/index.htm*
Interactive tutorial for knee arthroscopy

Review

I. Medical Terminology Assessment

Match the following terms with the correct definition.

_____**1.** Patella

_____**2.** Metatarsals

A. bones of foot

B. thigh bone

_____3. Medial malleolus

_____4. Femur

_____5. Carpals

_____6. Metacarpals

C. wrist bones

D. kneecap

E. bones of hand

F. ankle bone

II. Case Studies

Case Study 3-1: Emergency Department Record

Chief Complaint: Injury to right fourth and fifth toes

History of Present Illness: Patient states that he was running for the phone, and he stubbed his toes on a piece of furniture. Did this yesterday and has marked ecchymosis noted in the fourth and fifth toes of the right foot, slight swelling also. He states he has been able to ambulate and that his foot does not hurt except for when he walks. He denies any numbness, tingling, or loss of sensation. He also has an abrasion noted to the distal aspect of the fourth toe. He denies any further injury.

Past Medical History: Noncontributory

Allergies: Patient has no known medication allergies.

Current medications: None

Review of Systems: Negative

Vital signs: Blood pressure, 145/89. Temperature, 97.7. Pulse, 76. Respirations, 16.

General: Patient is alert, oriented, and in no acute distress.

Extremities: Shows marked ecchymosis noted in the fourth and fifth toes and in the dorsal aspect of the foot adjacent to the fourth and fifth toes on the right foot. The patient is tender to palpation over the fourth and fifth digits proximal. Right foot is neurovascularly intact. Sensation is intact. Patient has an abrasion noted to the distal aspect of the right fourth digit. Range of motion is intact. Patient is able to ambulate with a slight limp due to pain. Remainder of physical exam is normal.

Emergency Department Course: An X-ray was taken and revealed a fracture of the fourth and fifth proximal phalanx. The patient's right fourth and fifth toes were digitally blocked with 2.5 cc of 2% lidocaine each. Fractures were reduced in the fourth and fifth digits and buddy taped. His post reduction film showed that the fractures were in better alignment. Patient was fitted for a post-op shoe.

Plan: Rest, ice, buddy tape for two weeks, elevate foot, and follow up with family medical doctor if needed. Disposition: Home.

Code(s) _____

2010 Current Procedural Terminology © 2009 American Medical Association. All Rights Reserved.

Case Study 3-2: Operative Report

Preoperative Diagnosis: Internal derangement medial meniscus, tear, and degenerative changes

Postoperative Diagnosis: Internal derangement medial meniscus, tear, and degenerative changes

Procedure: Arthroscopic debridement, partial medial meniscectomy

Clinical Note: This patient is a 70-year-old male who we have been following for some time with arthritic left knee. We have treated him with anti-inflammatories, physical therapy, and injections of cortisone. None of these have been helpful; therefore, he comes for an arthroscopic evaluation.

Procedure: The patient was brought to the operating room, and, once general anesthesia was obtained, 2 gram IV Kefzol was given, and his knee was prepped and draped in a sterile fashion. The arthroscope was introduced in the lateral portal after medial inflow cannula had been established, and the diagnostic procedure began. The under surface of the kneecap had a significant plical region, which was debrided for approximately 25 minutes. The femoral trochlea was much more damaged with grade III–IV full thickness loss of cartilage. It was debrided down to stable surfaces. The lateral joint line was viewed. He had some degenerative fraying of the lateral meniscus, and the lateral femoral condyle and tibial plateau also had some grade I-II changes, but nothing significant. The medial side had a significant degenerative medial meniscus tear. All surfaces were debrided down to the cartilaginous borders. Partial medial meniscectomy was performed with mechanical and handheld instruments. The knee was irrigated, and then the wounds were closed with nylon. The patient tolerated the procedure well.

Code(s) _____

Case Study 3-3: Operative Report

Preoperative Diagnosis: Left hand infection

Postoperative Diagnosis: Left hand infection

Indications: The patient is a 63-year-old farmer who got stuck in the hand by a tobacco stick four days previously. He removed what he thought was all of the splinter, but he subsequently developed swelling, pain, and fluctuance around the site of insertion, which was at the base of the fourth finger and into the third and fourth web spaces. He presented to the ED and had stab wound drainage with return of purulence. He was splinted and elevated and put on IV antibiotics. He was much improved from initial exam but continued to have erythema, edema, tenderness, and some fluctuance. He was brought to the operating room for formal irrigation and debridement.

Description of Procedure: After adequate anesthesia by mask was obtained, the left arm was placed on an arm table and a nonsterile tourniquet was placed over Webril on the left upper arm. The hand and arm were prepped and draped in the normal sterile fashion. The arm was held in an elevated position, and the tourniquet was put up to a pressure of 250 mmHg. The area of fluctuance was just proximal to the base of the fourth finger on the palmar side with extensions into the third and fourth web spaces and also edema dorsally. There was a drainage spot on the base of the fourth finger as well as one in the fourth web space. These were opened with a hemostat. The incisions were both extended with a knife. The wounds were easily opened merely by spreading the tissue bluntly. There was a return of a large amount of purulence. Cultures were taken. Dissection was carried out in all directions to release the purulence,

2010 Current Procedural Terminology © 2009 American Medical Association. All Rights Reserved.

including extensions in the dorsal direction. Wounds were irrigated with a total of 3 liters of irrigation using a Pulsavac system of irrigation. The wounds were then cleaned, and there were no remaining signs of purulence. There was, however, tissue and questionable viability as well as some dead skin. Grossly dead skin and tissue was debrided. The flexor tendon sheath of the fourth finger was located. There was no purulence expressed from it. Wounds were again irrigated. The wounds were packed with plain 1-inch new gauze. Fluff cotton dressings were placed over the hand and in between the fingers. The hand and arm were wrapped in Webril and then a volar plaster splint was placed and wrapped in place with an Ace wrap. The tourniquet was left down at the end of the case. The patient was sent to the recovery room in satisfactory condition.

Code(s) _____

Case Study 3-4: Operative Report

Preoperative Diagnosis: Sebaceous cyst, right posterior neck

Postoperative Diagnosis: Lipomatous lesion, approximately 1.5 cm right posterior neck, intramuscular

Procedure: Excision of lipoma, right neck

Procedure: The patient was brought to the operating suite and was placed in prone position on the operating table. The patient's right neck was prepped and draped in a sterile fashion. At this point, we suspected the patient to have a cyst. We subsequently decided to do a circumferential incision. The incision was marked, the area was draped, and a local anesthetic was used. The skin incision was made and carried down to the subcutaneous tissue. At this point, we recognized that this was not a cyst but a lipoma, which was actually deep into the muscle area. We excised down through the capsule of the lipoma, and then we were able to harvest this from its capsule within the muscle fibers. This was done with sharp dissection. Bleeding was controlled with cautery. The wound was then closed with 3-0 Vicryl subcutaneous sutures, and then a 4-0 Vicryl subcuticular stitch was placed. Wound edges were painted with benzoin, and Steri-Strips were applied. The patient tolerated the procedure well.

Code(s) _____

Case Study 3-5: Operative Report

Preoperative Diagnosis: Fracture of proximal shaft of left fifth digit

Postoperative Diagnosis: Fracture of proximal shaft of left fifth digit

Operation Performed: Open reduction and internal fixation using Kirschner wires of fracture, proximal phalanx

Details: Patient was transferred to the bed in a supine position. An ulnar block was performed, and his arm was then prepped and draped in the usual sterile fashion. A sterile tourniquet was placed and was inflated to 250 mm of pressure. Additional local 1% lidocaine without epi was injected for a total of 20 cc for the ulnar block. An incision was made along the lateral aspect of the left fifth digit from the PIP just proximal to the MCP. The extensor tendon was retracted away from the site of the fracture, and dissection was then carried down to the fracture site. Using periosteal elevator, the callus and periosteum were elevated around the site of the fracture. An Aaron saw was then used to clean up the splintered edges of the fracture site, both proximally and distally. A towel clip was used to stabilize the proximal portion of the proximal phalanx, and the fracture site was reduced. Once it was clear that an adequate reduction was possible, a K wire was placed through the proximal or through the distal portion of the fractured bone, the fracture was reduced, and K wires were then advanced proximally into the proximal portion of the P1 and through the MCP into the fifth metacarpal. Wires were clipped and capped after the reduction was assessed and found to be a good reduction of the fracture. Electrocautery was used at that point to attain hemostasis, and the wound was closed using #5-0 nylon. Alternating mattress and simple sutures were used to close the skin. Bacitracin and Adaptic were placed over the incision site, followed by Kling, and then a Webril and a splint were placed. He was transferred to recovery in satisfactory condition.

Code(s) _____

Case Study 3-6: Operative Report

Preoperative Diagnosis: Left distal radius fracture

Postoperative Diagnosis: Left distal radius fracture

Operation: Open reduction with internal fixation of the left wrist with Grafton bone grafting

Procedure: The patient was brought to the operating room and underwent general anesthesia. He was placed on the operating room table in the supine position with an armrest. A pneumatic tourniquet was applied to the left upper arm. The arm was scrubbed with Betadine followed by Betadine paint and draped sterilely. An Esmarch tourniquet was used to exsanguinate the limb. The pneumatic tourniquet was inflated to 250 mm of mercury. Total tourniquet time for this case was 58 minutes.

A dorsal incision was made over the distal forearm with dissection carried to the third dorsal compartment, and the EPL muscle and tendon were retracted radially.

The fracture was exposed subperiosteally and was reduced and held with a bone holding clamp and then was internally fixed with a spoon type plate or dorsal buttress plate. The plate was attached proximally with cortical bone screws distally with cancellous screws and was bone grafted using Grafton. Then the wound was irrigated and closed with #2-0 Vicryl in the subcutaneous and staples in the skin.

Code(s) _____

Case Study 3-7: Operative Report

Preoperative Diagnosis: Hallux abductovalgus with bunion deformity, left foot

Postoperative Diagnosis: Hallus abductovalgus with bunion deformity, left foot

Operative Procedure: McBride type bunionectomy, left foot

Indications: The patient has been bothered by bunion deformity for more than years, getting progressively worse to the point where she is unable to tolerate shoe gear for long periods of time. She has tried conservative treatment but wishes to have surgical intervention.

Procedure: The patient was brought to the operating room and placed on the operating table in supine position. Anesthesia is accomplished, and the patient's left foot is then prepped and draped in the usual sterile manner. The foot is elevated, exsanguinated with an Esmarch. Ankle tourniquet is inflated to 250 mmHg. Attention was then directed to the first metatarsophalangeal joint where a serpentine incision approximately 4 cm is made dorsally. Incision is carried down to the level of the joint capsule with care being taken to ligate and retract all vital structures. First interspace is entered. Abductor muscle belly is tenotomized along with a section of the extensor hallucis brevis removed in toto. Attention was then directed back medially. An inverted L type capsulotomy was performed. Capsular tissue was reflected, exposing the hypertrophied medial eminence. This is then removed in toto utilizing oscillating equipment. Foot is rasped smooth both dorsally and medially, utilizing the oscillating rasp and rongeured dorsally. It is noted to be completely smoothed. It is copiously flushed. Capsulorrhaphy is accomplished on the medial ring of the capsule. Capsular tissue is reposed utilizing 3-0 Vicryl. Subcutaneous tissue is reposed utilizing 4-0 Vicryl, and skin is reposed utilizing skin staples. The area is dressed with Xeroform, Betadine soaked 4 x 4 fluff, cling, and mildly compressive dressing. The ankle tourniquet is deflated, and normal pink color is noted to return to all five digits of the left foot. The patient tolerated the procedure well.

Code(s) _____

Case Study 3-8: Operative Report

Preoperative Diagnosis: Right knee degenerative joint disease with medial and lateral meniscal tears

Postoperative Diagnosis: Right knee degenerative joint disease with medial and lateral meniscal tears

Operation: Right knee arthroscopy, partial medial and lateral meniscectomy

Arthroscopic findings:

1. Patellofemoral. Grade 3 changes of the patellofemoral joint.

2. Medial joint. There were grade 3 changes of the entire medial femoral condyle. There was large posterior horn medial meniscal tear.

3. Intercondylar notch. Normal appearance to the ACL.

4. Lateral joint. There were grade 3 changes of the lateral femoral condyle with a small tear in the central portion of the lateral meniscus.

Indications for Operation: This 64-year-old gentleman has degenerative joint disease involving the right knee. He has had significant knee pain and documented medial and lateral meniscus tears. Arthroscopic intervention was therefore indicated for debridement of the meniscus.

Details of Procedure: The patient was taken to the operating room and placed in the supine position. After adequate general anesthesia had been obtained, the tourniquet was placed around the right proximal thigh and inflated to 300 mmHg. The leg was then placed in a well-padded leg holder and prepped and draped in the usual sterile fashion.

2010 Current Procedural Terminology © 2009 American Medical Association. All Rights Reserved.

Using the standard anterior, medial, and lateral intrapatellar portals, the knee was examined, and the above-mentioned findings was noted. Attention was first placed on the medial meniscus. Using a combination of straight biter and 4.5 full radius shaver, the posterior horn of the medial meniscus was debrided back to the stable base. There were grade 3 changes of the entire medial femoral condyle. This was gently debrided with the 4.5 full radius shaver so there were no loose or frayed cartilaginous fragments within the joint.

Attention was then placed on the lateral meniscus. Using a combination of straight basket and 4.5 full radium shaver, the lateral meniscus was debrided back to a stable base. The knee was then copiously irrigated with Ringer's lactate. The incisions were closed with 4-0 nylon interrupted suture. The knee was then injected with 30 cc of 0.5% Marcaine solution. The closed skin incisions were covered with Adaptic, sterile gauze, sterile Webril, an Ace wrap and Berg ice wrap. The patient was then extubated and transferred to recovery room.

Code(s) _____

Case Study 3-9: Emergency Department Record

This 14-year-old gymnast felt pain in her left leg after vaulting at practice. She is unable to bear any weight on her left leg. Impression: Left fibular fracture.

Physical examination revealed foot and ankle to be normal. The neurovascular status of the foot is normal. The ankle is nontender and not swollen. Findings are confined to the distal fibula, two inches proximal to the lateral malleolus. There is point tenderness in this area. X-ray of the tibia and fibula shows a displaced fracture of the distal fibula.

The closed treatment of the fracture was reduced, and the patient was put in a short leg splint with extensive padding placed over the fracture site. Crutches were provided, and she is instructed not to place any weight on the foot. She was given Tylenol #3 for the pain and told to follow up with her doctor in 10 days.

Code(s) _____

Respiratory System

Chapter Outline

Introduction
Nose
Sinus Endoscopy

Laryngoscopy
Bronchoscopy
Lungs and Pleura

Key Terms

bronchial biopsy
bronchioles
bronchus
direct laryngoscopy
ethmoid
flexible fiberoptic
  laryngoscopy
frontal sinuses

indirect laryngoscopy
inferior turbinates
laryngoscopy
larnyx
lobectomy
maxillary sinuses
middle turbinates
pharynx

pleura
pneumonectomy
pneumocentesis
segment resection
sphenoid sinus
superior turbinates
thoracentesis
thorax

trachea
transbronchial biopsy
transbronchial needle
  biopsy
turbinates
wedge resection

Chapter Objectives

At the conclusion of this chapter, the student should be able to:

- Differentiate between coding guidelines for inferior and superior or middle turbinates.
- Describe the organization of diagnostic and surgical codes for sinus endoscopies.
- Define indirect, direct, and flexible fiberoptic laryngoscopy.
- Distinguish between the biopsy codes for endoscopic bronchoscopy procedures.
- Distinguish between a segmental and wedge resection of the lung.
- Given a case scenario, accurately assign CPT codes and modifiers (if applicable).

2010 Current Procedural Terminology © 2009 American Medical Association. All Rights Reserved.

Introduction

The main function of the respiratory system is to supply the blood with oxygen to deliver throughout the body. The respiratory system consists of the nasal cavity, **pharynx** (throat), **larynx** (voice box), **trachea** (windpipe), bronchi, and lungs (Figure 4-1).

This chapter will highlight the most common surgical procedures associated with the respiratory system.

Nose

The inside of both the internal and external nose is divided into right and left nasal cavities by a partition called the nasal septum. The center area of the nasal cavity contains three pairs of turbinate bones. **Turbinates** consist of bone covered by soft tissue membrane, or mucosa (conchae). The **inferior turbinates** articulates with the ethmoid, lacrimal bone, maxilla, and palate. The **middle** and **superior turbinates** are part of the ethmoidal labyrinth (bone) protruding from the lateral wall of the nasal cavity. Patients seek treatment for enlarged turbinates (hypertrophy) and chronic infections.

> **Note:**
>
> *Submucous resection of nasal septum is reported with code 30520 and should not be confused with submucous resection of the inferior turbinates.*

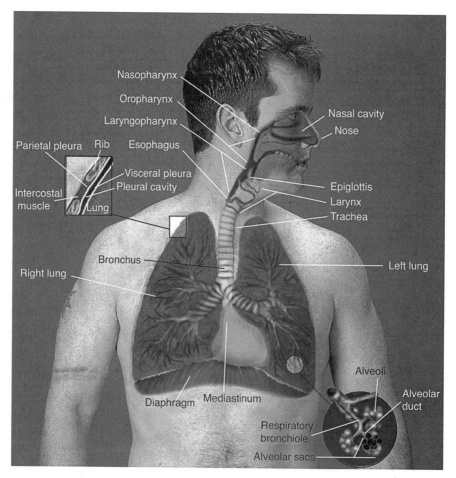

Figure 4-1 Respiratory system

2010 Current Procedural Terminology © 2009 American Medical Association. All Rights Reserved.

CPT codes 30130 (excision) and 30140 (submucous resection) are for surgical excision of inferior turbinates. In addition, codes 30801–30802 identify cautery and ablation of inferior turbinates. It is important to note several coding guidelines that appear after code 30140. Note that submucous resection or excision of superior or middle turbinates is reported with an unlisted code (30999). If the middle or superior turbinates are excised via endoscopic approach, then the sinus endoscopy codes (31254–31255) are appropriate.

> **Note:**
> Codes 30130 and 30140 are considered unilateral; therefore, modifier 50 would be reported for a bilateral procedure.

Documentation for submucous resection of inferior turbinate (code 30140) should reflect that the surgeon entered or incised the mucosa while removing or reducing a portion of the underlying bone.

Sinus Endoscopy

Endoscopic procedures of the sinuses are used to remove blockages due to infections, polyps, and tumors. There are four main sinus openings:

- **Maxillary**—in the cheekbones
- **Ethmoid**—between the eye sockets
- **Frontal**—in the forehead and above the eyebrows
- **Sphenoid**—deep in the head at the back of the nose (Figure 4-2)

The CPT code selection can be differentiated by diagnostic procedures (31231–31235) and surgical procedures (31237–31294). Coding professionals should carefully review the documentation (operative report) for detailed information about the procedures performed and sinuses explored. CPT coding guidelines state that any time a diagnostic endoscopic evaluation is performed on all the sinus/nasal areas, a separate code is not reported for each area.

> **Note:**
> Sinus endoscopy codes (31233–31294) are considered unilateral; therefore, modifier 50 would be reported for a bilateral procedure.

EXAMPLE: The surgeon performed a sinus endoscopy, which included removal of a polyp in the frontal sinus. Code 31267 would be reported.

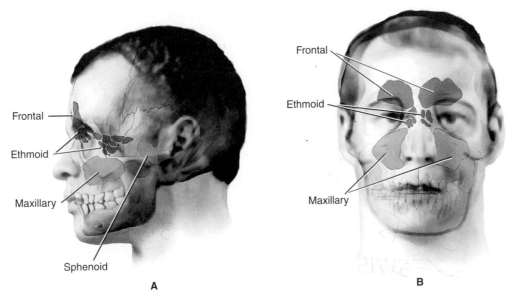

Figure 4-2 Paranasal sinuses. (A) Lateral view. (B) Anterior view.

2010 Current Procedural Terminology © 2009 American Medical Association. All Rights Reserved.

Exercise 4-1: Nasal Endoscopy Procedures

Assign CPT codes to the following procedures. Append CPT/HCPCS Level II modifiers if applicable. Concentrate on application of coding guidelines, and do not focus on sequencing codes or assignment of modifier 51.

1. The surgeon performs a bilateral endoscopic exploration of the nasal cavity.
Code(s) _____ 31231 ~~-50~~

2. The surgeon performs a bilateral nasal endoscopy with anterior and posterior ethmoidectomy.
Code(s) _____ 31255 -50

3. The surgeon performs a left nasal endoscopy with incision into the sphenoid for removal of a polyp.
Code(s) _____ 31288 - LT

Laryngoscopy

Laryngoscopy is an examination of the back of the throat, voice box (larynx), and vocal cords. CPT codes differentiate among three types of laryngoscopy procedures:

- **Indirect** (31505–31513): The physician uses a small hand mirror and a light to visualize areas of the throat and voice box. This procedure is typically performed in the doctor's office.

- **Direct** (31515–31571): With the use of a scope (flexible or rigid), the physician performs the endoscopic procedure.

- **Flexible fiberoptic** (31575–31579): The endoscopic procedure is performed with a thin, flexible instrument that contains fiberoptic cable that can be manipulated to examine areas not normally seen in traditional examination techniques.

  EXAMPLE: The surgeon performs a direct laryngoscopy to remove a piece of wire. The correct coding assignment is 31530.

> **Note:**
>
> Many laryngoscopy codes make reference to use of an operating microscope or telescope (e.g., 31531). The use of this technique helps the surgeon to visualize small or inaccessible parts of the body. Coding professionals should carefully review the body of the operative report for use of this equipment.

Exercise 4-2: Laryngoscopy Procedures

Assign CPT codes to the following procedures. Append CPT/HCPCS Level II modifiers if applicable. Concentrate on application of coding guidelines, and do not focus on sequencing codes or assignment of modifier 51.

1. Physician's office record: With the use of a laryngoscopic mirror, a biopsy of the vocal cord was performed.
Code(s) _____

2. With the use of an operating microscope, the surgeon removed a lesion from the vocal cord.
Code(s) _____ 31545 31541 ?

3. The surgeon performed a flexible fiberoptic laryngoscopy to diagnose the source of chronic hoarseness.
Code(s) _____

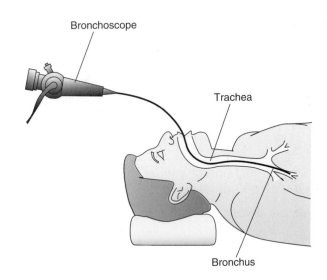

Figure 4-3 Bronchoscopy

Bronchoscopy

This endoscopic procedure permits the physician to view the throat, larynx, trachea, and lower airway via a long, thin, lighted tube (Figure 4-3). Each lung has one large bronchus, connecting it to the trachea. The **bronchus** is an airway in the respiratory tract where air travels into the lungs. Within the lung, the bronchus branches into smaller and smaller bronchi and finally into **bronchioles**. Several code ranges identify biopsy procedures:

- **Bronchial/endobronchial biopsy** (31625): A sample is removed from the bronchus or endobronchial tissue.

- **Transbronchial biopsy** (31628): Through the scope, biopsy forceps are passed through the bronchial wall to take tissue from a single lobe of the lung.

- **Transbronchial needle aspiration biopsy** (31629): With the use of a needle, the physician aspirates (withdraws) a sample of tissue or fluid from the trachea, main stem, or lobe of the bronchus.

> **Note:**
>
> *Code 31632 is reported for each additional lobe that is biopsied. It is not to be interpreted as each additional biopsy of the same lobe.*

Lungs and Pleura

The remainder of codes in this section identify procedures pertaining to the lungs, **pleura** (protective covering for lungs), or **thorax** (chest cavity). The challenge in this area of coding is to correctly assign codes that represent the procedure performed.

EXAMPLE: Pneumocentesis of lung for aspiration (32420)—puncture of pleural space to remove fluid or sample for cytology

Thoracentesis puncture aspiration (32421)—needle puncture of chest wall to remove fluid from the pleural cavity

Removal of Lung

The code range for removal of the lung or portion of the lung (32440–32540) references the terms resection of segment, pneumonectomy, and wedge resection. Note the following definitions:

- **Pneumonectomy**—removal of entire lung
- **Lobectomy**—removal of one lobe of the lung; removal of two lobes is called bilobectomy
- **Wedge resection**—removal of small, wedge-shaped portion of the lung
- **Segmental resection**—removal of a large portion of the lung lobe (larger than wedge resection)

Summary

- CPT provides a range of codes for excision of inferior turbinates; however, removal of superior and middle turbinates are assigned to an unlisted code.
- Nasal endoscopy procedures are distinguished by diagnostic/surgical and specific sinus opening (e.g., frontal, ethmoid).
- Laryngoscopy codes are provided for indirect, direct, and flexible fiberoptic procedures.
- Bronchoscopy codes differentiate among bronchial biopsies, transbronchial, and needle biopsies.
- Removal of a segment of the lung lobe is a larger specimen than a wedge resection.

Internet Links

University of Southern California School of Medicine: *http://www.cts.usc.edu/lpg-typesoflungsurgery.html*
Descriptions and illustrations of lung surgery

American Academy of Otolaryngology: *http://www.entnet.org*
Click "Health Information" on the tab across the webpage. From that link, click on the left side (e.g. ears) for fact sheets

Review

I. Medical Terminology Assessment

Multiple Choice:

Choose the best answer to the following.

1. The surgeon removes a cancerous lobe of the lung. This procedure is called:
   - a. pneumonectomy
   - b. thoracentesis
   - c. lobectomy
   - d. segmental resection

2. During a bronchoscopy procedure, the surgeon uses a needle to remove fluid from the lobe of the bronchus for diagnostic analysis. Which of the following accurately describes this procedure?
   - a. transbronchial needle aspiration biopsy
   - b. bronchial biopsy
   - c. transbronchial biopsy
   - d. pneumonectomy

3. Which of the following is the medical term for voice box?
   - a. trachea
   - b. larynx
   - c. pharynx
   - d. pleura

4. Which of the following is the sinus opening across the forehead above the eyebrows?
   - a. ethmoid
   - b. sphenoid
   - c. maxillary
   - d. frontal

5. The surgeon removes fluid from the pleural cavity with the use of a needle. This procedure is called:

  a. pneumectomy
  b. thoracentesis

  c. transbronchial needle aspiration
  d. lobectomy

II. Case Studies

Case Study 4-1: Operative Report

Preoperative Diagnosis: Bilateral chronic sinusitis

Postoperative Diagnosis: Bilateral chronic sinusitis

Procedure: Nasal endoscopy

Indications for Procedure: The patient is a 56-year-old gentleman who presented to the ENT clinic in March with a six-month history of left-sided nasal obstruction. The patient was treated for acute sinusitis times two, which had minimal improvement of his symptoms. The patient denied any signs of pressure, headaches, vision changes, or facial pain. A CT scan was performed by his primary care physician, which showed complete opacification of the left maxillary sinus with bony remodeling and erosion of the medial maxillary sinus wall and soft tissue extension to the left nasal passage and into the left inferior sphenoid and ethmoid sinus.

Procedures Performed:

1. Left maxillary sinusotomy

2. Left anterior ethmoidectomy

3. Removal of left nasal polyposis

Details of Procedure: The patient was brought to the operating room, and general anesthesia was induced. Bilateral nasal passages were injected with 1% lidocaine with 1:100,000 epinephrine, and injection included nasal septum, inferior turbinates, and superior turbinates as well as left uncinate process. After adequate decongestion, the left naris was suctioned and examined. Medial maxillary wall bulging into the nasal passage could be seen. Polyposis could be seen emanating from beneath the middle turbinate; using the shaver, polyposis was removed from the middle meatus. The shaver was then used to perform an uncinectomy. Upon performing the uncinectomy, thick yellow pus began to emanate from the maxillary sinus ostia. This was suctioned and sent for culture. Next, the maxillary sinus ostia were opened using the shaver. Maxillary sinus was then suctioned out, and all pus was removed. After an adequate maxillary antrostomy had been performed, anterior ethmoidectomy was performed. The shaver was used to enter into the anterior ethmoids. Some polypoid tissue could be seen emanating from the ethmoid, and this was removed. Next, the maxillary sinus was copiously irrigated with normal saline. Afrin-soaked nasal pledgets were then placed into the middle meatus to obtain hemostasis. The patient was then taken to the postanesthesia care unit (PACU) in good condition. After the patient was awake, the nasal Afrin-soaked pledgets were removed and no bleeding was noted. There were no apparent complications.

Code(s) _____ 31256 -LT   31254 - LT _____

Case Study 4-2: Operative Report

Preoperative Diagnosis: Left upper lobe lung mass

Postoperative Diagnosis: Left upper lobe lung mass

Procedures Performed: Flexible bronchoscopy with transbronchial biopsy with fluoroscopic guidance as well as bronchial washing and bronchial brushing.

Indications for Surgery: The patient is a 50-year-old man recently diagnosed with a left upper lobe lung mass. The PET scan was negative in his mediastinum and lit up only the mass as well as PFTs, and the patient was advised to undergo a bronchoscopy with biopsy.

Details of Procedure: The patient was brought to the operating room and placed in supine position on the operating room table. After general endotracheal anesthesia was performed, the Olympus bronchoscopy was placed in the ET tube down and into the patient's trachea. The carina was observed. The right upper, middle, and lower lobe was observed, and no lesions were observed. The bronchoscope was then removed and placed into the left main bronchus. Left main stem bronchus was inspected and found to be without deformities or mucosal irregularities. The left lower lobe was unremarkable. Attention was then turned to the left upper lobe. The lingular segment was inspected and was found to be without mucosal irregularities or intraluminal lesions. The left upper lobe superior posterior segment and superior anterior segments were then examined. The bronchial washings were obtained at this juncture with approximately 100 cc of warm saline, which was then instilled through the port and then aspirated and sent to cytology. Using fluoroscopic guidance to ensure that we were in the appropriate segment, after looking at the CT scan and the patient's chest X-ray, the tip of the bronchoscope was placed into the posterior segment of the left upper lobe bronchus, and the bronchial brush was run out into the periphery using fluoroscopic guidance several times. After this, the transbronchial biopsy forceps were used to biopsy this area. Using fluoroscopic guidance, three samples were obtained for frozen section, and three samples were obtained for permanent section. After removing the last specimen, the bronchoscope was then removed. The patient was extubated and sent to recovery in good condition.

Code(s) _____ 31628 _____ 31623 _____

Case Study 4-3: Operative Report

Preoperative Diagnosis: Left true vocal cord lesion, chronic hoarseness

Postoperative Diagnosis: Left true vocal cord lesion

Procedure: Microlaryngoscopy with excisional biopsy of lesion, flexible bronchoscopy

Anesthesia: General

Description of Procedure: The patient was brought to the operating room and placed in supine position and induced mask ventilated per anesthesia. Direct laryngoscopy was performed in standard fashion using Dedo laryngoscope. After inspecting the pyriform sinuses, post cricoids region, the vallecula, and supra glottis, a left true vocal fold lesion was noted. The patient was then intubated with 7-0 endotracheal tube through the Dedo laryngoscope. Tooke forceps were used to make an excisional biopsy. This was sent for frozen histopathologic diagnosis.

Attention was turned to the flexible bronchoscopy. This was performed through the endotracheal tube. Visualization was performed at the level of the tertiary bronchials with no bronchial lesions noted. The bronchoscope was removed.

At this point, the patient was suspended using the Dedo laryngoscope in standard fashion, exposing the left true vocal fold lesion. A microscope was brought into position, and the same lesion was excised using cold technique. Hemostasis was secured. The patient returned to the anesthesia care awake and extubated and then was taken to the recovery room in good condition.

Code(s) _____ 31541 _____ 31622 _____

Case Study 4-4: Operative Report

Preoperative Diagnosis: Acquired nasal deformity
                                         Nasal airway obstruction

Postoperative Diagnosis: Acquired nasal deformity
                                          Nasal airway obstruction

Procedure Performed: Septorhinoplasty

Indications for Procedure: This is a 34-year-old woman who, approximately 10 years ago, sustained nasal trauma. She had a resultant nasal airway obstruction with her breathing being obstructed on the left side. She also had an acquired nasal deformity with a depression and deficiency in the area of the right upper lateral cartilage. The patient was electively scheduled for a septorhinoplasty.

Anesthesia: General

Details of Procedure: The patient was brought to the operating room and placed on the operating table in supine position. Following induction of an adequate plane of general anesthesia, the patient was orally and endotracheally intubated by the anesthesia staff. Afrin-soaked pledgets were used to decongest the nose, and 1% lidocaine with 1:100,000 epinephrine was used for local anesthesia along the septum. A #15 blade was used to make a mucoperichondrial incision on the left aspect of the nasal septum. A Cottle elevator was then used to develop a mucoperichondrial flap. Dissection was carried back to the bony septum. The bony cartilaginous junction was separated, and the mucoperichondrium and mucoperiosteum on the right side of the septum was elevated. The bony septum was deviated toward the left; therefore, a section of the bony septum was removed using a swivel knife and Jansen-Middleton forceps. On the cartilaginous septum, it was apparent that the septum was pushed off of the maxillary crest to the left. Some redundant cartilage off of the maxillary crest was removed using the Cottle inferiorly. This allowed the cartilaginous septum to come into the midline. Fine scissors were used to develop a pocket in the midline of the columella for the caudal portion of the septum to rest in the midline. Following this, the patient's nasal airway appeared improved bilaterally. Next, to address the deficiency of the right upper lateral cartilage, an intercartilaginous incision was made and Joseph scissors were used to develop a pocket just superficial to the right upper lateral cartilage. A small piece of the previously resected cartilage was then fashioned into a graft and was placed into this pocket. The result was a more symmetric-appearing dorsum of the nose. At this point, a 5-0 chromic suture was used to close the intercartilaginous incision as well as the mucoperichondrial incision on the left portion of the septum. A 5-0 plain gut quilting stitch was then used across the septum. No significant bleeding was seen. The patient was taken to the postanesthesia care unit in good condition.

Code(s) _____ 30520 _____

Case Study 4-5: Operative Report

Preoperative Diagnosis: Bilateral vocal cord paralysis

Postoperative Diagnosis: Bilateral vocal cord paralysis

Operations Performed: Direct laryngoscopy

Carbon dioxide laser right cordotomy

Indications for Procedure: This is a 39-year-old man referred for evaluation of his airway. Approximately five years ago, he was in a motor vehicle collision, which resulted in the patient being intubated for six days. One month after discharge from the hospital, the patient began to have difficulty breathing. He was subsequently worked up and found to have bilateral true vocal cord paralysis. Soon after that, he had a tracheostomy tube placed due to increased breathing difficulties. This trach tube remained in place for six months, followed by decannulation. He did well for approximately one year, but then he began to have shortness of breath, and a tracheostomy tube was again placed. He now presents with increased dyspnea and stridor secondary to his bilateral true vocal cord paralysis. The decision was made to proceed to the operating room for laryngoscopy and possible cordotomy.

Description of Procedure: After adequate informed consent had been obtained, the patient was brought to the operating room and placed supine on the operating table. After general anesthesia was administered, the operating table was rotated to a 90-degree angle. A tooth guard was inserted. A Dedo laryngoscopy was inserted, and it was immediately apparent that the airway was widely patent. The patient was intubated with a #6 endotracheal tube through the Dedo laryngoscope. The Dedo laryngoscope was removed and then reinserted, and the patient was suspended. The presence of the endotracheal tube through the glottis precluded complete visualization with the operating microscope. Therefore, the decision was made to perform a cordotomy, apneic. The patient was extubated, the Dedo laryngoscope was inserted, and the patient was again suspended. The patient's oxygen saturations at no point dropped below 96%. Throughout the procedure, the patient was intermittently reintubated through the Dedo laryngoscope to allow for oxygenation. Evaluation of the true vocal cords was performed using the microlaryngeal instruments. The findings were that the left true vocal cord was stiffer, although it was more lateralized. The right true vocal cord was softer, but there was more significant amount of redundant mucosa overlying it, and this cord was more medial in nature. Given that nature that this patient's presentation was secondary to airway difficulties, the decision was made to perform a cordotomy on the right. The vocal process was identified. The Laser Safety Team was commenced. The patient was then prepped and draped with wet towel circumferentially around the head and face. All laser safety precautions including eye protection were followed by all operating room personnel. CO2 laser was set to 3 watts superpulsed continuous. The aiming beam was focused, and the right vocal process was identified. A right cordotomy was performed; 3 watts superpulse was not an adequate power for this, and the power was increased to 5 watts. So laser cordotomy continued. A releasing incision was made, and there was an immediate increase in caliber of the patency of the patient's airway. A small band of tissue in the crotch of the cordotomy was snipped, using microlaryngeal scissors. There was excellent hemostasis during the procedure.

The patient was re-evaluated with microscope and found to have a significantly larger caliber airway. The patient was unsuspended and transferred back to anesthesia's care. The patient tolerated the procedure well with no apparent complications.

Code(s) _____

31526   31599

Case Study 4-6: Operative Report

Preoperative Diagnosis: Left lower lobe lung nodule

Postoperative Diagnosis: Left lower lobe lung nodule

Operations Performed:

1. Left video-assisted thoracoscopy

2. Wedge resection biopsy, left lower lobe x 2

3. Bronchoscopy with the right upper lobe, transbronchial biopsy x 2

Indications for Procedures: The patient who has been followed by both the pulmonary services as well as seen in the thoracic surgery clinic had a long history of smoking. His chest CT had a nodule in the left lower lobe as well as an area in the right upper lobe that was consistent with some consolidation that had not increased in size. It was decided to perform a wedge biopsy of the left lower lobe lung nodule—since this is a discrete mass—and bronchoscopy for the right upper lobe. Patient understood the previously mentioned procedures and approach. Informed consent was obtained.

Details of the Procedure: Patient was brought into the operating room and placed on the operating table in supine position. After smooth induction of general anesthesia and endotracheal intubation, a Foley catheter was placed. The double-lumen endotracheal tube was placed. Patient was then turned into the left lateral decubitus position with the left side up and the right side down. We prepped and draped with Hibiclens, alcohol, and Loban. We then made a small incision in the posterior space with a scalpel, dissected down, bluntly entered into the chest cavity, and placed a 5 mm port that we then watched enter the anterior inferior area.

We then moved the camera to the anterior inferior portion and placed another 5 mm trocar posterior inferior. We then used gross inspection of the chest. There were no adhesions or pleural fluid to sweep out. No gross masses. Using a blunt grasper, we were able to palpate the mass in left lower lobe posteriorly. We then used graspers retracted to the lung specimen up and used the Endo GIA staplers to perform wedge biopsy. We could not get a specimen. In the second wedge biopsy attempt, we were able to get around from the green staple load and perform a biopsy, taking a wedge of the mass lesion. This was then placed in the EndoCatch bag and then removed. There was no bleeding to speak of. We removed our trocars under direct vision. Lung was allowed to reinflate. Chest tube was placed to suction 10 cm to close the 10-12 site with #2-0 Vicryl and #4-0 Vicryl followed by Dermabond. Other trocar sites were closed with #4-0 Monocryl and Dermabond. Once this was completed, the patient was turned supine. We then performed a bronchoscopy. While in bronchoscope, the trachea at the right appeared normal. On the right side, the bronchus intermedius appeared normal. We were able to cannulate the right upper lobe. We were able to use biopsy forceps to cannulate the apical segment of the right upper lobe. We sent several specimens with biopsy forceps to cytology as well as performed a biopsy with fluoroscopic guidance times two. We then removed the biopsy forceps.

We inspected the bronchus intermedius, the right medial lobe and right lower lobe orifices appeared normal. We then removed, pulled the scope back, and advanced down the left main stem bronchus. All segments and lobes appeared normal. Through the bronchoscope, this point of the procedure was terminated. Patient was extubated and transferred off the operating table to surgical intensive care unit (SICU).

Code(s) _____ 31526 _____ 31599 _____

32602   31628

5

Cardiovascular System

Chapter Outline

Introduction

Pacemakers and Automatic Internal
  Cardioverter-Defibrillator (AICD)

Valve Procedures

Coronary Artery Bypass Grafting

Review of Documentation

Aneurysms

Review of Documentation

Thromboendarterectomy

Review of Documentation

Central Venous Access Procedures

Review of Documentation

Arteriovenous Fistulas and Grafts

Varicose Veins

Key Terms

AICD	atherosclerosis	heart	thrombectomy
aneurysm	cardiac bypass	mitral valve	thrombus
aortic valve	capillaries	pacemaker	tricuspid valve
arteries	CVAD	PICC	varicose veins
arteriovenous fistula	embolus	pulmonary valve	vein

Chapter Objectives

At the conclusion of this chapter, the student should be able to:

- Identify anatomical structures of the cardiovascular system.
- Describe common surgical procedures of the cardiovascular system.
- Apply coding guidelines for reporting cardiovascular procedures.
- Distinguish between initial insertion and replacement of a pacemaker.
- Differentiate between open and endovascular aneurysm repairs.
- Use references to assist with coding assignment.
- Given a case scenario, accurately assign CPT codes and modifiers (if applicable).

2010 Current Procedural Terminology © 2009 American Medical Association. All Rights Reserved.

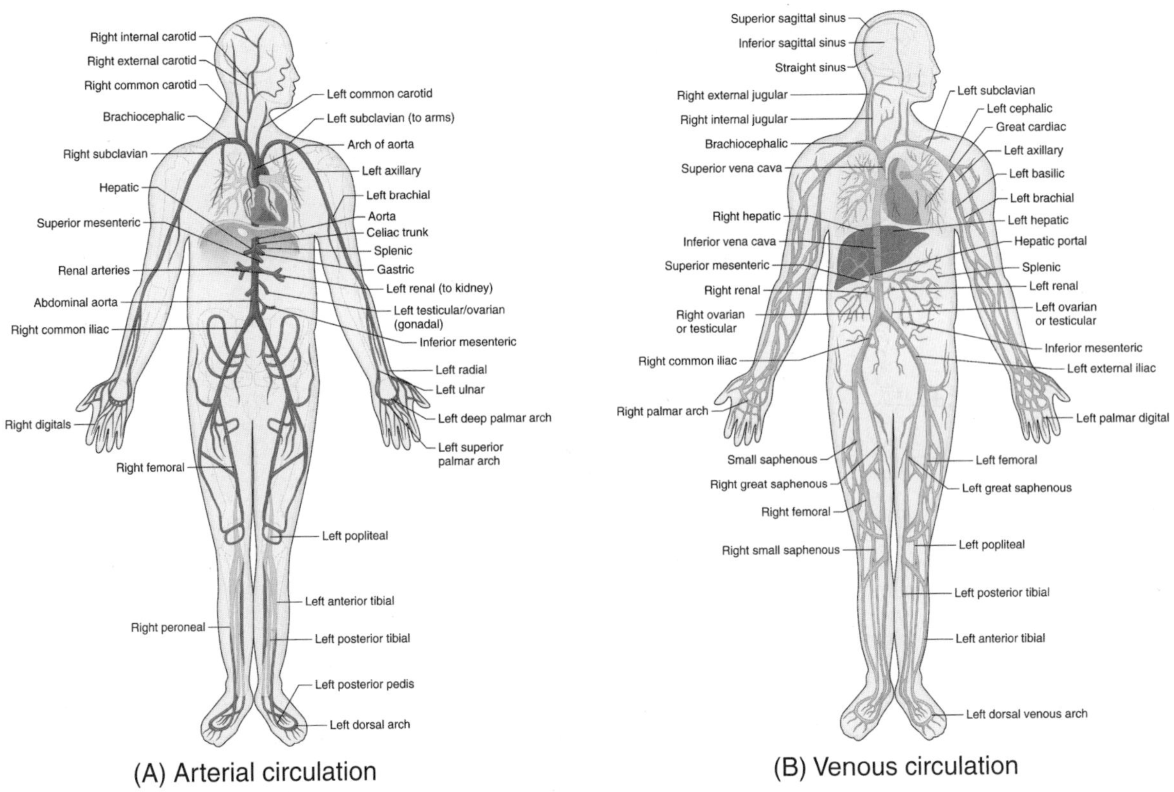

Figure 5-1 shows labeled diagrams of the circulatory system.

(A) Arterial circulation — labels include:
Right internal carotid, Right external carotid, Right common carotid, Brachiocephalic, Right subclavian, Hepatic, Superior mesenteric, Renal arteries, Abdominal aorta, Right common iliac, Right digitals, Right femoral, Right peroneal, Left common carotid, Left subclavian (to arms), Arch of aorta, Left axillary, Left brachial, Aorta, Celiac trunk, Splenic, Gastric, Left renal (to kidney), Left testicular/ovarian (gonadal), Inferior mesenteric, Left radial, Left ulnar, Left deep palmar arch, Left superior palmar arch, Left popliteal, Left anterior tibial, Left posterior tibial, Left posterior pedis, Left dorsal arch

(B) Venous circulation — labels include:
Superior sagittal sinus, Inferior sagittal sinus, Straight sinus, Right external jugular, Right internal jugular, Brachiocephalic, Superior vena cava, Right hepatic, Inferior vena cava, Superior mesenteric, Right renal, Right ovarian or testicular, Right common iliac, Right palmar arch, Small saphenous, Right great saphenous, Right femoral, Right small saphenous, Left subclavian, Left cephalic, Great cardiac, Left axillary, Left basilic, Left brachial, Left hepatic, Hepatic portal, Splenic, Left renal, Left ovarian or testicular, Inferior mesenteric, Left external iliac, Left palmar digital, Left femoral, Left great saphenous, Left popliteal, Left posterior tibial, Left anterior tibial, Left dorsal venous arch

© Delmar Cengage Learning.

Figure 5-1 Circulatory system. (A) Arterial circulation. (B) Venous circulation.

Introduction

The cardiovascular system consists of the heart, and arteries and veins throughout the body. (Figure 5-1)

The **heart** is the hollow muscular organ that pumps blood through the circulatory system. **Arteries** are the blood vessels that carry blood away from the heart to capillary beds throughout the body. **Veins** are blood vessels that carry blood from the body to the heart. **Capillaries** transport blood between small arteries and veins.

This chapter will focus on the most common surgical procedures of the cardiovascular system, such as pacemakers, coronary artery bypass, aneurysm repairs, thrombectomies, central venous access devices, and arteriovenous fistulas.

Pacemakers and Automatic Internal Cardioverter-Defibrillator (AICD)

A **pacemaker** is a device that includes a pulse generator containing electronics and a battery and one or more electrodes (leads). It is inserted to shock the heart electronically into regular rhythm (Figure 5-2).

An automatic internal **cardioverter-defibrillator (AICD)** includes a pulse generator and electrodes. They use a combination of anti-tachycardia pacing, low-energy cardioversion or defibrillating shocks to treat ventricular tachycardia or ventricular fibrillation (Figure 5-3).

A single-chamber device contains a single electrode that is positioned in the heart's right atrium or right ventricle.

A dual-chamber device contains two electrodes; one is placed in the right atrium, and the other is placed in the right ventricle.

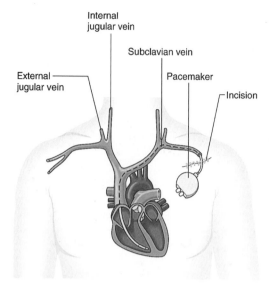

Figure 5-2 An artificial pacemaker is implanted under the skin.

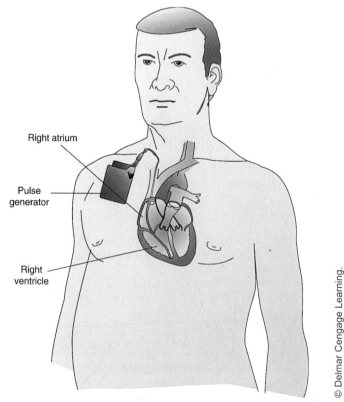

Figure 5-3 Implantable pacing cardioverter defibrillator (PCD)

Pacemaker/AICD Procedures

Before focusing on the specific pacemaker/AICD procedures, this overview will outline general coding guidelines that are applicable to all pacemaker/AICD procedures.

The following coding guidelines can be found in *CPT Assistant* (November 1999):

- Replacing the "battery"

When the "battery" of a pacemaker or a pacing cardio-defibrillator is changed, it is actually the pulse generator that is replaced. Two codes are necessary, one for the removal of the pulse generator and one for the insertion of the new pulse generator.

- 14-day rule

The procedure codes for insertion of a pacemaker or pacing cardio-defibrillator include repositioning or replacement within 14 days of the original insertion.

- Dual vs. single chamber

All devices being implanted currently have pacing capability that combines both a single- or dual-chamber pacemaker and a cardioverter defibrillator in device. While dual-chamber pacemakers require one lead in the atrium and the other lead in the ventricle, pacing cardioverter defibrillators may require multiple leads even in single-chamber devices.

Review of Documentation

During the review of the operative report for a pacemaker insertion, the coder will search for answers to the following questions:

- Was the pacemaker insertion initial, replacement, or repositioning?
- Was it temporary or permanent?
- Dual chamber? Single chamber?
- Epicardial or transvenous approach?
- Was the entire pacemaker system replaced or just the pulse generator?
- Was the pacemaker pocket revised?

This section is complicated by the fact that there are a variety of codes. Coding professionals must carefully abstract documentation and compare the key components of the code for accurate reporting. The following excerpts provide guidance for applying coding guidelines for this section of CPT.

Insertion and/or Replacement of Permanent Pacemaker (33206–33208)

These codes pertain to the initial insertion or replacement of a permanent pacemaker based on whether the electrode is placed in the atrium, ventricle, or both. The insertion of the pulse generator (battery) is included in this code selection. These CPT codes are the most commonly performed procedures for insertion of pacemakers.

Insertion or Replacement of Pacemaker Pulse Generator Only (33212–33213)

This code selection identifies single- or dual-chamber insertion or replacement of the pulse generator (battery). It is important to remember that the code for the removal of the pulse generator should be coded in addition to the insertion.

Repositioning of Pacemaker (33215)

The code describes repositioning of a previously implanted transvenous pacemaker or pacing cardioverter-defibrillator.

> **Note:**
>
> *If procedure description includes removal of an old pacemaker or its electrode(s), additional codes would be assigned to represent the work associated with the removal.*

2010 Current Procedural Terminology © 2009 American Medical Association. All Rights Reserved.

Insertion of Electrodes (33216–33217)

The code selection is based on single or 2 transvenous electrodes insertion of a permanent pacemaker or cardioverter-defibrillator.

Insertion of Electrodes for Left Ventricular Pacing (Biventricular Pacing) (33224–33225)

These codes are differentiated by whether the electrode was attached to a previously placed pacemaker (or cardioverter-defibrillator) pulse generator or attached at the time of insertion of the initial pacemaker generator (or pacing cardioverter-defibrillator).

> **Note:**
>
> Remember that when a replacement is performed, you will need one code for the removal and one code for the reinsertion.

Removal of Transvenous Pulse Generator (33233)

Code identifies removal of permanent pacemaker "battery" only; the leads are not removed.

The following examples will illustrate coding guidelines for accurate coding assignment.

EXAMPLE 1: During open heart surgery, a temporary single-chamber pacemaker is inserted to maintain normal heart rhythm.

> **Correct code assignment:**   33210

EXAMPLE 2: Patient presents with an infection of the pocket that his cardioverter-defibrillator resides in. The physician treated the area and revised the pocket for placement of pacing cardioverter-defibrillator.

> **Correct code assignment:**   33223

> **CODING TIPS:**
>
> - Cross-reference notes have been added to provide clarity in the appropriate use of these codes, based on the procedural technique and the device components involved.
> - Code ranges can be located in the alphabetic index under Pacemaker, Heart or Cardiology, Defibrillator, or Heart.
> - There is an extensive CPT note that describes the components of a pacemaker system and coding guidelines.

Exercise 5-1: Pacemaker Procedures

Directions: Assign CPT codes to the following procedures. Append CPT/HCPCS Level II modifiers if applicable. Concentrate on application of coding guidelines, and do not focus on sequencing or assignment of modifier of 51 (physician services).

1. Patient underwent subcutaneous insertion of permanent pacemaker pulse generator with transvenous placement of electrodes in the right atrium and right ventricle.

Code(s) _____

2. A patient came in for end-of-life pulse generator replacement on his single-chamber pacemaker. The existing pocket was reopened, and the pulse generator was disconnected from its electrode and removed. The new pulse generator was inserted into the pocket and connected to the electrode.

Code(s) _____

3. The patient presents to have his single-chamber pacemaker system upgraded to a dual-chamber system. New leads and a new pulse generator were inserted.

Code(s) _____

2010 Current Procedural Terminology © 2009 American Medical Association. All Rights Reserved.

Valve Procedures

The heart contains four valves that direct the flow of blood through the heart in the proper direction. They are the **aortic**, **mitral**, **tricuspid**, and **pulmonary valves**. When one or more of the valves is not functioning properly, the patient is diagnosed with valvular heart disease. The most common types of valvular heart disease are:

- Valvular regurgitation—backflow of the blood due to valvular prolapse
- Valvular prolapse—two valvular flaps do not close properly
- Valvular stenosis—narrowing of one or more cardiac valves

When coding procedures are performed on cardiac valves, note the following:

1. Determine which valve is being operated on:

- Aortic
- Mitral
- Tricuspid
- Pulmonary

2. Determine which type of procedure is being performed:

- Valvuloplasty—open heart surgery during which the surgeon removes the damaged valve and replaces it with a prosthetic, homograft or allograft, stented, or stentless valve
- Valvulotomy—open heart surgery in which an incision is made into a valve to repair valvular damage. This includes commissurotomy, in which narrowed valve leaflets are widened by carefully opening the fused leaflets with a scalpel

EXAMPLE 1: Patient underwent mitral valve replacement with cardiopulmonary bypass.

> Correct code assignment: 33430

EXAMPLE 2: Patient came into the hospital with aortic valve regurgitation. His physician determined that a valve replacement was necessary. He came into the hospital and had an aortic valve replacement with cardiopulmonary bypass, with a stentless valve.

> Correct code assignment: 33410

CODING TIPS:

- *The CPT book groups the procedure codes by the valve involved. Be sure you are in the right section!*
- *When a valve requires insertion of a prosthetic ring, report codes 33426–33427.*
- *Codes 33401–33403 include aortic valve valvotomy or commissurotomy.*
- *If multiple valve procedures are performed, append modifier 51 to secondary procedures (physician services only).*

Exercise 5-2: Valve Procedures

Directions: Assign CPT codes to the following procedures. Append CPT/HCPCS Level II modifiers if applicable. Concentrate on application of coding guidelines, and do not focus on sequencing or assignment of modifier of 51 (physician services).

1. The surgeon performs replacement of the tricuspid valve, with cardiopulmonary bypass.

Code(s) _____

2. Surgeon performed a valvulotomy of the pulmonary valve (cardiopulmonary bypass was not used).

Code(s) _____

3. Patient presents with supravalvular stenosis. The surgeon performed an aortoplasty.

Code(s) _____

4. A valvuloplasty of the aortic valve was performed using transventricular dilation. This was an open procedure using cardiopulmonary bypass.

Code(s) _____

Coronary Artery Bypass Grafting

The most common serious heart disease is hardening or narrowing of the coronary arteries by **atherosclerosis**. The narrowing causes reduced blood flow to the heart and can cause angina pectoris or myocardial infarction. Coronary artery **bypass** surgery removes the diseased portion of the coronary artery and replaces it with a segment of an artery or a vein. The surgeon takes a segment of a healthy vessel from another part of the body and makes a "detour" around the blocked part of the coronary artery (or arteries).

The most commonly used vessel for the bypass procedure is the saphenous vein from the leg. The surgeon sews the grafted vessel to the coronary arteries beyond the blockage and attaches the other end to the aorta.

In some cases, the surgeon uses an internal mammary artery to bypass the diseased vessel. Artery grafts are of limited length and can only be used to bypass vessels located near the beginning (proximal) of the coronary arteries (Figure 5-4).

For coding purposes, documentation should be reviewed to determine the number of bypasses performed and if they are combined arterial-venous or arterial or venous only.

The codes in the range 33510–33516 describe coronary artery bypass procedures using venous grafts only.

The codes in the range 33517–33530 describe coronary artery bypass procedures using a combination of arterial and venous grafts. These codes cannot be used alone and must be used with a code from the range 33533–33536 to describe the arterial graft.

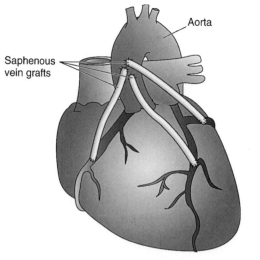

Aorta

Saphenous vein grafts

© Delmar Cengage Learning.

Figure 5-4 Coronary artery bypass graft (CABG) using saphenous vein grafts

2010 Current Procedural Terminology © 2009 American Medical Association. All Rights Reserved.

When performing a coronary artery bypass, the harvesting of the saphenous vein is included in the codes listed above. The harvesting of an artery is also included in the arterial codes listed above. However, if a vein from the upper extremity is being used (axillary, brachial, radial, or ulnar vein), code 35500 must be used also. If an upper extremity artery is being harvested (axillary, brachial, radial, or ulnar artery), code 35600 must also be used.

> **Note:**
>
> *Arterial graft codes and venous graft codes can be used alone, but the combined arterial-venous graft codes can never be used alone.*

Review of Documentation

During the review of the operative report for a coronary artery bypass procedure, the coder will want to use the following guidelines.

Type of Vessel Used	Code Range	Add-on Codes for Upper Extremity Veins or Arteries
Venous grafts	33510–33516	35500 (vein); artery not applicable 35572 (femoropopliteal vein segment)
Arterial and venous grafts	33517–33530	35600 (artery) or 35500 (vein) 35572 (femoropopliteal)
Arterial grafts	33533–33536	35600 (artery) or 35500 (vein) 35572 (femoropopliteal vein segment)

EXAMPLE 1: The patient underwent coronary artery bypass, during which a single arterial and single vein graft was performed.

    Correct coding assignment: 33533 and 33517

EXAMPLE 2: The patient was brought to the operating room, and a triple coronary bypass was performed using only venous conduits.

    Correct coding assignment: 33512

> **Note:**
>
> *Code ranges can be located in the alphabetic index under Bypass Graft, Coronary Artery, Arterial or Venous.*

Exercise 5-3: Coronary Artery Bypass Grafting

Directions: Assign CPT codes to the following procedures. Append CPT/HCPCS Level II modifiers if applicable. Concentrate on application of coding guidelines, and do not focus on sequencing or assignment of modifier of 51 (physician services).

1. Coronary artery bypass was performed using four coronary venous grafts. These grafts were harvested from the saphenous vein.

    Code(s) _____

2. The surgeon performed a coronary artery bypass using two coronary arterial grafts.

    Code(s) _____

3. Coronary artery bypass was performed using venous and arterial grafts. Two venous grafts and two arterial grafts were used.

    Code(s) _____

4. The surgeon performed a revision of a coronary artery bypass using two coronary venous grafts. This revision was performed three months after the original bypass.

    Code(s) _____

2010 Current Procedural Terminology © 2009 American Medical Association. All Rights Reserved.

Aneurysms

An **aneurysm** is a balloon-like dilation of a blood vessel that weakens the wall of the artery. Aneurysms occur most often in larger arteries such as the brachial artery, abdominal aorta, femoral artery, popliteal artery, and cerebral arteries. Arteriosclerosis is a common cause of aneurysms. In the case of the cerebral arteries, if the aneurysm bursts, a stroke is likely to occur (Figure 5-5).

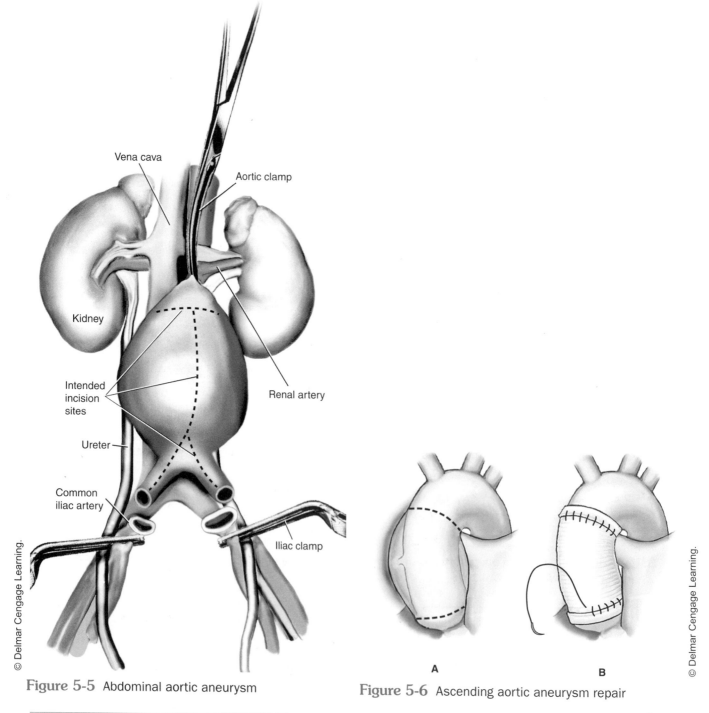

© Delmar Cengage Learning.

Figure 5-5 Abdominal aortic aneurysm

Figure 5-6 Ascending aortic aneurysm repair

© Delmar Cengage Learning.

2010 Current Procedural Terminology © 2009 American Medical Association. All Rights Reserved.

The following definitions of the most common ways to repair aneurysms can be found in *CPT Assistant,* December 2000:

- Open repair

This is the traditional method of repairing aneurysms. The patient is opened directly at the site of the aneurysm, blood flow is stopped with clamps, and a synthetic graft is sutured into the artery. The aneurysm sac is then wrapped around the graft and the incision is closed (Figure 5-6).

- Endovascular repair

This is a much less invasive procedure. An incision is made usually at the femoral artery, and a device (catheter) is inserted into the artery and guided up to the aneurysm. The graft is deployed from the device, and then a balloon is usually inserted to inflate the graft to its capacity.

Review of Documentation

During the review of the operative report for an aneurysm repair, the coder will search for the key terms listed in Figure 5-7.

EXAMPLE 1: Patient underwent descending thoracic aorta graft to repair thoracic aortic aneurysm. Cardiopulmonary bypass was used.

Correct coding assignment: 33875

EXAMPLE 2: Patient underwent direct repair with total excision of aneurysm and graft insertion to treat a radial artery aneurysm.

Correct coding assignment: 35045

> **CODING TIPS:**
>
> *The codes for endovascular repair of aneurysms include the following:*
> - *Device introduction*
> - *Manipulation*
> - *Positioning*
> - *Deployment*
> - *Distal extensions*
> - *Balloon angioplasty with the target treatment zone either before or after the graft deployment*

Exercise 5-4: Aneurysm Procedures

Directions: Assign CPT codes to the following procedures. Append CPT/HCPCS Level II modifiers if applicable. Concentrate on application of coding guidelines, and do not focus on sequencing or assignment of modifier of 51 (physician services).

1. The patient was diagnosed with an iliac aneurysm. An abdominal incision was made to expose the right iliac artery, and an endovascular graft was placed to repair right iliac aneurysm.

   Code(s) _____

2. A 67-year-old man presents with a carotid aneurysm. He underwent direct repair with partial excision of the aneurysm and graft insertion to treat the left carotid aneurysm.

   Code(s) _____

3. The physician performed an endovascular repair of a descending thoracic aorta aneurysm. To complete the repair, he had to place a proximal extension.

   Code(s) _____

4. The surgeon performed an endovascular repair of an abdominal aorta aneurysm using a bifurcated prosthesis.

   Code(s) _____

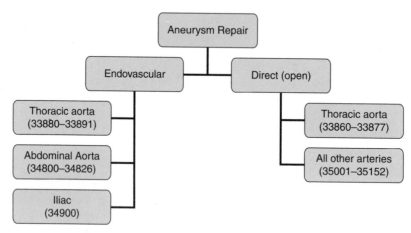

Figure 5-7 Aneurysm Decision Tree

Thromboendarterectomy

A **thrombus** is an abnormal blood clot obstructing a blood vessel or heart cavity, otherwise known as thrombosis. While most blood clots are a result of the body's natural ability to stop bleeding, sometimes it doesn't work correctly, resulting in blockage of blood flow to tissues in the body. The main contributors to abnormal thrombosis are atherosclerosis, hypertension, diabetes mellitus, a high-fat diet, smoking, lack of exercise, and oral contraceptives.

There are two types of thrombosis:

1. Arterial thrombosis: The clot is in an artery, usually the heart or brain, and causes a stroke or heart attack.

2. Venous thrombosis: The clot is in a vein, usually one of the deep vessels of the leg, causing swelling and pain.

> **CODING TIPS:**
>
> *The following must be coded IN ADDITION to the repair code:*
> - *Open arterial exposure and closure*
> - *Extensive repair or replacement of an artery*
> - *Proximal extensions*
> - *Introduction of guidewires and catheters*

If a piece of the clot breaks off and travels to another location in the body, it is called an **embolus.** Sometimes a physician will prescribe an anti-coagulant to prevent blood clots. The most common ones are Heparin, low molecular Heparin, and Warfarin. In some cases, the physician may choose to perform a thrombectomy.

The following guidelines can be found in *CPT Assistant* (January 2007) and (November 1998)

- Thromboendarterectomy

For codes 35301–35306, note the wording states "including patch graft, if performed."

- Thrombectomy of arterial/venous graft

Code 35875 was created to describe the thrombectomy of arterial or venous grafts other than hemodialysis grafts. This was needed to distinguish between the non-hemodialysis and hemodialysis graft thrombectomies because the non-hemodialysis graft thrombectomy is a more complicated procedure.

Review of Documentation

During the review of the operative report for a thrombectomy, the coder will search for answers to the following questions:

- Was the thrombus removed from an artery or a vein?

2010 Current Procedural Terminology © 2009 American Medical Association. All Rights Reserved.

- Was the artery lining removed along with the thrombus?
- Was a thrombolytic agent used along with a catheter?

A **thrombectomy** is the removal of a thrombus. When this procedure is performed, codes from the range 34001–34490 will be reported.

A thromboendarterectomy is the surgical excision of a thrombus (blood clot) and atherosclerotic inner lining from an obstructed artery. When this procedure is performed, codes from the range 35301–35372 will be reported.

A mechanical thrombectomy is the removal of a thrombus using a catheter and a thrombolytic agent. When this procedure is performed, codes from the range 37184–37188 will be reported.

> **Note:**
>
> *The injection of the thrombolytic is included in the mechanical thrombectomy code.*

> **Note:**
>
> *When using codes in the range of 35301–35372, harvesting of the saphenous or upper extremity vein is included.*

EXAMPLE 1: Patient underwent iliac thromboendarterectomy with patch graft.

   Correct coding assignment: 35351

EXAMPLE 2: Patient presents with a thrombus in the radial artery. A thrombectomy was performed.

   Correct coding assignment: 34111

Exercise 5-5: Thrombectomy Procedures

Directions: Assign CPT codes to the following procedures. Append CPT/HCPCS Level II modifiers if applicable. Concentrate on application of coding guidelines, and do not focus on sequencing or assignment of modifier of 51 (physician services).

1. The physician creates an incision in the neck to perform a direct thrombectomy of the subclavian vein.

   Code(s) _____34471_____

2. The surgeon performs a thromboendarterectomy with a patch graft of the tibial artery and the peroneal artery.

   Code(s) ____35305_____

3. The physician performs a thromboendarterectomy of the superficial femoral artery without a patch graft.

   Code(s) _____35302_____

4. A transcatheter mechanical thrombectomy was performed of the tibial artery using a thrombolytic agent.

   Code(s) _____

Central Venous Access Procedures

The insertion of a **central venous access device (CVAD)** involves the insertion of a catheter (small, flexible tube) into a blood vessel to provide a painless way of drawing blood or delivering drugs and nutrients into a patient's bloodstream repeatedly over a period of weeks, months, and even years. To qualify as a CVAD, the tip of the catheter/device must terminate in the subclavian, brachiocephalic, or iliac veins; the superior or inferior vena cava; or the right atrium.

The following are examples of uses of CVADs:

- Administration of medicines (e.g., long-term antibiotics or chemotherapy)

2010 Current Procedural Terminology © 2009 American Medical Association. All Rights Reserved.

- Long-term intravenous feeding for nutritional support
- Hemodialysis
- Blood transfusions

The CPT book divides venous access procedures into five categories:

- Insertion
- Repair
- Partial replacement
- Complete replacement
- Removal

Review of Documentation

During the review of the operative report for central venous access procedures, the coder will search for answers to the following questions:

- Was the catheter inserted centrally or peripherally?
- Was the catheter tunneled or nontunneled?
- Was a pump or port inserted?
- How old is the patient?

The following definitions will be helpful when coding CVADs:

- Central insertion: A centrally inserted catheter is placed in the jugular, subclavian, femoral vein, or the inferior vena cava.
- Peripheral insertion: A peripherally inserted catheter is typically inserted into the arm and advanced forward into the larger subclavian vein.
- Tunneled catheter: This catheter is inserted into a site (e.g., subclavian vein) and "tunneled" through skin and subcutaneous tissue to a great vein. Ultrasound guidance is usually used for this procedure. A code from the Radiology section would be applied for the ultrasound guidance.
- Nontunneled catheter: This catheter is inserted directly into a large vein such as the femoral vein.
- Port or pump: These devices are placed under the skin in a subcutaneous pocket. The blood is drawn or medication delivered through a needle into this device and then flows into the body. Tunneled venous access ports are typically used for long-term intravenous therapy, and they contain two parts: catheter and port.
- **Peripherally inserted central venous catheter (PICC):** This device is inserted into an arm vein and advanced over a guidewire to the large vein (usually the superior vena cava).

    EXAMPLE 1: Physician punctures the subclavian vein of a 4-year-old patient, passes a guidewire centrally, and inserts a central venous catheter.

    > Correct coding assignment: 36557

    EXAMPLE 2: Physician replaces the catheter portion only of a central venous access device with a port.

    > Correct coding assignment: 36578

CODING TIPS:

According to CPT coding guidelines, if an existing central venous access device is removed and a new one placed at a different site, two codes will be needed, one for the removal of the old device and one for the insertion of the new device.

Note:

Codes are provided for removal of obstructed material from central venous access devices. These codes are in the range 36593–36596. Codes 75901 or 75902 may need to be used in conjunction with these codes to identify the radiological supervision and interpretation.

Exercise 5-6: Central Venous Access Procedures

Directions: Assign CPT codes to the following procedures. Append CPT/HCPCS Level II modifiers if applicable. Concentrate on application of coding guidelines, and do not focus on sequencing or assignment of modifier of 51 (physician services).

1. A pocket is created under the skin in the subcutaneous tissues. The pump is inserted into the pocket, and the attached catheter is inserted into a nearby vein and directed into the central veins.

   Code(s) _____

2. A 68-year-old man comes in with a poorly functioning port. A catheter and guidewire are manipulated into the superior vena cava. A vascular snare is placed in the vena cava through the catheter, and the tip of the catheter is engaged with the snare. The fibrin sheath and thrombus are stripped from the catheter.

   Code(s) _____

3. The physician repairs a central venous access device, with a port, in the subclavian vein.

   Code(s) _____

4. The patient comes in to have his PICC line removed due to associated pain. The physician removes the tunneled device.

   Code(s) _____

Arteriovenous Fistulas and Grafts

Arteriovenous fistulas are created to provide access for hemodialysis. They are the most desirable method because they are less likely to clot or become infected than other methods. This procedure requires the surgeon to connect the artery to the vein, which allows more blood to flow from the artery directly to the vein. Over time, the vein becomes stronger and becomes thick-walled, making it the ideal target to place dialysis needles.

Codes 36800–36830 identify the following methods for creating a fistula. The following are some of the most common procedures:

- Direct arteriovenous anastomosis (36821)—an artery and vein are connected without the use of a graft. The artery and vein are located next to each other.

- Creation of arteriovenous (AV) fistula (36825)—a connection is made between two vessels using a graft from the patient's natural vein (autogenous).

- Creation of AV fistula (36830)—connection between two vessels using a synthetic graft such as Gortex (nonautogenous).

Codes 36831–36870 describe methods for correcting complications:

1. Thrombectomy
2. Plastic repair of arteriovenous aneurysm
3. Distal revascularization and interval ligation
4. External cannula declotting

> **Note:**
>
> *Arteriovenous hemodialysis access is created by using autogenous venous tissue or inserting a prosthetic graft.*

> **CODING TIPS:**
>
> *When coding a thrombectomy, be aware of whether the procedure includes a revision or not. For example, code 36833 includes both a revision and thrombectomy.*

EXAMPLE 1: Patient underwent forearm vein transposition between the elbow and the wrist.

   `Correct coding assignment:`   36820

EXAMPLE 2: Patient underwent open thrombectomy, without revision of the dialysis graft.

> Correct coding assignment: 36831

Exercise 5-7: AV Fistulas and Grafts

Directions: Assign CPT codes to the following procedures. Append CPT/HCPCS Level II modifiers if applicable. Concentrate on application of coding guidelines, and do not focus on sequencing or assignment of modifier of 51 (physician services).

1. A 57-year-old female on hemodialysis for one year developed increasing venous outflow pressures in her arteriovenous dialysis graft. The graft was dissected open followed by a balloon catheter thrombectomy. The graft was also revised.

Code(s) _____

2. Patient underwent a percutaneous thrombectomy of an autogenous arteriovenous fistula.

Code(s) _____

3. The physician created a direct arteriovenous anastomosis using the radial artery and cephalic vein for dialysis access.

Code(s) _____

4. The physician created an arteriovenous fistula using a synthetic graft.

Code(s) _____

Varicose Veins

Varicose veins are abnormally dilated and twisted veins, most often affecting the saphenous veins and their branches in the legs. Surgical treatment includes ligation, division, and stripping of the affected veins. While these procedures can be done on any veins, the saphenous veins are the most common.

In ligation and division, the surgeon ties off all tributaries and then ties off the saphenous vein below the tributaries and divides it between the ligatures. Stripping involves completely removing the vein from the leg (codes 37700–37760). A stab phlebectomy involves tiny stab incisions over multiple varicose vein sites. A vein is removed at each stab site (37765–37766).

> **CODING TIPS:**
>
> *Code 37785 is used for division and/or excision of varicose vein clusters. These are large varicose veins that cannot be removed via the traditional method because they require a larger incision.*

The following coding guidelines can be found in *CPT Assistant* (August 1996):

1. If only a portion of the long saphenous vein is stripped, use code 37700.

2. If only a portion of the short saphenous vein is removed, use code 37780.

3. To report complete stripping, codes 37718 and 37722 would be used.

EXAMPLE 1: The patient had a long saphenous vein stripping from saphenofemoral junction to below knee of left and right legs.

> Correct coding assignment: 37722–50

2010 Current Procedural Terminology © 2009 American Medical Association. All Rights Reserved.

EXAMPLE 2: Patient had ligation and excision of a varicose vein cluster.

    `Correct coding assignment:`   37785

Exercise 5-8: Varicose Vein Procedures

Directions: Assign CPT codes to the following procedures. Append CPT/HCPCS Level II modifiers if applicable. Concentrate on application of coding guidelines, and do not focus on sequencing or assignment of modifier of 51 (physician services).

1. Ligation and stripping of a short saphenous vein was performed.

    Code(s) _____ 37718 _____

2. The physician performed a ligation and division of a short saphenous vein at the saphenopopliteal junction.

    Code(s) _____ 37780 _____

3. The surgeon performed a ligation of perforator veins without a skin graft.

    Code(s) _____ 37761 _____

Summary

- When replacement of a pacemaker is performed, a code for the removal and a code for the insertion of the new device are needed.

- For heart valve procedures, the CPT book is divided into sections by the specific valve.

- Coronary artery bypass procedures are reported by the number of venous and arterial grafts performed. An add-on code is reported for combined arterial-venous grafting.

- There are two approaches to aneurysm repairs, open and endovascular.

- When coding a thrombectomy, determine if the procedure was performed on a vein or artery.

- Central venous access devices can be tunneled or non-tunneled.

- Arteriovenous fistulas can be created using synthetic grafts or autologous veins and arteries.

Internet Links

Food and Drug Administration (FDA): *http://www.FDA.gov*
Search website; picture and description of pacemakers

National Institutes of Health: *http://health.nih.gov/category/heartandcirculation*
Search for diseases and treatment pertaining to cardiovascular system

National Library of Medicine: *http://www.nlm.nih.gov/medlineplus/tutorial.html*
Many tutorials describing operative procedures

Radiology: *http://www.Radiologyinfo.org*
Information about vascular access procedures; treatment of varicose veins

---

2010 Current Procedural Terminology © 2009 American Medical Association. All Rights Reserved.

Review

I. Crossword Puzzle

Cardiovascular System

Across
3. device containing pulse generator
5. excision of blood clot
7. imaging of blood vessels
8. bulging artery

Down
1. remove plaque from artery
2. vessel that carries blood towards heart
4. widening a narrow blood vessel
6. vessel that carries blood from heart
9. detached blot clot

II. Case Studies

Case Study 5-1: Operative Report

Preoperative Diagnoses:

1. Status post implantable cardioverter-defibrillator implant

2. Atrial lead dislodgment

2010 Current Procedural Terminology © 2009 American Medical Association. All Rights Reserved.

Postoperative Diagnoses:

1. Status post implantable cardioverter-defibrillator implant

2. Atrial lead dislodgment

Procedure Performed:

1. Interrogation and reprogramming dual-chamber implantable cardioverter-defibrillator

2. Removal of implantable cardioverter-defibrillator generator

3. Revision of right atrial lead

4. Insertion of implantable cardioverter-defibrillator generator

Complications: None

Details of Procedure: After informed consent was obtained, the patient was brought to electrophysiology laboratory and conscious sedation was administered. The previously implanted Biotronik dual-chamber ICD was interrogated. The atrial lead was confirmed to be dislodged. The device was reprogrammed to disable tachycardia therapies for the duration of the case. After the area was draped and prepped and local anesthesia was administered, an incision was made and carried down to the device. The device was removed from the pocket. The atrial lead was freed and the screw retracted, New J stylet was advanced into the lead to reposition it to a secured position in the right atrium, where the lead screw was again deployed and the lead fluoroscopically viewed to be firmly fixed in place. The lead was then sutured to the surrounding tissue and tested, and it was found to be functioning properly. At this point, the lead was then attached to the previously implanted ICD, which was then placed back into the pocket. The pocket was irrigated with antibiotic solution, then closed with 2-0 Vicryl and 4-0 Monocryl and dressed with Steri-Strips, gauze, and Tegaderm. Testing of the device showed good function. The atrial lead had a P-wave of 1.8 mV with a capture threshold of 0.5 V at 01.4 ms and a placing impedance of 540 ohms. The patient tolerated the procedure well without complication.

Summary: Successful atrial lead revision.

Code(s) _____

Case Study 5-2: Operative Report

Preoperative Diagnoses:

1. Chronic renal failure

2. Thrombosed graft fistula

Postoperative Diagnoses:

1. Chronic renal failure

2. Thrombosed graft fistula

3. Venous outflow stenosis

Procedures Performed:

1. Graft thrombectomy

2. Angiogram

3. Angioplasty

4. Arthrectomy

Clinical Findings and Indications: This is a 52-year-old male with chronic renal failure, who presented with thrombosed graft fistula. The graft extends from the brachial artery up to the brachial vein. The patient was found to have a venous outflow stenosis extending from the graft to vein anastomosis up to the axilla. The whole length was angioplastied. The arthrectomy was performed on the arterial site for a retained clot. At the end of the procedure, the patient had a palpable thrill.

Details of Procedure: The patient's hand was prepped and shaved in the usual manner. Skin was infiltrated with Carbocaine 1%. An incision was made through skin and subcutaneous tissue midway into the graft, exposed with an 11-blade knife to open the graft. A Fogarty catheter was introduced in the arterial end. Good arterial inflow was obtained. An angiogram was performed. The graft was opened with an arthrectomy catheter. Heparinized saline was introduced in both ends. The venous end was compromised by stenosis. It was crossed with a Glidewire. A Conquest catheter 8×4 inflated to 23 atmospheres several times, with formation of waist and resolution of waist. Repeated angiogram showed improvement of this excellent back bleeding. The graftotomy was closed with interrupted 5-0 Prolene. Upon releasing the clamps, a palpable thrill was obtained. Incisions were closed in layers, subcutaneous tissue with 2-0 PDS and subcuticular 4-0 Monocryl. Steri-Strips were applied. The patient left the OR in stable condition.

Code(s) _____

Case Study 5-3: Operative Report

Preoperative Diagnosis: Chronic renal failure

Postoperative Diagnosis: Chronic renal failure

Procedure Performed: Insertion of right internal jugular Perm-a-Cath

Indications for Procedure: This patient is a 52-year-old female with chronic renal failure, presented for a nonworking left subclavian tunneled dialysis catheter. She also has a right internal jugular triple lumen for antibiotics. The subclavian line was removed to preserve the subclavian vein for access, and the right jugular Perm-a-Cath was placed under fluoroscopy guidance.

Details of the Procedure: The patient's neck was prepped and shaved in the usual manner. The triple lumen was accessed with a guidewire. Under fluoroscopy, this was removed over sheath, and, through this sheath and dilator, a guidewire was introduced. A cut down was made, sheath and introducer were placed, and the superior vena cava was accessed with this introducer. An Arrow-Cannon II was placed in the superior vena cava—right atrial junction. This was tunneled to the anterior chest wall, transected, attachments were placed, and flushed for inflow and outflow; it performed well. The catheter was fastened to the skin with 3-0 Prolene and the working incision with 4-0 Monocryl. Fluoroscopy was used to position. The catheter was in the right position. A temporary line was moved in, and the tunnel was closed with 3-0 Prolene. The patient left the OR in stable condition.

Code(s) _____

Case Study 5-4: Operative Report

Preoperative Diagnosis: Symptomatic third-degree heart block

Postoperative Diagnosis: Symptomatic third-degree heart block

Operation: Placement of permanent pacemaker with transvenous electrode

Anesthesia: Local infiltration of lidocaine 1%; total volume 13 cc

Complications: None

Indications: This 74-year-old gentleman was admitted with a diagnosis of third-degree heart block complicated by congestive cardiac failure. Patient is scheduled for placement of a permanent pacemaker today.

Procedure: With the patient supine on the operating table with a shoulder roll placed beneath the thoracic spine, the chest was prepped and draped in a sterile fashion. In the right infraclavicular region, a subcutaneous pocket was created for containing the pulse generator. Using an introducer guidewire, a sheath technique bipolar targeted lead was introduced into the right subclavian vein. Under fluoroscopy control, this was directed into the right ventricle. Two initial locations were not satisfactory for pacing parameters. Finally, the pacemaker was positioned in satisfactory position with the following parameters: at the threshold 0.4 volts, current 1.5 milliamps, and R wave 15. The pacing system analyzer was then turned to 10 volts output and the diaphragm observed for pulsations, which were not proven. The lead was then secured under the clavicle with a single suture of 2-0 Ethibond. It was then attached to a 5794 Medtronic low-profile VVI pacemaker programmed at 70 beats per minute. The pulse generator was then anchored in the subcutaneous pocket with a single 0 PDS suture. The subcutaneous tissue was then approximated with 2-0 PDS and the skin approximated with 4-0 Maxon. Sterile dressing was applied. A chest X-ray was obtained, which showed no pneumothorax and satisfactory position of the lead. The patient then returned to the coronary care unit in good condition.

Code(s) _____

Case Study 5-5: Operative Report

Preoperative Diagnosis: End-stage renal disease

Postoperative Diagnosis: End-stage renal disease

Procedure: Cimino right radiocephalic fistula with ligation of venous side of branches

Anesthesia: Local with monitored anesthesia care

Estimated Blood Loss: 10 cc

Drains: None

Specimens: None

Complications: None

Indications: Patient is a 69-year-old male with a history of hypertension and has developed end-stage renal disease and is in need of access for dialysis.

Details of Procedure: After explaining the potential risks and benefits of the procedure to the patient, a written consent was obtained. The patient was marked in the appropriate right arm. The patient was taken back to the operating room table in the supine position. Monitored anesthesia care was initiated. Patient's right upper extremity was prepped with DuraPrep and Betadine and draped in a standard sterile fashion. With the consent of anesthesia, we proceeded with the operation. A small incision was made on the lateral aspect of the distal forearm in between the cephalic and radial artery. This was preceded by the infusion of 1% lidocaine without epinephrine. The incision was made. Electrocautery was used to dissect down. A combination of electrocautery and blunt dissection was used to dissect out both the cephalic vein and radial artery. Once these were both sufficiently isolated, a vessel loop was passed around the radial artery distally. We then took the cephalic vein, padded off distally, and dissected it. Pott's scissors were then used to open the os of the vessel sufficiently. It was then brought to the radial artery, which was clamped off proximally with bulldogs. A small arteriotomy was made with a #11 blade. The Pott's scissors were then used to open up the same approximately. The arteriovenous anastomosis was accomplished with a running #7-0 Gore-Tex suture on both the posterior and anterior surfaces. Once these were tied down, the clamps were withdrawn, and the vein was felt appropriately. There was a palpable thrill midway up the forearm. Prior to the anastomosis being performed, a few small arterial branches and venous branches were tied off with a #4-0 silk suture. After completion of the arteriovenous anastomosis, we then proceeded further up the forearm, made a small incision over the branches of the cephalic vein, and tied them off with #4-0 silk. Hemostatis was assured in both operative sites. #3-0 Vicryl sutures were used to close the subcutaneous tissue, and a running #4-0 Prolene suture was used to close the epidermis of both operative sites. Again, in this procedure, the patient had a palpable radial pulse. He had a palpable flow approximately three-quarters of the way up the forearm over the cephalic vein. He was able to move all of his fingers and had good sensation. The patient was discharged to PACU in good condition.

Code(s) _____

Case Study 5-6: Operative Report

Preoperative Diagnosis: Kidney failure

Postoperative Diagnosis: Kidney failure

Procedure Performed: Left wrist forearm exploration for arteriovenous fistula creation, exploration only, no fistula formed because of obliterated vein

Estimated Blood Loss: Less than 20 cc

Indication: Patient is a 63-year-old male with chronic renal failure who required long-term dialysis. Patient has a history of IV drug use in the past, and we attempted to perform AV fistula in the forearm so as to allow him to dilate his venous sites and allow access for hemodialysis.

Details of the Procedure: Patient was brought to the operating room, given sedation, and then the left arm was thoroughly prepped and draped. We gave approximately 10 cc of combination of 1% lidocaine and 0.5% Marcaine in the subcutaneous tissue for about 3–4 cm longitudinal, 1 cm lateral to the radial pulse. We made a skin incision along the infiltrated area with a #15 blade and carried down dissection with electrocautery to the subcutaneous tissues. We then used Weitlaner, and we were able to carefully identify the distal cephalic vein, which was white and obliterated. We encircled it, examined it, and it was not useful for a dialysis access; in fact, it was felt to be chronically fibrotic. Therefore, a Cimino type AV fistula was abandoned, and we closed it with two layers with interrupted #3-0 Vicryl subcutaneously and a running #5-0 Prolene to re-approximate the skin edges. The patient tolerated the procedure well. Sterile dressing was applied. He was transferred to PACU in a stable condition. Estimated blood loss was less than 20 cc. Received 300 cc of crystalloids. No complications.

Code(s) _____

Digestive System

Chapter Outline

Introduction

Endoscopy Procedures

Upper Gastrointestinal (GI) Endoscopy
Procedures

Lower Gastrointestinal (GI) Endoscopy
Procedures

Hernia Repairs

Overview of Laparoscopic Procedures
in Digestive System

Laparoscopic Cholecystectomy

Nasogastric or Orogastric Tube Placement

Surgical Treatment of Hemorrhoids

Key Terms

ablation

bipolar cautery

cold biopsy

colonoscopy

EGD

epigastric

ERCP

esophageal dilation

esophagoscope

esophagus

femoral hernia

femoral hernia

hemorroidectomy

hemorrhoids

hernia

hot biopsy forceps

incarcerated hernia

incisional hernia

inguinal hernia

initial hernia repair

laparoscopic

large intestines

lumbar

mesh

percutaneous
endoscopic
gastrostomy (PEG)

proctosigmoidoscopy

recurrent hernia

reducible hernia

rubber band
ligation

sigmoidoscopy

sliding hernia

small intestines

snare

spigelian hernia

strangulated
hernia

suture ligation

umbilical hernia

upper GI system

Chapter Objectives

At the conclusion of this chapter, the student should be able to:

- Identify anatomical structures of the digestive system.
- Describe common surgical procedures of the digestive system.
- Explain coding guidelines applicable to digestive system coding.
- Differentiate between methods for esophageal dilation.

2010 Current Procedural Terminology © 2009 American Medical Association. All Rights Reserved.

- Describe coding guidelines for incomplete colonoscopies.
- Apply guidelines for coding hernia repairs.
- Differentiate among the surgical methods for treating hemorrhoids.
- Use references to assist with coding assignment.
- Given a case scenario, accurately assign CPT codes and modifiers (if applicable).

Introduction

The digestive system is a series of organs and glands that process foods (Figure 6-1).

The **esophagus** is the hollow tube that connects the pharynx with the stomach. The sac-like stomach leads to the small intestines. The **small intestines** begin at the pyloric sphincter and are composed of three contiguous sections: duodenum, jejunum, and ileum. The **large intestines** (colon) include the cecum, ascending colon, transverse colon, descending colon, and sigmoid colon. The rectum is continuous with the sigmoid colon, and it passes through a funnel-shaped pelvic diaphragm to join the anus.

This chapter will focus on the most common surgical procedures of the digestive system, such as colonoscopy, esophagogastroduodenoscopy (EGD), endoscopic retrograde cholangiopancreatography (ERCP), and hernia repairs.

Endoscopy Procedures

Before focusing on specific endoscopic procedures of the digestive system, this overview will outline general coding guidelines that are applicable to all endoscopic procedures. The following coding guidelines can be found in *CPT Assistant* (October 2001):

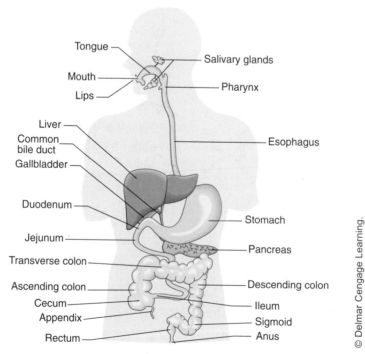

Figure 6-1 Digestive system organs

2010 Current Procedural Terminology © 2009 American Medical Association. All Rights Reserved.

- Surgical & Diagnostic Endoscopy
  Surgical endoscopies always include diagnostic endoscopies. In these cases, the diagnostic endoscopy is not reported as a separate procedure. During the endoscopic session, surgical techniques may include such procedures as biopsies, control of bleeding, or dilation.

- Biopsy and Removal of Lesion
  If a single lesion is biopsied and then subsequently removed during the same operative session, only the code for removal is reported. If a separate lesion is biopsied and another lesion is removed, then both procedures are coded.

- Multiple Codes from Same Family
  Multiple codes from the same family can be reported if performed in the same session by the same physician.

- Control of Bleeding
  Several endoscopic procedures describe control of bleeding by any method. These codes are intended for use when the control of bleeding was required for spontaneous hemorrhage or because of a traumatic injury, not the result of another type of operative intervention.

Review of Documentation

During the review of the operative report for an endoscopic procedure, the coder will search for answers to the following questions:

- Was the procedure diagnostic or surgical?
- What was performed? What was visualized?
- What (if anything) was removed (e.g., polyp)?
- What technique was used to remove tissue (e.g., snare)?

Upper Gastrointestinal (GI) Endoscopic Procedures

The **upper GI system** consists of the esophagus, stomach, and duodenum (first portion of the small intestines). This section will highlight common upper GI endoscopic procedures that help to diagnosis and treat abnormalities: esophagoscopy, esophagogastroduodenoscopy, and endoscopic retrograde cholangiopancreatography.

Esophagoscopy (43200–43232)

An **esophagoscope** is inserted as a means to treat and diagnose diseases and disorders of the esophagus. Most digestive system endoscopic procedures list the diagnostic code first in the family of codes.

43200 esophagoscopy, rigid or flexible; diagnostic, with or without collection of specimen(s) by brushing or washing (separate procedure)

43201	With directed submucosal injection(s),any substances	
43202	With biopsy, single or multiple	Family of codes
43204	With injection sclerosis of esophageal varices	
43205	With band ligation of esophageal varices	

If the surgeon performed a flexible esophagoscopy with washings and band ligation of esophageal varices, the correct code assignment would be 43205.

2010 Current Procedural Terminology © 2009 American Medical Association. All Rights Reserved.

Esophageal Dilation

CPT provides for two methods for **esophageal dilation:**

NOTE:

Hurst and Maloney are common types of bougies used for esophageal dilation (code 43450). A bougie is a slender, flexible instrument used for exploring or dilating.

- **Endoscopic**: through the endoscope the physician selects a dilating balloon (43220) or plastic dilators over the guiding wire to stretch the esophagus (43226)
- **Manipulation** (not during scope): surgeon sprays the throat with local anesthesia to pass a tapered dilating instrument through the mouth and guided to the esophagus (43450–43458)

Esophagogastroduodenoscopy (EGD) (43235–43259)

An **EGD** is performed by inserting a thin tube in the mouth to view the esophagus, stomach, and duodenum (first part of small intestines) (Figure 6-2).

NOTE:

Code ranges can be located in the alphabetic index under Endoscopy, Gastrointestinal, and Upper. There is no alphabetic entry for the abbreviation EGD.

When the endoscope passes through the diaphragm into the stomach, the procedure is an esophagogastroscopy. When the scope extends through the pyloric channel, then it is described as an EGD.

In the CPT format for upper GI endoscopic procedures, the diagnostic procedure is listed first, and following is a list of descriptions for surgical treatment. According to CPT endoscopy guidelines, it is appropriate to list multiple codes if the documentation supports the coding selection.

During the EGD, the surgeon performs a removal of a polyp by hot biopsy forceps and removal of a foreign body.

```
Correct coding assignment:    43250 Snare removal
                              43247 Removal of foreign body
```

Note: For physician services, modifier 51 (multiple procedures) would be appended to the second code to indicate that the same physician performed multiple procedures at the same session.

Endoscopic Retrograde Cholangiopancreatography (ERCP)

An **ERCP** combines the use of X-rays and an endoscope to visualize the liver, gallbladder, bile ducts, and pancreas. Through the endoscope, the physician can see the inside of the stomach and duodenum and

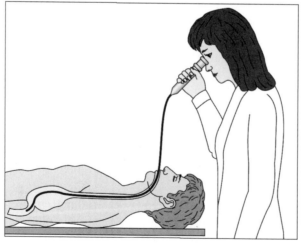

© Delmar Cengage Learning.

Figure 6-2 Esophagogastroduodenoscopy (EGD)

2010 Current Procedural Terminology © 2009 American Medical Association. All Rights Reserved.

can inject dyes into the ducts in the biliary tree and pancreas so they can be seen on X-rays. ERCP is primarily used to diagnose and treat conditions such as gallstones, strictures, and cancer.

Similar to the format of other endoscopies, the coding selection describes the diagnostic ERCP followed by a family of surgical descriptions (CPT codes 43260–43272).

Exercise 6-1: Upper Gastrointestinal Endoscopy Procedures

Assign CPT codes to the following procedures. Append CPT/HCPCS Level II modifiers if applicable. Concentrate on application of coding guidelines, and do not focus on sequencing or assignment of modifier 51 (physician services).

1. The surgeon inserted the scope in the esophagus and removed some cell specimens via brushing. After the scope was removed, the surgeon dilated the esophagus over a guide wire.

Code(s) _____ 43200 , 43226 _____

2. The physician performs an EGD with a biopsy of a polyp. After the biopsy, the physician elects to remove the same polyp via hot biopsy forceps.

Code(s) _____

3. The surgeon performed an EGD with dilation of the esophagus over a guide wire.

Code(s) _____

4. The surgeon performed an esophagoscopy for removal of a piece of chicken bone. Upon removal of the bone, a sharp piece perforated the lining of the esophagus, and the bleeding required use of cautery.

Code(s) _____

Lower Gastrointestinal (GI) Endoscopy Procedures

Lower GI endoscopies can be classified by the area of the intestine examined, as follows:

- **Proctosigmoidoscopy:** Examination limited to the rectum and sigmoid colon (45300–45327).

- **Sigmoidoscopy:** Examination of entire rectum and sigmoid colon, which may include a portion of the descending colon (45330–45345). The depth of visualization is typically 35 or 60 cm, depending on the instrument used.

- **Colonoscopy:** Examination of entire colon, from rectum to cecum, which may include the terminal ileum (45355–45392). In general, a colonoscopy examines the colon to a level of 60 cm or higher (Figure 6-3). Indications for performing lower GI procedures include an abnormal barium enema, lower gastrointestinal bleeding, and diarrhea. They may also be performed for follow-up examination after removal of a neoplastic growth.

Removal of Tumors and Polyps

Endoscopic removal of tumors and polyps can be accomplished with several techniques. The CPT codes differentiate among the following methods (Figure 6-4).

- **Hot Biopsy/Bipolar Cautery (45384)**

  Hot biopsy forceps resemble tweezers connected to an electrosurgical unit. Grasping the polyp, the physician pulls the growth away from the wall of the structure. The remaining portion is destroyed with the electrocoagulation current. Bipolar cautery also uses electrical current to remove the polyp.

2010 Current Procedural Terminology © 2009 American Medical Association. All Rights Reserved.

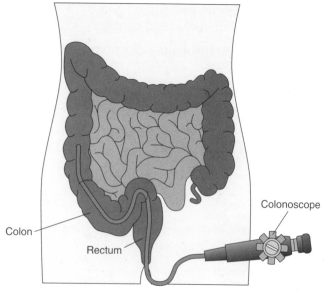

Figure 6-3 Colonoscopy (posterior view)

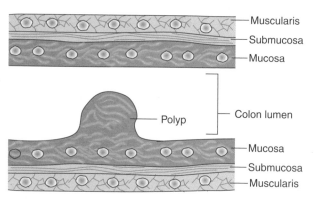

Figure 6-4 Colon polyp

© Delmar Cengage Learning.

© Delmar Cengage Learning.

- **Snare Technique (45385)**

  A wire loop is slipped over the polyp or tissue. The stalk is then cauterized, and the growth is removed. Snare devices may also be used without electrocautery to "decapitate" small polyps. Larger lesions may be removed with a single application of the snare or can be removed with several applications of the snare in pieces frequently described as "piecemeal." Examples of snare devices include hot snare, monopolar snare, cold snare, and bipolar snare.

- **Other Ablation (45383)**

  The **ablation** (removal) of the tissue can be performed with many different types of devices (heater probe, bipolar cautery probe, argon laser, etc.) whether or not a sample was obtained with biopsy forceps before the ablative device is applied. When another method is used (e.g., laser) during the endoscopy, the coder should assign the code for the endoscopy that states "with ablation of tumor(s), polyp(s), or other lesion(s) not amenable to removal by hot biopsy forceps, bipolar cautery, or snare technique."

- **Cold Biopsy (45380)**

  The cold biopsy technique is used with forceps to grasp and remove a small piece of tissue without the application of cautery. The biopsy may be from a lesion that is too large to remove, from a suspicious area of abnormal mucosa, or from a lesion or polyp so small that it can be completely removed in the performance.

Control of Bleeding (during Colonoscopy)

Control of bleeding that occurs because of removing a polyp, etc., and controlled by any method is considered part of the treatment and would not be assigned a separate code.

If a patient has spontaneous bleeding (e.g., angiodysplasia), then an additional code would be appropriate. Note that if a report describes an injection in conjunction with attempts to control spontaneous bleeding, then the correct code would be 45382, not 45381.

> **Coding Tips:**
>
> *It is common for surgeons to remove remnants of a lesion; this is an integral part of the procedure. Report only the CPT code that identifies the technique used to remove the polyp or tumor, not the remnants.*

> **Note:**
>
> *For physician services, CPT guidelines state (read note before code 45300) to use modifier 52 (reduced services) for an incomplete colonoscopy with full preparation. However, CMS directs the coder to use modifier 53 (discontinued procedure).*

2010 Current Procedural Terminology © 2009 American Medical Association. All Rights Reserved.

Incomplete Colonoscopies

There are several guidelines for coding discontinued procedures for physicians and hospitals. In the case of a colonoscopy, the procedure may be attempted, but circumstances may prevent the entire colon from being visualized (e.g., poor prep).

> **Note:**
>
> *For facility services, use modifiers 73 or 74 as appropriate (discontinued outpatient procedures) (CMS Transmittal 442, January 2005).*

Exercise 6-2 Colonoscopy Procedures

Assign CPT codes to the following procedures. Append CPT/HCPCS Level II modifiers if applicable. Concentrate on application of coding guidelines, and do not focus on sequencing or assignment of modifier 51 (physician services).

1. During a colonoscopy, the surgeon removed a polyp at the hepatic flexure via hot biopsy. A second polypectomy was performed in the sigmoid colon, and it was removed with the use of a snare. With the snare removal, a small amount of bleeding was noted, and it was cauterized.

   Code(s) _____

2. During the colonoscopy, the surgeon injected the polyp with India ink and subsequently removed the polyp via hot biopsy forceps.

   Code(s) _____

3. Operative note states that the patient had a lower GI endoscopy that extended from the anus to the cecum. A snare removal of a polyp in the sigmoid colon was performed. In addition, remnants of the polyp were removed via electrocautery.

   Code(s) _____

4. Patient was taken to the endoscopy suite for a colonoscopy. IV sedation was administered, and the video colonoscope was inserted through the anus and advanced to the sigmoid colon. The anatomical distortion of the colon prevented the scope from being advanced further, and it was elected to terminate the procedure. (Note codes for physician services and hospital outpatient services.)

   Code(s) _____

Hernia Repairs

Hernias occur when the muscles become weak and push through a spot creating a bulge. CPT codes 49491–49659 describe procedures related to hernia repair (Figure 6-5).

To assign a code from this range, a coder will need to answer one or more of the following questions:

- *Was the repair performed via laparoscope?* CPT offers a separate range of codes for laparoscopic repairs (49650–49659).

- *What is the type of hernia (e.g., inguinal, incisional)?*

- *What is the age of the patient (several codes specify age)? Initial* inguinal hernia repair codes differentiate between the ages of the patients.

- *What was the clinical presentation (sliding, incarcerated)?*

- *What is the history related to the hernia (recurrent, initial)?*

> **Note:**
>
> **Initial repair** is defined as the first surgical repair of the hernia. **Recurrent** means the hernia has been surgically repaired previously.

2010 Current Procedural Terminology © 2009 American Medical Association. All Rights Reserved.

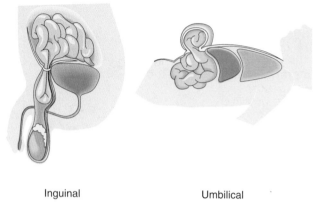

Inguinal   Umbilical

© Delmar Cengage Learning.

Figure 6-5 Hernias: inguinal and umbilical

Location and Clinical Presentation of Hernias

The following terms are used to describe the type and location of the hernia:

- **Inguinal:**   inguinal canal in the groin area
- **Lumbar:**   lumbar region of torso
- **Incisional:** site of previous surgical incision
- **Femoral:**   femoral canal in groin area
- **Epigastric:** above the navel
- **Umbilical:** at the navel
- **Spigelian:** after the inferior epigastric vessel along the outer border of the rectus muscle

> **Note:**
>
> Diaphragmatic and hiatal hernias are not assigned to the digestive system. See code range 39502–39541.

A number of terms are used to describe the clinical presentation of hernias. These include:

- **Reducible:**   Protruding organs can be returned to normal position by surgical (not medical) manipulation.
- **Sliding:**   The colon or cecum is part of the hernia sac. In some cases, the urinary bladder may also be involved.
- **Incarcerated:** Hernia cannot be reduced without surgical intervention.
- **Strangulated:** Blood supply to the contained organ is reduced. This may present a medical emergency.

Diagnosis: Recurrent, sliding inguinal hernia

Summary of procedure: 34-year-old patient underwent a repair of an inguinal hernia.

CPT code: 49525 Repair inguinal hernia, sliding, any age

Implantation of Mesh

During a hernia repair, if the defect is large and muscles cannot be sutured, the surgeon may elect to place a mesh (or other prosthesis) to cover the defect. **Mesh** is a synthetic path used to strengthen and close the incision site. Commonly used meshes are Marlex and Prolene.

> **Note:**
>
> CPT code 49568 for implantation of mesh is only to be used as additional code for incisional and ventral hernia repairs. The use of mesh with other hernia repairs is not coded. Insertion of mesh during a laparoscopic repair is considered part of the procedure and would not warrant an additional code.

2010 Current Procedural Terminology © 2009 American Medical Association. All Rights Reserved.

Surgeon performs an incisional hernia repair with mesh for a patient with a recurrent, incarcerated hernia.

Code assignment: 49566 Repair, recurrent, incisional, incarcerated

49568 Implantation, mesh

Laparoscopic Hernia Repairs

A laparoscopic repair is commonly performed to repair bilateral and recurrent hernias. Less discomfort and faster recovery are the main advantages of this approach. As with other endoscopies, a surgical laparoscopy includes a diagnostic laparoscopy.

Exercise 6-3: Hernia Repairs

Assign CPT codes to the following procedures. Append CPT/HCPCS Level II modifiers if applicable. Concentrate on application of coding guidelines, and do not focus on sequencing or assignment of modifier 51 (physician services).

1. The surgeon performed a laparoscopic hernia repair on a 44-year-old male who had the diagnosis of recurrent, incarcerated incisional hernia. The repair includes implantation of mesh.
Code(s) _____

2. The surgeon performed an umbilical hernia repair on a 34-year-old male. The size of the defect required implantation of mesh.
Code(s) _____

Overview of Laparoscopic Procedures in Digestive System

Laparoscopic procedures are minimally invasive, requiring less recovery time than traditional open procedures.

Laparoscopy was long used by gynecologists for the diagnosis of diseases of the ovary and uterus. Technological improvements, such as use of video cameras, have permitted procedures on the smallest of structures, and the use of laparoscopy has been extended to surgical procedures involving the appendix, colon, and more.

In earlier editions of CPT, laparoscopic procedures were consolidated into one section. Today, laparoscopic procedures have their own headings in the various surgical sections.

Note the following sampling of laparoscopic procedures in the digestive system:

```
43280    Laparoscopic fundoplasty
44970    Laparoscopic appendectomy
45400    Laparoscopic proctopexy
```

> **Note:**
>
> *The format of CPT provides for an "unlisted procedure" code in each of the laparoscopic code ranges. Due to the advancements of surgical practice and technology, it is common for unlisted procedures to be assigned for new procedures.*

Laparoscopic Cholecystectomy

With traditional surgery (open treatment), the gallbladder is removed through an incision into the abdomen. The **laparoscopic** approach (a small, thin tube with a scope on the tip) removes the gallbladder through a small incision in the umbilicus (Figure 6-6).

This procedure is less invasive since it does not require a major incision; it is performed with three or four tiny puncture holes.

The coding selection for laparoscopic cholecystectomy includes the following excerpt:

47562   Laparoscopic cholecystectomy

47563   with cholangiography *(cholangiography is the radiological study for visualization of the bile ducts)*

47564   with exploration of common bile duct *(the exploratory procedure is used to see a stone or some obstruction that is blocking the flow of bile from the liver and gallbladder to intestine)*

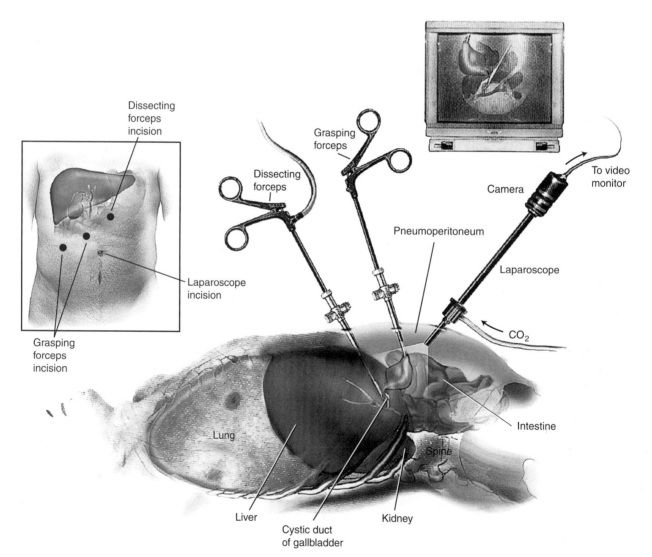

Figure 6-6 Laparoscopic cholecystectomy: lateral view

© Delmar Cengage Learning.

Nasogastric or Orogastric Tube Placement

Putting in a feeding tube, medically known as a **percutaneous endoscopic gastrostomy** (PEG), is a way to provide food, liquids, and medications (when appropriate) directly into the stomach through a tube placed in the abdomen.

The procedure is performed on patients who are having difficulty swallowing and can't consume enough food or liquids by mouth to maintain adequate nutrition.

The endoscope is passed through the mouth and then advanced through the esophagus into the stomach. To ensure correct positioning of the PEG tube, radiological images are obtained. The feeding tube, which is inserted through an incision in your abdomen, rests in the stomach and exits through the skin.

CPT provides a range of codes (43752–43761) for placement, changing and repositioning of the tube.

> **Note:**
>
> *Use code 43761 (repositioning of the gastric feeding tube through the duodenum for enteric nutrition) after (not at the same session) as placement of the feeding tube. Any repositioning to reach the final site for enteric nutrition is included in the initial placement procedure and is not coded separately.*

> **Note:**
>
> *Placement of a PEG tube during an EGD procedure is assigned CPT code 43246.*

Surgical Treatment of Hemorrhoids

There is a variety of CPT codes dedicated to the treatment of hemorrhoids. **Hemorrhoids** are swollen and inflamed veins in the anus and rectum (Figure 6-7).

They may result from straining during bowel movements or the increased pressure on these veins during pregnancy. Treatment includes the following:

- **Incision of Thrombosed Hemorrhoid (external)** (46083)

  A scalpel blade is used to make an incision along the long axis of the thrombosed hemorrhoid. A clamp is used to grasp the thrombus (clot) for removal.

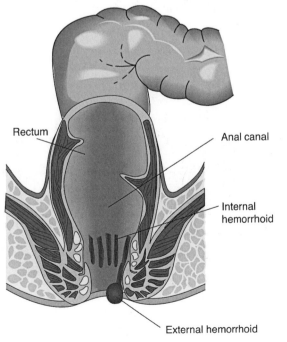

Rectum

Anal canal

Internal hemorrhoid

External hemorrhoid

© Delmar Cengage Learning.

Figure 6-7 Hemorrhoids: internal and external

2010 Current Procedural Terminology © 2009 American Medical Association. All Rights Reserved.

- **Rubber Band Ligation** (46221)

  Hemorrhoidectomy is a treatment for internal hemorrhoids that is sometimes referred to as "banding." The physician attaches tiny rubber bands to the base of hemorrhoids. With their circulation cut off, the hemorrhoids painlessly fall away after 7 to 10 days and are expelled with stool.

- **Destruction of Internal Hemorrhoid(s) by Thermal Energy** (46930)

  Thermal energy ablation (e.g., infrared coagulation) is applied to remove the hemorrhoid(s). Infrared coagulation involves a small probe with a light source that coagulates the veins above the hemorrhoid causing it to shrink and recede.

- **Suture Ligation** (46945–46946)

  Suture ligation differs from hemorrhoidectomy by simple ligature in that the physician isolates the hemorrhoid and ties suture material to its base. Codes are differentiated by single hemorrhoid column/group versus 2 or more hemorrhoid column/groups.

- **Hemorrhoidectomy** (46250–46262)

  The surgical excision codes are differentiated by whether the hemorrhoids were internal, external, or both. In addition, the coding selection is based on the number of hemorrhoidal columns/groups removed.

- **Destruction by Cryosurgery** (46999)

  Coders are instructed to report as unlisted code 46999 for destruction of hemorrhoids by cryosurgery.

> **Note:**
>
> *Code 46221 is only assigned once per operative session regardless of how many hemorrhoids the physician bands at a time.*

Summary

- The digestive system includes numerous endoscopic procedure codes.
- Unless coding guidelines (or NCCI edits) specify otherwise, multiple codes from the same family can be reported.
- Control of bleeding during an operative procedure may or may not be assigned a separate code depending on the circumstances.
- Read the operative reports carefully to determine what procedures were performed during the operative episode (do not rely on surgical procedures section).
- There are two methods for coding esophageal dilations (via scope and not via scope).
- Technique used for removing colon polyps dictates the code assignment.
- If a lesion is biopsied and the **same** lesion is subsequently removed, just code the removal.
- If a lesion is biopsied and **another** lesion is removed, then code both the biopsy and removal of lesion.
- Removal of remnants of lesion is integral to the procedure and does not warrant a separate code.
- Several coding guidelines exist for coding incomplete colonoscopies.
- The only code for laparoscopic hernia repairs is for inguinal hernia. Other types of laparoscopic hernia repairs will require an unlisted code.
- Several coding selections exist for reporting removal of hemorrhoids.

Internet Links

National Library of Medicine: *http://www.nlm.nih.gov/medlineplus/digestivesystem.html*
Overview of the anatomy of the digestive system and associated diseases and disorders

2010 Current Procedural Terminology © 2009 American Medical Association. All Rights Reserved.

National Digestive Diseases Information Clearinghouse: *http://digestive.niddk.nih.gov/ddiseases/pubs/yrdd/*
Digestive system overview

National Cancer Institute: *http://training.seer.cancer.gov/module_anatomy/unit10_5_quiz_dd_1.html*
Interactive quiz for identifying digestive system organs

National Library of Medicine: *http://www.nlm.nih.gov/medlineplus/tutorials/uppergiendoscopy/htm/index.htm*
EGD interactive tutorial

National Digestive Diseases Information Clearinghouse: *http://digestive.niddk.nih.gov/ddiseases/pubs/ercp/index.htm*
Diagram and description of ERCP

National Library of Medicine: *http://www.nlm.nih.gov/medlineplus/tutorials/*
Series of tutorials including sigmoidoscopy and colonoscopy

CMS: *http://www.cms.hhs.gov/transmittals/downloads/R442CP.pdf*
Transmittal from January 2005 explains use of modifiers 52, 73, 74

Review

I.   Medical Terminology Assessment

Match the following terms with the correct definition:

D	1. cecum	A. last part of the small intestine
F	2. rectum	B. organ that stores bile and releases it into the small intestines
E	3. duodenum	C. tube between the stomach and mouth
B	4. liver	D. first part of the large intestines
C	5. esophagus	E. first part of the small intestines
A	6. ileum	F. lower part of the large intestines

II.   Case Studies

Case Study 6-1: Operative Report

Preoperative Diagnosis: Dysphagia

Postoperative Diagnosis: Hiatal hernia

Procedures Performed: Esophagogastroduodenoscopy with esophageal dilation

Details of Procedure: The Olympus video endoscope was inserted per orally and advanced to the descending duodenum. The descending duodenum and duodenal bulb are both normal. The pylorus is normal. The cardia is normal. The patient does have a moderate-sized sliding hiatal hernia, but there is no evidence of esophageal stricture or ring. The patient's esophageal mucosa appears normal. The scope was removed. Because of the patient's dysphagia to solids, I did pass a 50 French Maloney dilator to be sure there were no areas of relative narrowing unappreciated on endoscopy. This dilator passed quite easily, meeting no resistance. The procedure was then terminated.

Assessment: I suspect the patient's dysphagia is based on an esophageal motility disorder.

Code(s) _____

2010 Current Procedural Terminology © 2009 American Medical Association. All Rights Reserved.

Case Study 6-2: Operative Note

Procedure Performed: Colonoscopy

Indications for Procedure: Polyp in colon

Anesthesia: Demerol 50 mg. Versed 5 mg. Intravenous

Findings: The videocolonoscope was inserted into the rectum and advanced to the cecum. It was noted that a 1.5 to 2 cm ascending colon polyp was in the ascending colon, which was biopsied. Subsequently, a contact YAG laser probe was used to vaporize the polyp. Photographs were taken before and after. There were no apparent complications. As mentioned, biopsies were taken before the YAG laser was used. There were no other polyps in the colon or rectum. No masses noted.

Code(s) _____

Case Study 6-3: Operative Report

Procedure: Endoscopic Retrograde Cholangiopancreatography (ERCP)

Medication: Cetacaine local, Versed 4 mg. Demerol 50 mg. Glucagon 0.7 mg. IV.

Indication: This is a 71-year-old female who is status post cholecystectomy. The patient had a choledochotomy with expression of several stones from the common duct, followed by Fogartization with another 16 small stones removed. A T tube was placed at the time of the procedure, and the postoperative course went without incident. However, the patient had a recurrent attack of abdominal pain similar to her gallbladder attacks, and liver function tests were elevated. This procedure was done to rule out retained common duct stone.

Procedure: Following informed consent, the patient was placed on her stomach, and the side-viewing duodenoscope was passed per os through the upper esophageal sphincter and into the small bowel. The ampulla was identified and appeared normal. Selective cannulation of the pancreatic and common bile duct was performed for administration of dye.

Findings: Pancreatogram—the pancreatic duct appeared normal in caliber, contour, and course. Cholangiogram—the common bile duct, common hepatic duct, intrahepatic duct, and cystic duct remnant appeared normal. No evidence of intrahepatic filling defects present. The procedure was terminated. The patient tolerated the procedure well without any obvious complications.

Impression: Normal postcholecystectomy ERCP. It is possible that the patient has recently passed a stone, but no intrinsic filling defects were noted with careful examination and magnification.

Code(s) _____

Case Study 6-4: Operative Report

Procedure: EGD

Indications: The patient has had several episodes of hematemesis. The patient is now finally up for endoscopy to assess the cause of the hematemesis. This was particularly important, given the potential ongoing need for nonsteroidal anti-inflammatory drugs.

2010 Current Procedural Terminology © 2009 American Medical Association. All Rights Reserved.

Procedure: The endoscope was inserted into the esophagus without difficulty. There were two small ulcerations located just above the Z line, which were biopsied. Some erythema was noted. There were no mechanical obstructions and no other inflammatory changes. The stomach, duodenal bulb, and descending duodenum were normal. Impression: distal reflux esophagitis.

Code(s) _____

Case Study 6-5: Operative Note

Postoperative Diagnosis: Right inguinal hernia

Operation: Repair of right inguinal hernia

History: This 46-year-old male has a large symptomatic right inguinal hernia. No previous history of hernia repair.

Procedure: The patient was brought to the operating room; spinal anesthesia was administered. The patient was prepped and draped in the usual sterile fashion, and 0.5% Marcaine was infiltrated in the right inguinal region. The right inguinal region was explored. The external ring was dilated, and the external oblique was opened. A large indirect sac was carefully dissected from the spermatic cord. The sac was opened; there was no evidence of intra-abdominal contents at this time. High ligation of the sac was carried out with #0 silk placed in a purse-string fashion. A second silk tie was placed slightly distally and a redundant sac removed. The floor overall was strong. Bassini repair was performed approximating the conjoin tendon to the shelving border of the inguinal ligament with interrupted #0 silk sutures. The internal ring was tightened minimally. The spermatic cord was placed in its normal position. The external oblique was approximated with interrupted #3-0 silk sutures and the external ring loosely re-created. Irrigation was again carried out. Hemostasis was excellent. Scarpa's fascia was approximated with #3-0 plain sutures. Skin was approximated with staples. Sterile compression dressing was applied. The patient was sent to the recovery room in good condition.

Code(s) _____

Case Study 6-6: Endoscopy Report

Brief History: The patient is a 56-year-old female who was referred for an age-appropriate cancer screen. She has no abdominal pain, change in bowel habit, weight loss, rectal bleeding, or other symptoms. She has had no previous abdominal surgery

Procedure: Colonoscopy with polypectomy

Details of Procedure: Conscious sedation was administered, and the patient was carefully monitored throughout the procedure and recovery period, including oxygen saturation, vital signs, and cardiac rhythm. She tolerated the procedure well and recovered uneventfully. The patient was placed in left lateral decubitus position, and a digital rectal examination was performed, which was normal. The scope was inserted through the anal canal and advanced through the rectum and sigmoid colon. In a well-prepped bowel, it could be advanced to the cecum, which was identified by visualization of the ileocecal valve and cecal ring. The cecum was normal, and the scope was slowly withdrawn through the ascending, transverse, and descending colons, which were normal. Withdrawal through the sigmoid colon revealed a polyp in the distal sigmoid colon measuring approximately 1 cm. This was snared and removed. The rectal mucosa was normal. Withdrawal from the anal canal was unremarkable. The patient tolerated the procedure well.

Impression: 1 cm sessile polyp in the distal sigmoid colon.

Pathology Report: Tubular adenoma

Code(s) _____

Case Study 6-7: Operative Report

Preoperative Diagnosis: Dysphagia secondary to oropharyngeal cancer and radiation therapy

Postoperative Diagnosis: Dysphagia

The Olympus video gastroscope was introduced into the posterior pharynx and passed easily to the esophagus with swallowing. The scope was advanced under direct vision to the esophagus into the stomach and through the pylorus into the duodenal bulb in the second portion. The duodenal bulb appeared normal. The endoscope was withdrawn into the stomach. The stomach was normal in appearance. The esophagus was judged normal in appearance. The satisfactory site for a placement of a gastrostomy tube was identified in the lower body of the stomach. The skin was anesthetized with infiltration of local lidocaine, a needle catheter was introduced transcutaneously into the gastric lumen, and suture material was introduced through this catheter. The suture material was grasped with the endoscopic snare and pulled through the esophagus and out the mouth. This suture material was affixed to the leading edge of the gastrostomy tube, which was pulled down through the esophagus and into the stomach and out the cutaneous tract leaving only the internal bolster of the gastrostomy tube present in the stomach. The endoscope was placed into the stomach, and the bolster was noted to be in appropriate position endoscopically. External bolsters were applied at the level of the skin. The scope was withdrawn, and the patient tolerated the procedure well.

Findings:

1. Normal EGD

2. PEG with satisfactory placement

Code(s) _____

Case Study 6-8: Operative Report

Preoperative Diagnosis:

1. Foreign body of the distal esophagus

2. Hiatal hernia

3. Esophageal stricture

4. Peptic esophagitis

Postoperative Diagnosis:

1. Foreign body of the distal esophagus

2. Hiatal hernia

3. Esophageal stricture

4. Peptic esophagitis

Operation:

1. Esophagoscopy

2. Removal of foreign body (roast beef)

3. Esophageal dilation

Operative Indications: This 54-year-old male has had a known hiatal hernia and a history of having food lodged in the distal esophagus. This happened approximately 10 years ago. He was eating roast beef last night, and the meat became lodged in the distal esophagus. This persisted and so the patient went to the emergency department. Dr. Blevins was called, and he tried to take the food out or push it down, but he was unsuccessful, in spite of giving the patient 250 mg of Demerol and glucagon. I was asked to see him and schedule an esophagoscopy and dilation under anesthesia.

Operative Technique: The patient was brought to the operating room and prepped and draped in the usual fashion. A large Jesberg esophagoscope was introduced into the esophagus without difficulty. The esophagoscope was advanced down into the distal esophagus. The meat was removed, and the area was irrigated with saline. The esophagoscope was then gradually removed. On the way out, no other abnormalities were noted. An esophageal dilatation using Maloney Mercury bougies were used. The Maloney dilator was left in the esophagus for approximately three minutes to keep it dilated. It was gradually removed without difficulty. The patient was transferred to the postanesthesia care unit in satisfactory condition.

Code(s) _____

Case Study 6-9: Colonoscopy Report

Indications: GI bleeding

Procedure: The patient was placed in the left lateral decubitus position and IV sedation was administered. The scope was passed into the anal canal and the rectal mucosa was visualized and appeared normal. The scope was then passed to the rectosigmoid junction, where there were exudative changes with erythematous mucosa extending approximately 10 cm proximally into the sigmoid colon. Beyond this region, the mucosa appeared normal with abnormal mucosal vascular pattern. I was able to advance the colonoscope up to the splenic flexure, but the procedure had to be terminated due to a poor prep.

Impression: Changes suspicious for ischemic colitis

Code(s) _____

Case Study 6-10: Operative Report

Procedure: Colonoscopy

Instrument Used: Olympus Pentax colonoscopy

Premedications: Fentanyl, 100 micrograms, and Versed, 4 mg intravenously

Indications: The patient presents for colonic polyps follow-up

Procedure: The digital and anal exams were normal. The colonoscopy was inserted to the cecum. The prep unfortunately was only fair with a lot of retained thick brown liquid stool scattered throughout the colon. Most of this could be suctioned away, and I think an overall adequate examination was obtained. A total of four polyps were identified, located in the sigmoid and descending colon regions. The largest measured 1.25 cm in diameter. Three of these polyps were large enough to be snared and removed. Two of the three snared polyps were retrieved. The third polyp was lost in a collection of liquid stool and could not be located. This was the smallest polyp. This polypectomy site was also noted to be bleeding following removal of the polyp. The bleeding was bright red and somewhat pulsatile. This polypectomy site was injected with 6.0 cc of a 1/10,000 epinephrine solution with cessation of the bleeding. Finally, one smaller sessile and diminutive polyp was identified, and this was removed with hot biopsy forceps. No other mucosal lesions were identified, though small polyps could conceivably have been missed due to a marginal prep.

Impression: Colonic polyps, removed, path pending. One of the polypectomy sites required injection with epinephrine to control post-polypectomy bleeding.

Code(s) _____

Case Study 6-11: Operative Report

Preoperative Diagnosis: External hemorrhoids

Postoperative Diagnosis: External hemorrhoids

Procedure: Hemorrhoidectomy

Indications: The patient is a 55-year-old male who presented to the surgery center with a chief complaint of prolapsing, itching, bleeding hemorrhoid tissue. Physical examination disclosed the presence of a grade 4 mixed internal and external right posterior hemorrhoid associated with a sizable left internal hemorrhoid as well. He was scheduled for elective hemorrhoidectomy.

Operative Procedure: The patient was brought to the operating room and placed in a sitting position on the transport gurney. A subarachnoid block anesthesia was administered. The patient was transferred to the operating room table on a prone-jackknife position.

After ensuring an adequate level of regional anesthesia, the patient's perineal tissues were prepped and draped in a clean fashion.

A Hill-Ferguson anal speculum was used to examine the patient's anal canal. This examination revealed a large, grade 4 chronically prolapsed right posterior hemorrhoid, a grade 3 left hemorrhoid, and a grade 2 right anterior hemorrhoid.

Based on these findings, it was elected to perform an excisional hemorrhoidectomy on the right posterior column, as this appeared to be the most symptomatic of his lesions.

A #3-0 chromic figure-of-eight suture was placed at the apex of the right posterior hemorrhoidal column. An Allis clamp was used to grasp the anoderm at the external edge of the hemorrhoid and retracted laterally. A diamond-shaped mucosal incision was outlined over the surface of the hemorrhoid.

The mucosal incision over the top of the hemorrhoid was opened from the apex of the hemorrhoid to the anal verge. Superior and inferior flaps of mucosa were elevated.

The hemorrhoid itself was then elevated off the underlying internal sphincter beginning at the anal verge and worked toward the apex of the hemorrhoid. When the apex of the hemorrhoid was reached, it was amputated and passed off the operative field. Bleeding points along the sphincter and underneath the hemorrhoidal column were controlled with cautery. The wound was irrigated, and, when hemostasis was felt to be complete, the mucosa over the right posterior hemorrhoidal defect was closed using a running #3-0 chromic suture. As this suture was brought across the anal verge, the mucosa was packed to the underlying internal sphincter to prevent postoperative mucosal prolapse.

The left group was examined and felt to be amenable to treatment with placement of hemorrhoidal bands. The left hemorrhoidal group was elevated into a McGilvery hemorrhoidal-banding gun. The hemorrhoid was seen to engorge over the top of these bands.

The right posterior hemorrhoidal incision was again examined for hemostasis, which was felt to be complete. The rectum was irrigated a final time, and the incision was covered with Polysporin ointment. A sterile gauze was placed over the anus. Surgical underwear was used to hold the gauze in place. The patient was then transferred back to the transport gurney in supine position and taken to the recovery area in stable condition.

Code(s) _____

Case Study 6-12: Operative Report

Preoperative Diagnosis: Chronic cholelithiasis

Postoperative Diagnosis: Chronic cholelithiasis and subacute cholecystitis

Operation: Laparoscopic cholecystectomy

Procedure: The patient was brought to the operating room, placed in supine position, and underwent general endotracheal anesthesia. After adequate induction of anesthesia, the abdomen was prepped and draped in the usual fashion. The patient had several previous lower midline incisions and right flank incisions; therefore, the pneumoperitoneum was created to epigastric incision to the left of the midline with a Veress needle. After adequate pneumoperitoneum, the 11 mm trocar was placed through extended incision in the left epigastrium just to the left of the midline. The trocar was placed, and the laparoscope and camera were in place. Inspection of the peritoneal cavity revealed that the right upper quadrant was free, but there were several adhesions in the umbilical region where the patient's previous incisions were as well as to the right lower quadrant. Two 5 mm trocars were placed in the right subcostal region, and the adhesions to the right lower quadrant and midline were taken down with a combination of sharp and blunt dissection; most adhesions were flimsy and were just fat and omentum with bowel being adhered. After adhesions were freed in the umbilicus, the umbilical region was free, and an 11 mm trocar was then placed under direct vision through a small infraumbilical incision. The scope and camera were then moved to this position, and the gallbladder was easily visualized. The gallbladder was elevated, and Harman's pouch was grasped. Using a combination of sharp and blunt dissection, the cystic artery was identified. The gallbladder was somewhat tense and subacutely inflamed. A needle was passed through the abdominal wall into the gallbladder, and the gallbladder was aspirated free until it collapsed. One of the graspers was held over this region to prevent any further leakage of bile. Again, direction was turned to the area of the triangle of Calot. The cystic duct was dissected free with sharp and blunt dissection. A small opening was made in the duct, and the cholangiogram catheter was passed. The cholangiogram revealed no stones or filling defects in the bile duct system. The biliary tree was normal. There was good flow into the duodenum, and the catheter was definitely in the cystic duct. The catheter was removed, and the cystic duct was ligated between clips, as was the cystic artery. The gallbladder was then dissected free from the hepatic bed using electrocautery dissection, and it was removed from the abdomen through the umbilical port. Inspection of the hepatic bed noted that hemostasis was meticulous. The region of dissection was irrigated and aspirated dry. The trocars were removed, and the pneumoperitoneum was released. The incisions were closed with Steri-Strips, and the umbilical fascial incision was closed with 2-0 Maxon. The patient tolerated the procedure well, and there were no complications. She was returned to the recovery room awake and alert.

Code(s) _____

Urinary System

Chapter Outline

Key Terms

bladder
calculi
cystoscopy

glomerulus
kidney
nephrons

urea
ureter
ureteral stent

urethra
urolithiasis

Chapter Objectives

At the conclusion of this chapter, the student should be able to:

- Differentiate among the various methods for removing stones in the urinary system.
- Apply general use of modifiers guidelines.
- Distinguish between an indwelling and temporary ureteral stent.
- Apply coding guidelines for urinary system procedures.
- Given a case study, correctly assign CPT codes for surgical cases.

Introduction

The organs, tubes, muscles, and nerves that work together to create, store, and carry urine comprise the urinary system. The urinary system includes two kidneys, two ureters, the bladder, two sphincter muscles, and the urethra. See Figure 7-1.

The kidneys are bean-shaped organs about the size of your fists. They are located in the middle of the back, below the rib cage. The kidneys and urinary system filter waste substances from the blood and eliminate them in urine.

The urinary system removes a type of waste called **urea** from your blood. Urea is carried in the bloodstream to the **kidneys**. The kidneys remove the urea from the blood through the tiny filtering units

2010 Current Procedural Terminology © 2009 American Medical Association. All Rights Reserved.

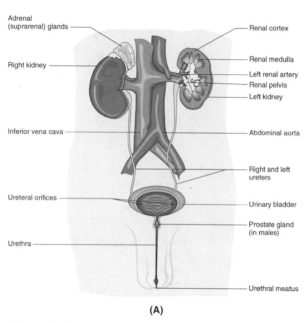

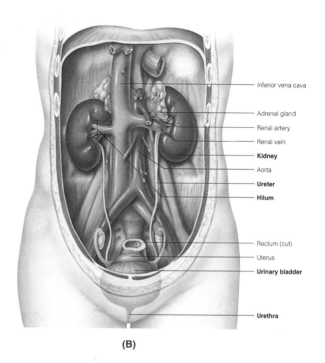

(A)

(B)

© Delmar Cengage Learning.

Figure 7-1 Urinary system. (A) Male. (B) Female.

called **nephrons**. Each nephron consists of a ball formed of small blood capillaries, called **glomerulus**, and a small tube called a renal tube. Urea, together with water and other waste substances, forms urine as it passes through the nephrons and down the renal tubes of the kidney. From the kidneys, urine travels down two thin tubes called **ureters** to the bladder. The **bladder** is a hollow muscular organ that stores urine. Circular muscles called sphincters help keep urine from leaking. The urine exits the bladder through the **urethra**.

Radiological Guidance

Although this textbook chapter focuses on application of surgical coding guidelines, it is important to note that many codes in the urinary system are performed with radiologic guidance. The choice of codes is based on what was done and documented in the medical record.

General Use of Modifiers

Several codes in this section identify that the procedure may be *unilateral or bilateral*; it does not affect the assignment.

    52290   Cystourethroscopy, with ureteral meatotomy unilateral or bilateral

In other codes, it is inherent that they *bilateral*; therefore, appending modifier 50 would not be appropriate.

    52000   Cystourethroscopy (separate procedure)

Other codes are considered *unilateral*; therefore, use of modifiers LT, RT, and 50 would be appropriate.

    52320   Cystourethroscopy (including ureteral catheterization), with removal
             of ureteral calculus

Table 7-1 provides guidance for use of modifiers.

Table 7-1: Use of Modifiers (*CPT Assistant*, May 2001)

Codes That Read Unilateral or Bilateral	Inherent Bilateral Procedures	Unilateral Procedures
• 52290 • 52300 • 52301	• 52000 • 52010 • 52204–52285 • 52305–52318	• 52005 • 52007 • 52320–52355
Do not append modifier 50	Do not append modifier 50	Appropriate to use LT, RT, and 50

Removal of Urinary Stones

Stones (**calculi**) are hard buildups of mineral that form in urine that has stagnated or become concentrated. Stones (**urolithiasis**) can be located in the urethra, bladder, ureter, or kidneys (Figure 7-2).

Surgical treatment includes several methods, some of which require no surgical incision. Some of the common treatments are outlined below:

* Cystoscope can be used in conjunction with a laser lithotripsy to mechanically crush or break up the stones in the bladder. The result is "gravel" type material that can be flushed out of the system. This procedure is called a cystolitholapaxy. A variety of codes are provided for the various

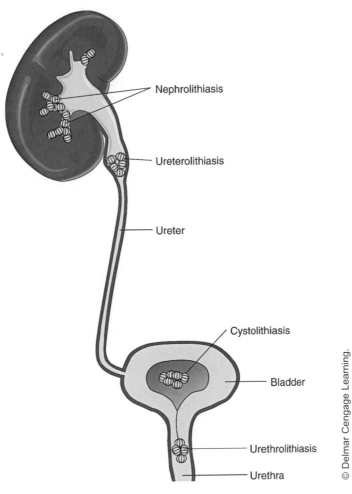

© Delmar Cengage Learning.

Figure 7-2 Common locations of urinary calculi (stone) formation

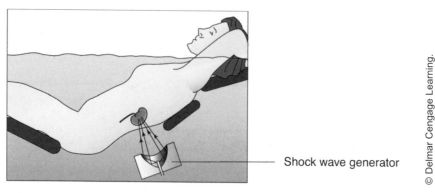

Shock wave generator

© Delmar Cengage Learning.

Figure 7-3 Extracorporeal shock wave lithotripsy (ESWL)

procedures performed for removal of stones in bladder. Accurate code assignment depends on matching the code descriptions with documentation in the health record.

52352   Cystourethroscopy, with ureteroscopy and/or pyeloscopy; with removal or manipulation of calculus

52317   Litholapaxy: crushing or fragmentation of calculus by any means in bladder and removal of fragments; simple or small (less than 2.5 cm)

- Stones may be fragmented from outside the body using sound shock waves. This method, known as extracorporeal shock-wave lithotripsy (ESWL), uses X-rays to locate the stone. At this point, high-power sound waves are focused on the stone and shatter it (Figure 7-3).

50590   Lithotripsy, extracorporeal shock wave

In the Kidney heading, the removal of urinary calculi is coded according to the anatomic site and approach.

50060   Nephrolithotomy; removal of calculus

Cystoscopy

Cystoscopy (or cystourethroscopy) is a procedure where the surgeon uses a thin, lighted instrument (cystourethroscope or resectoscope) to view the urethra and bladder. Physicians commonly refer to this procedure as a "cysto." A review of the structure of code descriptions will reveal a range of codes for diagnostic/routine procedural cystourethroscopy (52000–52010), cystourethroscopy (bladder and urethra) 52204–52318 and (ureter and pelvis) 52320–52355, and vesical neck and prostate (52400–52402). Coders are instructed to review the documentation to determine if an ureteroscopy was performed in addition to the cystoscopy because it has an impact on accurate coding selection. Before coding these procedures, it will be necessary to review coding notes that appear before codes 52000 and 52320.

Cystourethroscopy for removal of calculus   52310

Cystourethroscopy, ureteroscopy for removal of calculus   52352

Ureteral Stents

A **ureteral stent** is a thin, flexible tube that is threaded into the ureter to help drain from the kidney. Stents can be used for patients with active kidney infections or diseased bladder or to manipulate kidney stones. Typically, the stents are inserted via a cystoscope. In some instances, a guidewire is inserted into the ureter under the aid of a fluoroscope. The guidewire provides a path for placement of the stent. Once the stent is in place, the guidewire and cystoscope are removed. For coding purposes, there are two kinds of stents: temporary and indwelling. Stents that are left in place for the duration of a particular intervention are classified as temporary. A self-retaining (indwelling) catheter is intended to remain in the ureter beyond the intraoperative period. Placement and removal of a temporary ureteral stent is integral to the cystoscopy procedures 52320–52339; therefore, an additional code would not be reported. However, if the physician inserts an indwelling ureteral stent, it should be reported (52332). This code is considered to be unilateral; therefore, if bilateral ureteral stents were placed, modifier 50 (bilateral) would be appropriate.

Exercise 7-1: Cystoscopy Procedures

Directions: Assign CPT codes to the following procedures. Append CPT/HCPCS Level II modifiers if applicable. Concentrate on application of coding guidelines, and do not focus on sequencing codes or assignment of modifier 51. For appropriate appending of modifiers to CPT codes, students should have access to software that has up-to-date editing features.

1. The surgeon performs a cystoscopy with laser lithotripsy of ureteral calculus with ureteroscopy and ureteral catheterization.

Code(s) _____

2. The physician performs a cystoscopy and resection of a 1.0 cm bladder tumor and administration of a steroid injection into a urethral stricture.

Code(s) _____

3. The surgeon performs a cystourethroscopy with balloon dilation of left ureteral stricture. In addition, due to reports of pain on the right side, a diagnostic cystourethroscopy with ureteroscopy of right ureter was performed.

Code(s) _____

Summary

- Endoscopic procedures dominate the urology section of CPT.

- A variety of methods and codes are used to describe removal of urinary stones.

- Indwelling ureteral stents are in place after intraoperative episode.

Internet Links

The Kidney: *http://www.thekidney.com*
Educational site with links

WebMD: *http://www.webmd.com*
General topics

Urology Health: *http://www.urologyhealth.org*
Click Patient Information link (extensive list of diseases, anatomic diagrams)

Review

I. Image Labeling

Label the following diagram with the correct anatomic descriptions.

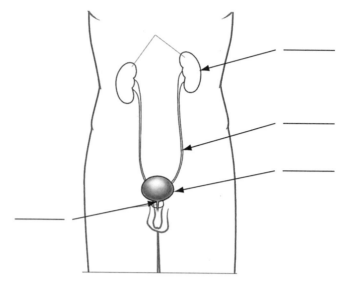

© Delmar Cengage Learning.

Figure 7-4 Urinary system

II. Case Studies

Case Study 7-1: Operative Report

Preoperative Diagnosis: Indwelling right ureteral stent

Postoperative Diagnosis: Indwelling right ureteral stent

Procedures:

1. Cystoscopy

2. Removal of right ureteral stone

Findings: Right ureteral stent was removed without difficulty.

Indication for Operation: Patient is a 60-year-old gentleman who has a known bilateral ureteral stone, which is status post right ureteroscopy with stone extraction. There was a remaining left ureteral renal stone. The patient had a right ureteral stent placement at that time. He is here for the stent removal.

Operation in Detail: Patient was taken to the Cystoscopy Suite and placed in the supine position. His genitalia were prepped and draped in the sterile surgical fashion after which 2% lidocaine jelly was infused into the penile urethra. A #19 French variable flexible cystoscope was inserted into the urethra. It should be noted that prior to this, he was noted to have meatal anastomosis and had to be dilated with Van Buren sounds starting at #12 French going to #20 French without difficulty. The scope was able to be reinserted. The pendulous urethra appeared normal. The prostatic urethra had some moderate enlargement of lateral lobes and high median bar. The scope was passed easily into the bladder. Once inside the bladder, the right ureteral stent was easily visualized, and a grasper was used to remove the stent under direct vision. The patient was then taken to PACU and recovered and was given gatifloxacin 500 mg p.o. q.d. × three days. We will follow up the intervention for his remaining left renal stone.

Code(s) _____

Case Study 7-2: Operative Report

Preoperative diagnosis: Recurrent bladder cancer

Postoperative diagnosis: Recurrent bladder cancer

Procedure Performed: Cystoscopy with bladder biopsies and fulguration

Anesthesia: General

Procedure: The patient has prior transitional cell carcinoma of the bladder and also carcinoma in situ. He has received MVAC therapy and BCG. Surveillance cystoscopy demonstrated a lesion of the bladder wall. He is being admitted for cystoscopy, bladder biopsy, and fulguration. Procedure, reasons, risks, and complications were reviewed, and consent was granted.

He was brought to the operating room under general anesthesia, placed in the dorsolithotomy position, and prepped and draped in a sterile manner. A #21 French cystoscope was inserted; urethra was normal, verumontanum intact. Prostate revealed evidence of prior transurethral resection and moderate outlet obstruction. There was a small lesion (0.3 cm) noted. Both ureteric orifices were normal size, shape, and caliber with clear efflux. The lesion was then biopsied with flexible biopsy forceps. After obtaining biopsies, the area was then fulgurated with Bugbee electrode. Re-inspection was carried out; no gross bleeding was noted. The bladder was drained, cystoscope was withdrawn, and the patient was transferred to the recovery room in satisfactory condition with all vital signs stable.

Pathology Report

Final Diagnosis: urothelial carcinoma in situ, focal; chronic nonspecific cystitis

Code(s) _____

Case Study 7-3: Operative Report

Preoperative Diagnosis: Left nephroureteral lithiasis

Postoperative Diagnosis: Left nephroureteral lithiasis

Operation Performed: Cystoscopy with bilateral retrograde pyelograms and left ureteral stent placement.

Findings: Right retrograde ureteral pyelogram was negative; left ureteral retrograde pyelogram showed a large filling defect in the mid-ureter consistent with a large renal ureteral calculi.

Indications for Operation: Patient is a 48-year-old gentleman who had symptomatic left flank pain. The patient was found to have a 0.9 × 0.7 cm stone in his left upper pole of his kidney; it was nonobstructive. There were several other small stones in the lower pole of his left kidney. The patient was also noted to have a small 3 mm stone in his right kidney. The patient was electively scheduled for a cystoscopy with bilateral retrogrades for evaluation of microscopic hematuria.

Operation in Detail: The patient was brought into the operating room after appropriate consent was obtained; he was given gatifloxacin 500 mg IV perioperatively. He was then induced under general anesthesia and was placed in the dorsal lithotomy position. His genitalia were prepped and draped in the sterile surgical fashion. After which, a #22 French cystoscope was inserted into the penile urethan. The pendulous urethra appeared normal. The prostatic urethra appeared normal. Once inside the bladder, a thorough inspection revealed no abnormal lesions. Then, a #6 French cone-tip catheter was inserted

2010 Current Procedural Terminology © 2009 American Medical Association. All Rights Reserved.

through the scope, and the right ureteral orifice was cannulated. A retrograde pyelogram was performed using fluoroscopy, which showed no filling defects. No hydronephrosis and the left ureteral orifice was cannulated; left ureteral retrograde pyelogram was performed using fluoroscopy. It showed a large filling defect in the mid-ureter. We were able to get contrast past this filling defect; however, we were unable to appreciate the renal pelvis in detail. It should be noted that there was clear urine coming from the left ureteral orifice and clear urine from the right ureteral orifice. After which a 0.35 guidewire was placed into the left ureteral orifice and advanced up to the left kidney without difficulty and a #6 French variable length stent was placed over the guidewire. The position of the indwelling ureteral stent was confirmed. The bladder was emptied, and the scope was removed. The patient was taken to the PACU, recovered, and was sent home.

Code(s) _____

Case Study 7-4: Operative Report

Preoperative Diagnosis: Left ureteral calculus

Postoperative Diagnosis: Left ureteral calculus

Procedure: Cystoscopy, right retrograde pyelogram, right ureteroscopic stone extraction and placement of right double-J ureteral stent

Procedure: The patient was taken to the operating room suite and placed in supine position. He was given IV sedation and switched to the dorsolithotomy position and prepped and draped in the usual sterile fashion. Cystoscopy was performed using 21 French cystoscopic sheath and 30-degree lens. The cystoscopy revealed the bladder mucosa to be smooth without evidence of tumors, stones, or foreign bodies. The right ureteral orifice was seen and engaged with the 5 French open-tip ureteral stent, and right retrograde confirmed calculus in the distal ureter right over the bony pelvis. This was difficult to see. We were unable to place a guidewire by this calculus. The small rigid ureteroscope was then passed under direct vision. The stone was encountered. It was a fairly large stone, but a guidewire was able to be manipulated by this stone using ureteroscopy. The ureteroscope was removed and over this guidewire a Microvasic dilating balloon was used to dilate the intramural orifice up to the level of the stone, up to 6 mm. The dilating balloon was removed, and the larger rigid ureteroscope was passed under direct vision.

The stone was encountered in the distal ureter and grasped with grasping forceps. It was broken into a couple of pieces, and the largest piece was then retrieved. Multiple small fragments were then irrigated down into the bladder. The largest piece was sent for pathological analysis. Further ureteroscope up to the renal pelvis identified no further evidence of stones. The ureteroscope was removed. The cystoscope and sheath were replaced over the guidewire. Over this guidewire, a 7 French × 26 cm double-J stent was passed with the proximal end lying within the renal pelvis and the distal end lying within the bladder. The guidewire was removed, leaving the stent in place. Fluoroscopy revealed a good curl within the renal pelvis, and direct cystoscopy revealed a good curl within the bladder. The bladder was drained. The cystoscope and sheath were removed. Final KUB documented placement of stent. There were no complications to the procedure.

Code(s) _____

Case Study 7-5: Operative Report

Procedure Note:

History: Indwelling left nephrostomy

Nephrostomy Tube Change: The patient was placed on the table and prepped and draped in the usual sterile fashion. A 14-gauge needle was advanced into the left nephrostomy tube, and a straight wire was advanced into the collecting system. The catheter was then cut and removed. An 8.5 French nephrostomy catheter was replaced and locked. The procedure was then terminated. There were no apparent complications, and the patient was sent to the floor with stable vital signs.

Impression: Successful left nephrostomy tube replacement

Code(s) _____

Case Study 7-6: Operative Report

Preoperative Diagnosis: Status postcystoscopy plus fulguration of bladder tumor with persistent hematuria

Postoperative Diagnosis: Status postcystoscopy plus fulguration of bladder tumor with persistent hematuria

Operation:

1. Cystoscopy

2. Transurethral fulguration of bladder tumor

3. Clot evacuation

Indications for Procedure: Patient is an 86-year-old male who recently underwent a cystoscopy with fulguration of bladder tumor. Patient was previously diagnosed with a bladder tumor. Postoperatively, the patient was left with a catheter placed for urinary retention issues. Patient was then discharged home, and, two days later, the patient was admitted to a local outlying hospital for complaints of hematuria and clogged Foley catheter clots. The patient was admitted to that outlying hospital, and apparently bladder irrigation was continued on the patient. Patient remained in the hospital for a period of almost two weeks, during which time the patient continued to have hematuria. Patient had a #16 French catheter in place and also developed pneumonia while in the hospital. Patient's care was then transferred to us. We admitted the patient and noted a three-way irrigation catheter (#24 French) was placed, and the patient was left to continuous bladder irrigation. Patient was then preoperatively considered for cysto with clot evacuation and possible fulguration of bladder tumor.

Details of Procedure: After obtaining informed consent, the patient was brought to the operating room and placed on the OR table in supine position. The patient was anesthetized and sedated with local MAC. Patient was then placed in dorsal lithotomy position. Patient's perineum and genitalia were then prepped and draped in the usual sterile fashion. Next, 20 cc of 2% local lidocaine was instilled per urethra, left in place for a period of 5–10 minutes. Next, a #22 French cystourethroscope with a 30-degree lens was placed within the urethra and advanced into the bladder. No abnormalities were noted within the urethra. No bladder outlet obstruction could be noted cystoscopically. Cystoscope was then passed into the bladder. All aspects of the bladder were visualized, the lateral walls, the base, dome and UOs bilaterally, posterior wall, and trigone. Of note, there was a significant amount of clot within the bladder. This was evacuated with the use of the Ellik evacuator. Because there was an apparent clot that could be very well irrigated out with this #22 French cystourethroscope, a #26 French resectoscope and sheath were placed within the urethra and advanced into the bladder after removing the #22 French cystourethroscope. This allowed us thorough access to the clots. With the use of the Ellik evacuator and the loop of the resectoscope, we were able to mobilize and evacuate all clots within the bladder. After clot evacuation was performed, the #26 French sheath resectoscope with a loop was used to electrocoagulate/fulgurate the areas of active bleeding. Of note, very little of the active bleeding was seen, and this was coagulated immediately. After the fulguration procedure, the bladder was again visualized, and all aspects were visualized. No areas of active bleeding could be seen within the bladder or at the prostatic urethra or at the bladder neck. The #26 French resectoscope and sheath were then removed. Following this, #24 French three-way irrigation Foley catheter was placed into the urethra and left to continuous bladder irrigation. Patient was transferred to recovery in good condition.

Code(s) _____

Case Study 7-7: Operative Report

Preoperative Diagnosis: Right kidney mass

Postoperative Diagnosis: Right renal mass

Procedure: Right nephrectomy

Indications for Procedure: The patient is a 58-year-old male who was referred to the clinic last month with a suspicious enhancing right renal mass. A metastatic workup was negative with the exception of slight elevated AST and ALT. His alkaline phosphatase was normal. He has consented for a laparoscopic versus open right radical nephrectomy accordingly.

Findings: Although the patient had a previous laparoscopic cholecystectomy and open appendectomy for a ruptured appendix, there were very few adhesions encountered. The kidney was able to be mobilized superiorly and inferiorly without difficulty. There was a single renal vein and a single renal artery. The renal artery was ligated with clips times two proximally and times one distally. The renal vein ligated with a vascular GIA 35 stapler. The kidney was removed in an EndoCatch bag in its entirety.

Details of Procedure: After informed consent was obtained and the patient received 1 g of Ancef IV, the patient was brought to the operating theater placed in the supine fashion. Preoperatively, he had already had an epidural placed for pain control. After a smooth induction of general anesthesia, the patient was placed in the modified left lateral decubitus position with all areas padded. The patient's right flank, in the up position, was then prepped and draped in the usual sterile fashion. An incision was carried out in the midclavicular line approximately the size of Dr. Lee's fist from superior to inferior fashion. This incision was deepened down to the level of the anterior rectus fascia, which was incised with curved Mayo scissors. The lateral aspect of the rectus muscle was then found, and the posterior rectus sheath was identified. This was incised in the superior to inferior fashion. #2-0 PDS stay sutures were placed medially and laterally on the cut ends. The hand-assist port was then placed into the peritoneum.

A #11 mm port was then placed approximately 4 cm inferior to the costal margin of the midclavicular line. Exactly halfway between this and the superior end of the hand-assist incision, a 12 mm working port was inserted. These two ports were placed under direct vision with Veress needle after infiltrating the skin and subcutaneous tissue with 2% lidocaine with epinephrine.

Once established, visualization occurred with both 30-degree and 45-degree lenses. Using both blunt dissections with a Kittner as well as sharp dissection with the harmonic scalpel, the posterior peritoneum was incised and the kidney was mobilized. After mobilization superiorly and inferiorly, attention was turned to the vessels. The duodenum was retracted medially. The inferior vena cava was visualized, and the gonadal vein was identified. The right renal vein was then easily identified and dissected free from its surrounding tissues. After further dissection, the single right renal artery was identified. A right angle was passed posterior to the artery and the vein to make sure that they were completely mobilized. Vascular clamps were placed on the renal artery in the above described fashion. Scissors were then used to transect the renal artery. As described above, the vascular GIA 35 stapler was used to transect the renal vein. Complete hemostasis was achieved at the conclusion of taking the vessels of the hilum. Dissection was then carried out superiorly and posteriorly using the harmonic scalpel as well as blunt dissection until the kidney was completely free. The kidney was then placed in an EndoCatch bag, which was brought out through the hand-assist port. After the kidney was removed, visualization was carried out in the area of the previous dissection. Irrigation was used, and there was no active venous or arterial bleeding noted. The port sites were closed with single #2-0 PDS suture using a laparoscopic needle passer. The hand-assist port was closed in the following fashion. The posterior sheath was closed with a running #0 looped Maxon. The anterior sheath was closed with a running #0 looped Maxon as well. The apical sutures of #2-0 PDS were used to approximate the apices. The previously placed stay sutures in the posterior rectus sheath were tied together. The wounds were then copiously irrigated with warm saline. Subcuticular sutures of interrupted #3-0 Vicryl were then placed in all of the incisions. The hand-assist incision was then closed with a running subcuticular #3-0 Vicryl suture. All incisions were closed with Dermabond. The patient tolerated the procedure well and was awakened in the operating room prior to being taken to SICU for recovery in satisfactory condition.

Code(s) _____

8 Male Genital System

Chapter Outline

Key Terms

circumcision
epididymis
glans penis
orchiectomy
orchiopexy

penis
perineal prostatectomy
prepuce
prostatectomy
prostate gland

radical orchiectomy
scrotum
simple orchiectomy
subcapsular
  orchiectomy

testes
transurethral
  prostatectomy

Chapter Objectives

At the conclusion of this chapter, the student should be able to:

- Define key terms.
- Differentiate between destruction of lesion codes that are assigned from the integumentary system versus those from the anatomic site.
- Distinguish among the descriptions for coding circumcisions.
- Describe types of orchiectomy and orchiopexy procedures.
- Identify the techniques for performing prostatectomy procedures.
- Apply coding guidelines for male genital system procedures.
- Given a case study, correctly assign CPT codes for surgical cases.

2010 Current Procedural Terminology © 2009 American Medical Association. All Rights Reserved.

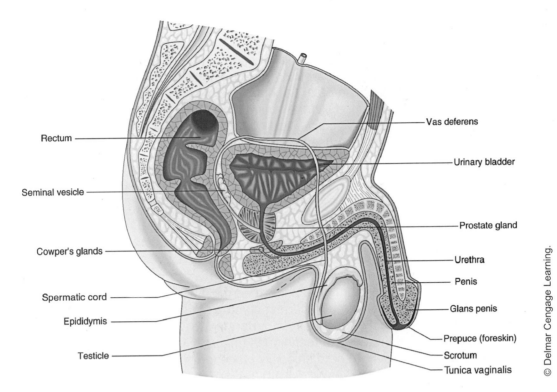

Figure 8-1 Male genital system.

Introduction

The male genital system includes procedures performed on such structures such as the penis, scrotum, testis, epididymis, and prostate (Figure 8-1). The **penis** is used to introduce or deliver spermatozoa into the female reproductive tract. The distal end of the penis is called **glans penis**. Covering the glans penis is a section of loose skin called **prepuce**. The **testes** produce sperm and the male sex hormones. The **scrotum** is the external sac of skin that is the supporting structure for the testes. The **epididymis** is a structure within the scrotum that serves to store, mature, and transport spermatozoa between the testis and vas deferens. The **prostate gland** surrounds the superior portion of the urethra just below the bladder. The main function is to store and secrete alkaline fluid that contributes to the volume of semen (along with spermatozoa and seminal vesicle fluid).

Destruction of Skin Lesions—Penis (54050–54065)

As demonstrated in this subsection, removal of skin lesions may be classified in the anatomic sites instead of in the integumentary system. Instructional parenthetical notes are found below code 54065 and before 17000.

Circumcision

A **circumcision** is removal of the foreskin covering the glans penis. Typically, the procedure is performed on newborns using either local or no anesthesia. However, the American Academy of Pediatrics endorses use of regional anesthesia (dorsal nerve block or ring block). Older children and adults are more commonly operated on under general anesthesia. The range of codes differentiates between surgical techniques (clamp, or excision), use of regional block (54150), and/or age.

> **Note:**
>
> *An instructional parenthetical note appears after code 54150 to direct the coder to report the code with modifier 52 if the procedure was performed without a nerve block.*

Orchiectomy

Orchiectomy (54520–54535) is the surgical removal of one or both testes, which produces the majority of the body's testosterone. The main reason for this procedure is to treat cancer; it stops the production of testosterone, which the cancer needs in order to continue growing. In a **simple orchiectomy** (54520), the surgeon removes the testicles and parts of the spermatic cord through the incision. The procedure is commonly performed for orchitis, prostatic cancer and chronic pain. A **subcapsular orchiectomy** is similar to a simple procedure except the glandular tissue is removed from the lining of each testicle rather than the entire gland being removed. A partial orchiectomy (54522) describes the removal of a benign cyst or tumor.

A **radical orchiectomy** (54530–54535) removes the entire spermatic cord as well as the testicles themselves. This procedure is commonly performed for removal of malignant tumors.

Orchiopexy

An **orchiopexy** (54640–54650) is surgery performed to fasten undescended testicles inside the scrotum. It is performed most often in male infants or very young children to correct cryptorchidism (undescended testicles). In adults, the procedure is performed to treat testicular torsion. In CPT, there are two techniques (inguinal and abdominal approach) that describe the orchiopexy procedure. Laparoscopic orchiopexy codes reported using 54690–54692.

> **Note:**
>
> *If an inguinal hernia repair is performed with the inguinal orchiopexy, coders are instructed to report the codes for both procedures.*

Prostatectomy Procedures

Prostatectomy procedures involve removing part of all of the prostate gland. Symptoms of an enlarged prostate are commonly the cause of painful and potentially health-threatening conditions. The prostate gland lies under the bladder and surrounds the first part of the tube (the urethra) that carries urine to the penis. When the prostate becomes enlarged, it may obstruct the urethra, which makes urination difficult. The following describes methods for prostatectomy procedures:

Transurethral Prostatectomy

The **transurethral prostatectomy** is a procedure performed using a straight, narrow, tubular structure (rectoscope) that passes through the opening of the tip of the penis. The surgeon uses the edge of the resectoscope to cut away the urethral wall in order to reach the interior of the prostate gland. Most rec-toscopes use a small loop of tungsten wire that can be made red hot by electric current to cut away the redundant prostate tissue. In addition, some surgeons may use laser beams for the same purpose. Transurethral resection of the prostate (TURP) is reported with code 52601 (from the Urinary System chapter) (see Figure 8-2). Note that visual laser ablation of the prostate (VLAP) is reported with code 52647 or 52648. These codes reflect new alternatives for surgical treatment of benign prostatic hypertrophy (BPH).

Perineal Prostatectomy

In a **perineal prostatectomy**, the surgeon makes a curved incision between the back of the scrotum and the anus and cuts straight down to the underlying prostate. Potentially cancerous lymph nodes may also require removal. This approach is reported using codes from the 55801–55815 range.

Suprapubic and Retropubic Prostatectomy

These procedures require a larger incision in the lower abdomen, through which the prostate and nearby lymph nodes can be removed. Codes are selected from the range of 55821–55845 for these procedures.

2010 Current Procedural Terminology © 2009 American Medical Association. All Rights Reserved.

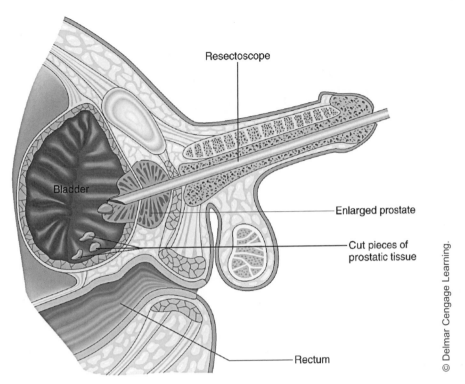

Figure 8-2 A transurethral prostectomy (TURP) is performed to treat benign prostatic hypertrophy.

Biopsy of Prostate (55700–55706)

A prostate gland biopsy is a test to remove a small sample of tissue to be examined under a microscope by the pathology department. The procedure is used to verify the presence of cancer. Code 55700 describes a needle or punch biopsy. Another code (55706) is used to report transperineal stereotactic template-guided saturation prostate biopsies. The procedure includes systematic collections of samples in those areas of the prostate gland where tumors are most frequent. Incisional biopsy procedures are reported with code 55705.

Summary

- Destruction of skin lesions of penis is located in the male genital system.
- Circumcision codes are distinguished by technique, age, and use of regional block.
- Most procedures in the male genital system are differentiated by surgical technique.

Internet Links

Medline Plus (National Library of Medicine): *http://www.nlm.nih.gov/medlineplus/tutorials/turp/htm/index.htm*
Tutorial describes TURP procedure

2010 Current Procedural Terminology © 2009 American Medical Association. All Rights Reserved.

Review

I. Medical Terminology Assessment

Match the following terms with the correct definition:

_____ 1. testes	A. fold of skin covering penis
_____ 2. orchiopexy	B. sac containing testes
_____ 3. orchiectomy	C. surgical treatment of undescended testicle
_____ 4. scrotum	D. male gonads
_____ 5. prostatectomy	E. removal of one or more testes
_____ 6. prepuce	F. removal of gland that surrounds beginning of urethra

II. Case Studies

Case Study 8-1: Operative Report

Preoperative Diagnosis: Elevated prostate-specific antigen

Postoperative Diagnosis: Elevated prostate-specific antigen

Procedure: Transrectal ultrasound-guided prostate needle biopsy

Findings: The patient had approximately 40g prostate. It was smooth, symmetric, soft, and nontender.

Indications for Procedure: Patient is a 72-year-old gentleman who was found to have an elevated PSA of 4.1 with a benign digital rectal exam. The patient has been on finasteride in the past as well as terazosin for obstructive voiding symptoms. He is currently simply on terazosin. Patient was scheduled for prostate needle biopsy secondary to elevated PSA.

Procedure in Detail: Patient was brought to the operating room after he was given gatifloxacin p.o. q. d. He was then placed in left lateral decubitus position. A digital rectal exam was performed, which showed approximately a 40g prostate. It was smooth, symmetric, soft, and nontender. After which, an ultrasound probe was inserted into the rectum, and approximately 12 prostate needle biopsy cores were taken from the right and left base, midsection, and apex. There was minimal bleeding, and then the probe was removed. We will follow up with the patient with his pathology.

Code(s) _____

Case Study 8-2: Operative Report

Preoperative Diagnosis: Left groin condyloma

Postoperative Diagnosis: Left groin condyloma

Operation: Fulguration of left groin condyloma

Indications: This is a 47-year-old male who presents to the clinic with a complaint of groin lesion in his left groin area, on his inner thigh facing the scrotum. He first noticed it a couple of years ago, but it suddenly became larger. He will have intermittent bleeding from the site, but there is no pain and no itching. He was scheduled for removal of the condyloma on an outpatient basis.

Details of Procedure: After identifying the operative site and consenting the patient for the procedure, the patient was brought to the operating room and placed on the table in supine position. He legs were frog legged, and he was given Versed for anesthesia. His left groin was prepped and draped in sterile fashion and upon the injection of approximately 12 cc of 1% lidocaine with 0.5% Marcaine. The 2 ×4 cm area of condyloma located in his left groin was excised with the use of electrocautery. Hemostasis was obtained. Attention was turned to a single lesion approximately 1 × 1 cm that was located just lateral to the previously mentioned lesion that was removed. This lesion was just removed using electrocautery. During this entire procedure of electrocautery, the high-pressure air vacuum was used as prophylaxis for the spreading of any viral particles. The sites of each lesion were then approximated using interrupted #4-0 nylon sutures. The area was dressed with Polysporin ointment. Dry gauze was placed, and mesh underwear was placed on the patient. The patient awoke without any difficulty from his Versed administration, and he was taken to the postanesthesia unit.

Code(s) _____

Case Study 8-3: Operative Report

Preoperative Diagnosis: Right undescended testis

Postoperative Diagnosis: Recurrent indirect right inguinal hernia and undescended testis

Procedure: Repair of recurrent indirect right inguinal hernia and right orchiopexy

Operative Findings: At time of operative procedure, the patient has had a previous right inguinal hernia repair done at another institution. His right testis is stuck in the right external ring with massive scarring. The cord structures are scarred. The tunica over the testis is scarred, so the right testis could not be seen under direct visualization. The right cord structures were stuck, and there was a recurrent indirect right inguinal hernia.

Procedure: Under general laryngeal mask airway anesthesia, preparation of the lower abdomen and scrotum was done with Betadine solution, and draping was performed.

About 5 cc of 0.25% Marcaine solution was used to do the ilioinguinal nerve block. An additional 5 cc of 0.25% Marcaine was given into the upper scrotum and subcutaneous tissue. The previous incision, which was about 3 cm long, was opened up in the right inguinal region. The skin and subcutaneous tissues were divided along the same line. The external oblique aponeurosis was divided along its fibers. Because of the scar, the right ilioinguinal nerve could not be identified. The cord structures were fed up from the surrounding tissues as well as the testis, which was scarred to the pubic tubercle and was freed up. There was an indirect right inguinal hernia, which was dissected away from the cord structures and high ligated at the internal ring using two transfixion sutures of 4-0 Vicryl. A piece of hernial sac was sent to pathology.

An incision was made in the right scrotum about 2 cm long. The skin was separated from Dartos muscle, and an opening was made in the Dartos muscle. The right testis was brought through the opening in the Dartos muscle. The tunica, which was scarred over the testis, was then sutured to the Dartos muscle edges using 4-0 Vicryl interrupted sutures.

The skin over the testis was closed with 4-0 chromic interrupted skin sutures. The external oblique aponeurosis was closed with 4-0 Vicryl interrupted sutures. The skin subcutaneous tissue was closed with 4-0 Vicryl continuous sutures. The skin was closed with 4-0 Vicryl continuous sutures in subcuticular fashion. Incidentally, the right testis seems to be much smaller than the left testis. Dermabond was applied over both inguinal and scrotal incisions.

Postoperative Condition: The patient tolerated the procedure well.

Code(s) _____

Case Study 8-4: Operative Report

Preoperative Diagnosis: Prostate cancer

Postoperative Diagnosis: Prostate cancer

Procedure: Iodine-125 seed implant

This patient was taken to the Cysto Suite after adequate general anesthesia was obtained. The patient was prepped and draped in the usual manner. The ultrasound probe was placed in a similar position in his rectum after the scrotum was sutured anteriorly to the anterior abdominal wall. Then, iodine seed implant was done. The patient had a total of 52 seeds that will be 36 rapid strand seed strength 0.729 millicuries per seed and 16 loose seeds 0.383 millicuries per seed with a total of 16 needles. The patient tolerated the procedure well. After the procedure, the scrotum was released, and the patient had trouble with urinary stricture, therefore a Foley catheter could not be placed. We will monitor his urine through a urinal system in PACU. The patient was taken to the PACU in good condition.

Code(s) _____

Case Study 8-5: Operative Note

Procedure: Circumcision

Indications: Elective

Description of Procedure: The 6-month-old infant was cleaned and draped in sterile fashion and was first numbed at the base of the penis with 1% lidocaine without epinephrine, after which time it was noted that the meatus was at the tip of the penis. Adhesions were then lysed. The dorsum of the foreskin was then clamped, and an incision was made along the clamp line. The foreskin was then retracted, and the adhesions were further lysed. Gomco bell, size #2, was placed over the tip of the penis, and the foreskin was retracted over the bell and secured with a safety pin. The clamp was then placed and secured. It was held for approximately 5 minutes until appropriate devascularization was obtained. The foreskin was then removed with a #11 blade. The Gomco bell and clamp were then removed. There was minimal bleeding. The patient was then dressed with sterile Vaseline gauze, and the Betadine was also cleaned from the area. He was returned to the newborn nursery, fairly quiet, for observation. The mother was spoken with after the procedure and told that the patient tolerated it well, and she was satisfied.

Code(s) _____

Case Study 8-6: Operative Report

Preoperative Diagnosis: Necrotizing fasciitis

Postoperative Diagnosis: Necrotizing fasciitis

Procedure: Groin/scrotal debridement; resection of scrotum

Indications for Procedure: The patient is a 58-year-old male with complaints of a perineal area infection. He was noted to have a 6-week history of "being sick." The patient noted that the initial groin infection began with a simple "pimple" and readily grew over the past six weeks. Upon presentation, he was noted to have frank pus and gas and air coming out of multiple areas of his perineal and groin area. He was then scheduled for an emergency operating room radical debridement and dissection of this necrotizing fasciitis.

Description of Procedure: The patient was prepped and draped in the normal sterile fashion in the lithotomy position in the operating room. The patient was noted to have pus out of multiple sites in the perineal area, an area around the perineum and groin, which measured from the mid-inguinal area onto the medial scrotal line. A 10-blade knife was used to make the initial incision through skin. Operative findings showed a dark black gray purulent material, which extended deep into the fascial planes. With further dissection with the Mayo scissors and a Bovie, it was noted that the necrotizing fasciitis extended deep into the scrotum and into the tissues surrounding the right lateral side of his penis. Upon further dissection around the testicles, it was noted that the fasciitis did not extend into the testicle and simply remained around the sheath. Mayo scissors, a Bovie, and a 15-blade knife were used to excise all the necrotic tissue. All devascularized skin edges were removed, and the incision was extended to the area of the perineum and the groin until viable noninfected tissue was easily observed. The wound was then irrigated with 6 liters of normal saline. Hemostasis was maintained, and the wound was packed with Dakin's half-strength solution and a Kerlix and then dressed with a mesh-pad, which was stapled in. The patient received 4 liters of intraoperative normal saline and was extubated safely and taken to the surgical intensive care unit.

Code(s) _____

Case Study 8-7: Operative Report

Preoperative Diagnosis: Benign prostatic hypertrophy with obstructive voiding symptoms

Postoperative Diagnosis: Benign prostatic hypertrophy with obstructive voiding symptoms

Procedure Performed: Cystoscopy with transurethral resection of prostate

Anesthesia: Spinal

Complications: None

Estimate Blood Loss: 10 mL

Specimens: Prostate chips

Indications for Procedure: The patient is an 82-year-old gentleman with a history of transurethral resection of prostate several years ago. He developed worsening obstructive voiding symptoms. He had cystoscopy performed, which showed lateral lobe hyperplasia. He consented for transurethral resection of the prostate.

2010 Current Procedural Terminology © 2009 American Medical Association. All Rights Reserved.

Details of Procedure: The patient was given preoperative antibiotics. He was taken to the operating suite and moved onto the table in the supine position. Spinal anesthesia was induced. His position was changed to lithotomy position. His genitalia was prepped and draped in a simple fashion. A 22.5 French rigid cystoscope sheath with a 30-degree lens was advised through the urethra into the bladder. There was found to be lateral lobe hyperplasia of the prostate. There was really no median lobe. There was some trabeculation with some cellules within the bladder. Both ureteral orifices were visualized and were normal in position and caliber. We then switched off to the 24 French resectoscope and began resecting the lateral lobe of the prostate. We started with the patient's left lateral lobe, which was resected from the level of the bladder neck down to the verumontanum. We then moved to the patient's right lateral lobe and again resected from the level of the bladder neck down to the verumontanum. At the end of the procedure, the prostatic fossa was wide open. Bleeding was controlled with electrocautery. A 24-French three-way catheter was placed. The patient was awakened from anesthesia and transferred to the postanesthesia care unit in stable condition.

Code(s) _____

Female Genital System

Chapter Outline

Introduction
Destruction and Excision of Lesions
   of Vulva
Colposcopy
Hysteroscopy

Hysterectomy
Other Laparoscopic Procedures
Dilation and Curettage (D&C)
Lysis of Adhesions
Maternity Care and Delivery Subsection

Key Terms

adhesiolysis

adhesions

cervix

colposcopy

conization

dilation and curettage
  (D&C)

endometrium

fallopian tubes

hysterectomy

hysteroscopy

laparoscopic assisted
  vaginal hysterectomy
  (LVAH)

loop electrode excision
  procedure (LEEP)

lysis

ova

ovaries

oviducts

perineum

supracervical
  hysterectomy

total abdominal
  hysterectomy (TAH)

total laparoscopic
  hysterctomy

uterus

vaginal hysterectomy

vulva

Chapter Objectives

At the conclusion of this chapter, the student should be able to:

- Identify anatomical structures of the female genital system.
- Describe common surgical procedures of the female genital system.
- Explain coding guidelines applicable to female genital system coding.
- Distinguish between colposcopy procedures.
- Differentiate among hysterectomy procedures.
- Use references to assist with coding assignment.
- Given a case scenario, accurately assign CPT codes and modifiers (if applicable).

2010 Current Procedural Terminology © 2009 American Medical Association. All Rights Reserved.

Introduction

The female genital system consists of the ovaries, uterine ducts, uterus, vagina, and external genitalia (Figure 9-1)

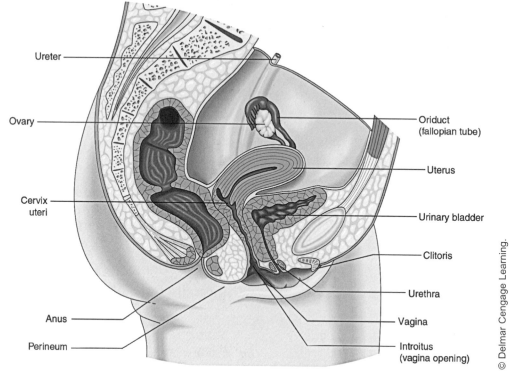

Figure 9-1 Female genital system

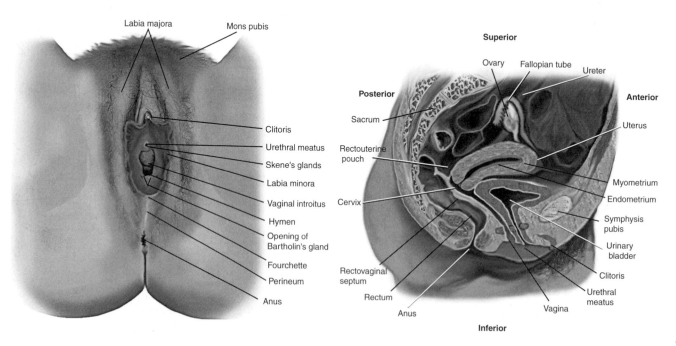

External genitalia   Cross-section of internal structures

Figure 9-2 The female reproductive system

2010 Current Procedural Terminology © 2009 American Medical Association. All Rights Reserved.

The **ovaries** are paired organs that are the size of an unshelled almond. These organs produce eggs (**ova**) and hormones such as estrogen. The egg is transported to the uterus via the **fallopian tubes** (**oviducts**). The womb (**uterus**) is where the fertilized egg is implanted. When a woman is not pregnant, the lining of the uterus (**endometrium**) is shed, and menstruation occurs. The vagina serves as a passageway for menstrual flow or as the birth canal. Between the uterus and the vagina is a small cylindrical organ called the **cervix**. The **vulva** is a general term often referred to as the external genitalia, which is composed of the mons pubis, the labia majora and minora, the clitoris, the vestibule of the vagina and its glands, and the opening of the urethra and of the vagina. The **perineum** is the area between the vulva and the anus (Figure 9-2).

The most common procedures performed in this specialty include dilation and curettage (D&C), hysterectomies, and hysteroscopies. In addition to these frequently performed procedures, this chapter will also include a focus on colposcopies, excision of lesions, and lysis of adhesions.

Destruction and Excision of Lesions of Vulva

Depending on the nature of the lesion, the diagnosis and treatment of vulvar lesions may be approached in several ways. If a diagnosis needs to be confirmed, then the surgeon may elect to take a small piece of tissue (biopsy) and send it to the pathology department for an analysis. CPT codes 56605–56606 identify biopsies. Note that both code descriptions include the phrase "separate procedure," indicating that the coder should determine if this procedure was an integral component of another procedure. If so, then the "separate procedure" code would not be assigned. If the "separate procedure" code is unrelated or distinct from the other procedures, then the code should be additionally reported (append modifier 59).

The surgeon may elect to remove the lesions by excision or destruction. Codes for excision of local vulva skin lesions are from the Integumentary System. Destruction codes (56501–56515) include treatment using laser, electrosurgery, cryosurgery, or chemotherapy.

Simple Destruction vs. Extensive Destruction

Codes 56501 and 56515 differentiate between a simple and extensive destruction of vulvar lesions. This is one of those situations where CPT does not provide a definition of simple or extensive to help differentiate between the codes. The decision is determined by the physician with supportive documentation. Documentation stating that a single lesion was destroyed with cryosurgery would indicate the assignment of 56501 (simple). The physician would have to consider time, effort, and complexity of the case before making the decision to document "extensive."

Colposcopy

A **colposcopy** is a procedure used to examine the vulva, vagina, and cervix. The procedure is often used to evaluate patients with an abnormal Pap smear combined with a normal appearing cervix on visual exam. Note the following code selections for colposcopy procedures:

- Colposcopy of entire vagina with cervix   57420–57421
- Colposcopy of cervix   57452–57461
- Colposcopy of vulva   56820–56821

Loop Electrode Biopsy (57460) vs. Loop Electrode Conization of Cervix (57461)

The **loop electrosurgical excision procedure (LEEP)** uses a thin, low-voltage electrified wire loop to cut out abnormal tissue

> **Note:**
>
> *Codes 57420–57421 include an examination of the cervix along with the entire vagina; therefore, an additional colposcopy code from the cervix examination family of codes would not be appropriate. If the focus of the endoscopy was on the cervix, then codes from 57452–57461 are appropriate. It is important to note that an examination of the entire cervix may extend into the upper portion of the vagina.*

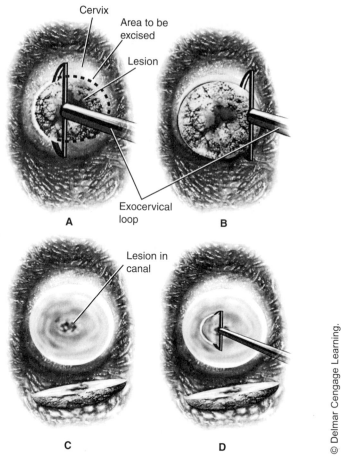

© Delmar Cengage Learning.

Figure 9-3 Cervical conization—LEEP technique: (A) Path of electrosurgical loop through distal cervix, (B) loop near completion of excision, (C) lesion identified in cervix, (D) loop excision of lesion

(CPT code 57420). **Conization** excises the tissue in a cone fashion. The procedures help to diagnosis intraepithelial neoplasia. The key fact is that code 57460 describes a procedure where the physician removes tissue (specimen) for examination by the pathologist. Code 57461 identifies the removal of a portion of the endocervix or transformation zone (Figure 9-3).

Conization (CPT code 57421) can be performed with a scalpel (cold-knife conization), laser, or electrosurgical loop. The surgeon will take a small amount of normal tissue around the cone-shaped wedge of abnormal tissue so that a margin free of abnormal cells is left in the cervix.

> **Note:**
>
> *If endocervical curettage is performed at the same time as a conization of the cervix, only report 57461.*

Hysteroscopy

Hysteroscopy (58555–58565), or visualization of the uterine cavity, has long been used to diagnose and treat conditions such as polyps, fibroids, and excessive bleeding. The scope is inserted through the cervix into the uterus. Unlike a dilation and curettage (D&C), this endoscopic procedure allows the surgeon to visually examine the uterus. Note the main surgical hysteroscopy descriptor states "with or without D&C," meaning that an additional code for a D&C is not warranted.

> **Note:**
>
> *If the surgeon performs two distinct procedures indented under the "family of codes," it is appropriate to assign both codes. For example, if the surgeon performed a hysteroscopy for removal of leiomyomata and endometrial ablation, then codes 58561 and 58563 may be assigned.*

2010 Current Procedural Terminology © 2009 American Medical Association. All Rights Reserved.

Hysterectomy

Hysterectomy removes the patient's uterus and, in some situations, the fallopian tubes and ovaries. The procedure is performed to treat conditions such as gynecological cancer, fibroids, endometriosis, and uterine prolapse.

CPT codes differentiate between the open method and laparoscopic removal of the uterus. The following definitions will assist when reviewing the documentation in the health record:

- Supracervical hysterectomy—Removal of uterus but cervix is left intact.

- Vaginal hysterectomy—The surgeon operates entirely through the vagina, pulling the uterus down through the vagina into view, disconnecting the cervix and then the rest of the uterus.

- Laparoscopic assisted vaginal hysterectomy (LAVH)—Removal of the pelvic organs through the vagina but includes starting with cutting the ovarian attachments laparoscopically. It is done this way because of suspicions that the ovaries probably cannot be disconnected by operating only through the vagina.

- Total laparoscopic hysterectomy—The entire uterus is disconnected (other structures as needed) laparoscopically.

- Total abdominal hysterectomy (TAH)—An abdominal incision is made in order to remove the uterus (also, tubes and ovaries if needed).

Depending on the code selection, additional documentation may be needed (e.g.. size of uterus).

Exercise 9-1: Hysterectomy and Hysteroscopy Procedures

Assign CPT codes to the following procedures. Append CPT/HCPCS Level II modifiers if applicable. Concentrate on application of coding guidelines, and do not focus on sequencing or assignment of modifier of 51 (physician services).

1. Operative Note: Diagnosis: menorrhagia, anemia. A laparoscopic hysterectomy is performed. Procedure notes: Laparoscope inserted, uterus and attached tubes and ovaries are ligated and transected. Uterus 200 g

Code(s) _____

2. Surgeon performs a hysteroscopy with biopsy of endometrium and D&C.

Code(s) _____

3. Surgeon performs a laparoscopic supracervical hysterectomy (uterus 270 g).

Code(s) _____

4. Vaginal hysterectomy performed with removal of oviducts, ovaries, and repair of enterocele (uterus 280 g).

Code(s) _____

Challenge Question

5. The surgeon performs a total abdominal hysterectomy and bilateral salpingo-oophorectomy with omentectomy and radical dissection for debulking for primary ovarian cancer. What is the correct code assignment?

Code(s) _____

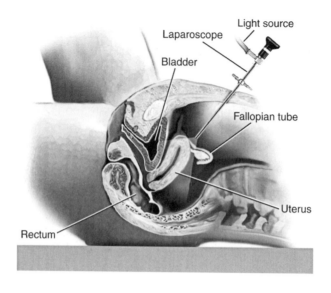

© Delmar Cengage Learning.

Figure 9-4 Laparoscopy

Other Laparoscopic Procedures

Laparoscopic procedures are located throughout CPT (Figure 9-4).

In addition to the laparoscopic hysterectomy codes listed above, another category of codes is located in the Female Genital System for procedures such as:

- 58660 Laparoscopy, surgical; with lysis of adhesions (salpingolysis, ovariolysis) (separate procedure)

- 58661 with removal of adnexal structures (partial or total oophorectomy and/or salpingectomy)

- 58662 with fulguration or excision of lesions of the ovary, pelvic viscera, or peritoneal surface by any method

Careful examination of the note that follows code 58679 reveals that additional laparoscopic codes for aspiration of an ovarian cyst and biopsy of ovary/fallopian tube can be found in the Digestive System category.

Dilation and Curettage (D&C)

A **D&C** requires the surgeon to dilate the cervix to allow the lining of the cervix to be scraped using instruments called "curettes." The scrapings are sent to the pathologist for testing. This procedure is commonly performed to diagnose and treat such conditions as abnormal bleeding and polyps.

In CPT, the procedure for a D&C of a nonobstetrical patient is represented by code 58120. Although this code description does not include the phrase "separate procedure," a D&C is often included as part of the surgical package for many gynecological procedures. For example:

57520 Conization of cervix, with or without fulguration, **with or without dilation** and curettage, with or without repair; cold knife or laser.

> **Note:**
>
> *In the Alphabetic Index of CPT, if a coder searches for the nonobstetrical D&C code, the subterm "corpus uteri" is the correct entry. It is interesting to note that the main alphabetic entry for Dilation and Curettage with no subterms is 59840, which is a D&C after an abortion.*

2010 Current Procedural Terminology © 2009 American Medical Association. All Rights Reserved.

Lysis of Adhesions

An **adhesion** is a band of scar tissue that binds surrounding tissues. Adhesions form because of surgery, infection, trauma, or radiation. The tissue develops when the body's repair mechanisms respond to any tissue disturbance, such as surgery, infection, trauma, or radiation. Patients having adhesions may be asymptomatic, but they also can be the cause of abdominal pain, cramping, or obstruction. The term for surgical treatment of freeing the adhesions is called **lysis** or **adhesiolysis**. The surgeon will cut the abnormal connections between the intra-abdominal organs to separate them.

> **Note:**
>
> CPT code 58660 is a "separate procedure"; therefore, it would not be assigned if it was an integral part of a larger procedure (e.g., laparoscopic removal of ovaries).

CPT provides several code selections for lysis of adhesions:

58660   Laparoscopy, surgical; with lysis of adhesions (salpingolysis, ovariolysis) (separate procedure)

58740   Lysis of adhesions (salpingolysis, ovariolysis)

CPT code 58740 is not designed as a "separate procedure" code, but close attention to NCCI edits will reveal that this code is often bundled with other related procedures.

Maternity Care and Delivery Subsection

Surgical services in this subsection relate to the care and treatment during pregnancy and delivery. Coding selections are provided for vaginal delivery, cesarean delivery, and abortions. Notes in this subsection provide guidance for coding physician services. For example, a normal, uncomplicated maternity case includes antepartum care, delivery, and postpartum care.

Summary

- Excision of vulvar lesion codes are located in the Integumentary System.
- There are three sets of codes for colposcopy procedures.
- Coding for hysterectomy procedures requires attention to details to reveal method, technique, and structures removed.
- Laparoscopy procedures are located throughout CPT. For example, laparoscopic removal of ovarian cyst is found in the Digestive System.
- D&C is often included in surgical descriptions; therefore, it is not assigned a separate code.
- Lysis of adhesions codes provide for open procedure and laparoscopic. NCCI edits will provide a guide for use as an additional code.

Internet Links

MEDLINE PLUS, National Library of Medicine: *http://www.nlm.nih.gov/medlineplus/tutorials/colposcopy/htm/index.htm*
Interactive video for colposcopy

MEDLINE PLUS: *http://www.nlm.nih.gov/medlineplus/tutorials/dilatationandcurettage/htm/index.htm*
Interactive video for dilation and curettage (D&C)

MEDLINE PLUS: *http://www.nlm.nih.gov/medlineplus/tutorials/hysterectomy/htm/index.htm*
Interactive video for hysterectomy

2010 Current Procedural Terminology © 2009 American Medical Association. All Rights Reserved.

eMedicine: *http://www.emedicine.com/obgyn/index.shtml*
Numerous articles about gynecological diseases and procedures

American College of Obstetricians and Gynecologists: *http://www.acog.org*
Patient education and links to coding information

Review

I. Crossword Puzzle

Female Genital System

Across
1. inflammatory bands
4. destroy tissue with electric current
8. examinine vulva, vagina and cervix
9. surgical repair of uterus
10. located between uterus and vagina

Down
2. exam of uterine cavity
3. excision of cone of tissue
5. freezing to destroy tissue
6. extermal genital
7. between vulva and anus in female

II. Case Studies

Case Study 9-1: Operative Report

Preoperative Diagnosis: Desires sterilization

Postoperative Diagnosis: Desires sterilization

Procedures Performed: Bilateral laparoscopic tubal banding under general anesthesia

Anesthesia: General

Details of Procedure: The patient was taken to the operating room, where general anesthesia was administered with endotracheal intubation without difficulty. She was placed in the dorsal lithotomy position. Her vagina, perineum, and abdomen were prepped and draped in a sterile fashion with Betadine solution.

2010 Current Procedural Terminology © 2009 American Medical Association. All Rights Reserved.

A weighted speculum was put in place in the posterior wall of the vagina. The anterior lip of the cervix was grasped with a single-tooth tenaculum. A HUMI uterine elevator was placed into the uterine cavity after dilatation of the cervical os. A red rubber catheter was placed in the bladder for drainage during the procedure.

Attention was turned to the abdomen, where an infraumbilical incision was made with a knife, through which Veress needle was inserted. Thorough insufflation of the abdominal cavity was carried out with 2.5 L of carbon dioxide gas. Veress needle was then removed, and the Surgipro trocar was inserted.

Scope was inserted. Exploration of the abdomen revealed essential normal pelvis and abdominal anatomy. Uterus, tubes, and ovaries were all normal with no evidence of infection or inflammation and with no evidence of infection or inflammation or endometriosis. Appendix was visualized and appeared normal.

A second incision was made in the midline just above the symphysis through which the laparoscopic banding instrument was inserted. This instrument and each of the tubes were identified bilaterally and banded with Silastic bands. Each knuckle of tube was isolated with blanching, indicating good ischemia at the close of the procedure.

At this time, the instruments were removed from the abdomen. The abdomen deflated of gas, and the incisions closed with interrupted stitches of 3-0 undyed Vicryl. Sterile dry dressings were then placed. The vaginal instruments were removed.

The patient was moved to the recovery room in stable condition without complication. The estimated blood loss was less than 50 cc.

Code(s) _____

Case Study 9-2: Operative Report

Preoperative Diagnosis: Chronic pelvic pain, menometrorrhagia

Postoperative Diagnosis: Chronic pelvic pain, menometrorrhagia, pelvic adhesions, left ovarian cyst, suspected endometriosis, and adenomyosis.

Gross Findings: With the patient in the dorsolithotomy position, under general anesthesia, a bimanual abdomino-vaginal examination revealed a symmetrically enlarged, somewhat boggy uterus. The uterus sounded to a depth of 10.5 cm. Under direct vision with the hysteroscope, the endometrial canal was noted to be regular in shape. The canal was cavernous, but no evidence of uterine fibroids, polyps, or other intrauterine pathology was readily apparent. Under direct vision with the laparoscope, the symmetrically enlarged boggy uterus was confirmed. The uterus was approximately 12 weeks gestational size. Observation of the anterior cul-de-sac revealed multiple adhesions of the anterior surface of the uterus to the parietal peritoneum. These were lysed and excised. Observation of the adnexal structures revealed the right ovary to be within normal limits. The left ovary demonstrated a cyst, measuring approximately 2–3 cm in diameter, which, when opened, extruded clear, straw-colored fluid. Inspection of the posterior cul-de-sac reveals some stellate scarring, neovascularization, and the evidence suggestive of endometriosis located to the right of the midline, just beneath the right uterosacral ligament. A representative biopsy of this area was obtained and then the area was fulgurated. Inspection of the sigmoid colon and cecum revealed them to be within normal limits. The appendix was not visualized. The liver and the gallbladder were also visually normal, and no perihepatic adhesions were detected.

2010 Current Procedural Terminology © 2009 American Medical Association. All Rights Reserved.

Operative Procedure: With the patient in the dorsolithotomy position under general anesthesia, the abdomen and perineum were sterilely prepped and draped in the usual manner. A bimanual abdominovaginal examination was performed with results noted above. A weighted vaginal speculum was inserted, and a self-retaining cervical cannula applied for uterine manipulation. The vaginal speculum was removed, and the perineum was sterilely draped. Attention was then directed to the abdomen, where an infraumbilical incision was made, through which a Veress needle was inserted and a pneumoperitoneum of 3 liters of carbon dioxide gas created. The needle was removed, and an appropriate disposable trocar with protective sleeve was inserted without difficulty. With the sleeve remaining in place, the trocar was replaced with the laparoscope, and the pelvis was entered under direct vision. Accessory trocar sites were established in the lower quadrants under direct vision with the laparoscope. The pelvic and abdominal viscera were then inspected with the results as noted above. Instruments were removed from their respective trocar sleeves, and the pneumoperitoneum was allowed to evacuate. The sleeves were subsequently removed, and the incisions were reapproximated with simple inverted stitches of 5-0 undyed delayed absorbable suture. Sterile dressings were applied, and then attention was redirected to the perineum. The self-retaining cervical cannula was removed, and the weighted vaginal speculum reinserted. The continuous flow hysteroscope was removed, and the endocervical canal circumferentially curetted. The cervix was then sequentially dilated and the uterus sounded. The corpus of the uterus was then systematically curetted, beginning in the uterine fundus. This material was labeled separately as a pathological specimen. All instruments were removed from the vagina, and the patient was undraped and taken to the recovery room in good condition.

Code(s) _____

Case Study 9-3: Operative Report

Preoperative Diagnosis: Vulvar intraepithelial neoplasia III

Postoperative Diagnosis: Vulvar intraepithelial neoplasia III

Anesthesia: Continuous lumbar epidural

Specimens:

1. Left labia minora lesion

2. Posterior perineum with suture tacked at 9 o'clock position

3. Perianal condyloma

Findings:

1. A 1 x 1 cm broad-based raised lesion protruding from the left labia minora.

2. An area of whitish and reddish skin changes on the posterior portion both left and right of the perineum

3. Multiple perianal condylomas mixed with areas that appeared to be hemorrhoids.

Indications: This patient is a 48-year-old nulligravida woman who had a five-year history of an increasing size of a left vulvar mass. Upon evaluation, the labial lesion on the left appeared to be a condyloma; however, there were both reddish and white skin changes that were of concern. A vulvar biopsy was performed in the clinic, which demonstrated VIN III. The patient agreed to treatment of wide local excision.

2010 Current Procedural Terminology © 2009 American Medical Association. All Rights Reserved.

Procedure: Patient was taken to the operating room, and adequate lumbar epidural anesthesia was applied by the anesthesiologist service. The patient was placed in the dorsal lithotomy position using Allen's stirrup and prepped and draped in the normal sterile fashion. The vulvar lesions were identified and, using a marking pen, were circumscribed with a knife to achieve a 1 cm border and then incised the depth of the dermal layer. This was first done to the left labial lesion and then done at the perirectal lesion. The excised diameter of the labial lesion was 2.5 cm × 1.0 cm × 0.2 cm. The excised diameter of the perineum lesion was 4.2 cm × 2.1 cm × 0.5 cm. The perineum lesion could not be appropriately performed without getting into the anal wall. So, this lesion being quite large, was removed at its base by incising the skin and then using cautery to go through its stalk. Hemostasis was achieved using electrocautery. The right labial lesion was closed using a #4-0 Vicryl suture in a subcuticular fashion. The perirectal lesion was closed using a single #4-0 stitch to reapproximate the skin. The posterior perineum lesion was closed similar to that of an episiotomy. The deep tissue was reapproximated using #2-0 chromic sutures of a crown stitch. Then using #3-0 Vicryl sutures starting from the hymenal ring, a posterior limit of the incision was reached; the skin was then closed in a subcuticular fashion using the same #3-0 Vicryl stitch repair. Hemostasis was assured. All sponge, needle, and instrument counts were correct. The patient was taken out of dorsal lithotomy position, placed in a supine position, and taken to the recovery room in stable condition.

Pathology Report

Specimen A: Clinically, left labia minora lesion excision: Squamous cell carcinoma in situ with mild dysplasia present at the margin.

Specimen B: Clinically, posterior perineum: Squamous cell carcinoma in situ

Specimen C: Clinically, perianally condyloma: Squamous cell carcinoma in situ. Margin appears free of squamous cell carcinoma in situ

Code(s) _____

Case Study 9-4: Operative Report

Preoperative Diagnosis:

1. Dysfunctional uterine bleeding

2. Anemia

Postoperative Diagnosis:

1. Dysfunctional uterine bleeding

2. Anemia

Operation:

1. Fractional D&C

2. Thermachoice balloon endometrial ablation

Anesthesia: General with endotracheal tube intubation

Specimens to lab: Endocervical curettings, endometrial curettings

Operative Procedure: The patient was taken to the operating room and put under adequate general anesthesia; she was prepped and draped in the dorsolithotomy position for a vaginal procedure. The uterus was sounded to approximately 9–10 cm. Using Pratt cervical dilators, the cervix was dilated to the point that a Sims sharp curette could be inserted. A Kevorkian curette was first used to obtain endocervical curettings, and the Sims sharp curette was passed to obtain endometrial curettings. After the curettings were obtained, the Thermachoice system was assembled and primed. The catheter with the balloon was placed inside the endometrial cavity and slowly filled with fluid until it stabilized at a pressure of approximately 175 to 180 mmHg. The system was then preheated, and, after preheating to 87 degrees C, 8 minutes of therapeutic heat was applied to the lining of the endometrium. The fluid was allowed to drain from the balloon, and the system was removed. The procedure was then discontinued.

At the end of the procedure, the sponge, instrument, and needle counts were all correct. The patient tolerated the procedure well and was taken to the recovery room.

Code(s) _____

Case Study 9-5: Operative Report

Preoperative Diagnosis: Menorrhagia

Postoperative Diagnosis: Menorrhagia

Operation Performed: Hysteroscopy with D&C

Anesthesia: General

Details of Operation: Under adequate general anesthesia, the patient was placed in the dorsolithotomy position. She was prepped and draped in the usual fashion. Examination under anesthesia revealed a mildly enlarged uterus, approximately 10 to 11 weeks size with regular contour. Adnexal regions were negative.

The cervix was visualized and grasped with Allis clamp, and the uterine cavity was sounded to a depth of approximately 10.5 cm without difficulty. The os was dilated without difficulty. A 3 mm hysteroscope was inserted using a distention medium of Ringer's lactate. We were able to visualize the entire uterine cavity. There appeared to be no irregularities, fibroids, polyps, etc. The uterine surface looked pretty much within normal limits as well. A sampling of endometrial tissue was obtained. Instrumentation was withdrawn. The patient tolerated the procedure without complications and left the operating room in good condition.

Findings: Mildly enlarged uterus, 10–11 weeks size; cavity sounded to 10.5. Tissue specimen minimal.

Estimated Blood Loss: Approximately 20–25 cc.; approximately 30–40 cc old blood from uterus and vagina.

Code(s) _____

Case Study 9-6: Operative Report

Preoperative Diagnosis: Dysmenorrhea, dyspareunia, menorrhagia, endometriosis

Postoperative Diagnosis: Dysmenorrhea, dyspareunia, menorrhagia, endometriosis, and right ovarian adhesion (path pending)

Specimen: Uterus, ovaries, tubes, and adhesion from right ovary

Findings: The uterus appeared normal, and there was no evidence of endometriosis implants anywhere in the pelvis. The right ovary was adherent to the right pelvic sidewall with adhesions bridging the distance between. Otherwise, the ovaries and tubes appeared normal.

Procedure: The patient was placed in the dorsal spine position and given general anesthesia. The abdomen, vagina, and external genitalia were then prepped and draped in the usual sterile fashion using Povidone iodine. A Foley catheter was inserted into the bladder and attached to gravity drainage. A previous wide midline lower abdominal scar was outlined with a marking pen. The scar was then excised, and cautery of bleeding vessels in the subcutaneous tissue was then accomplished. The subcutaneous tissue was then divided into the midline, using a second scalpel and the fascia scored. The fascial incision was extended vertically and the rectus muscles then divided from the fascia. The peritoneum was sharply entered and the peritoneal incision then extended vertically.

The abdomen and pelvis were visually and manually explored. The patient was placed in Trendelenburg position, and the bowel packed away cephalad using moist laparotomy pads. An O'Connor-O'Sullivan self-retaining retractor was placed into the wound.

The uterus was placed on traction, and the left round ligament then skeletonized, doubly clamped, divided, and suture ligated with 0-Vicryl suture material. The anterior leaf of the broad ligament was then sharply divided across the lower uterine segment to the right round ligament, which was skeletonized, doubly clamped, divided, and the suture ligated with 0-Vicryl suture material. The vesicouterine space was then developed by sharp dissection.

The left infundibulopelvic ligament was then skeletonized, doubly clamped, divided, and suture ligated with 0-Vicryl suture material. The right infundibulopelvic ligament was then skeletonized, doubly clamped, divided, and suture ligated with 0-Vicryl suture material.

The posterior uterine serosal peritoneum was then sharply divided down to the uterosacral ligaments, and the uterine vessels then skeletonized. The uterine vessels were bilaterally clamped, divided, and suture ligated with 0-Vicryl suture material. The remainder of the broad ligaments, cardinal ligaments, uterosacral ligaments, and ultimately the lateral vaginal fornices were clamped, divided, and suture ligated with 0-Vicryl suture material. The cervix was then circumcised from the vaginal cuff and the uterus removed. It should be noted that, prior to the division of the right infundibulopelvic ligament, the right ovary had been sharply released from the pelvic peritoneum by sharply lysing the adhesions involved. The vaginal cuff was made hemostatic by the placement of a running nonlocking Meigs suture closure of 0-Vicryl suture material.

The pelvis was irrigated with Ringer's lactate solution and found to be hemostatic. The remainder of the adhesion, which had extended from the right ovary, was excised. The posterior peritoneum was then approximated in running nonlocking fashion using 2-0 chromic suture material attaching this suture to the cuff suture in the midline to diminish dead space. Again, the pelvis was irrigated with Ringer's lactate solution and found to be hemostatic.

All sponge, instrument, and needle counts were found to be correct. The O'Connor-O'Sullivan self-retaining retractor was removed, as were the three laparotomy pads. The small bowel and omentum were anatomically placed. The peritoneum was closed in nonlocking fashion using 2-0 chromic suture material. The rectus fascia was then approximated in interrupted figure-of-speed Jones fashion using 0-Vicryl suture material. The subcutaneous tissue was approximated in interrupted fashion using 3-0 plain suture material. The skin was then approximated in running nonlocking subcuticular fashion using 3-0 Prolene suture material. A dressing was applied to the wound. The patient was awakened from general anesthesia and taken to the recovery room in good condition.

Code(s) _____

2010 Current Procedural Terminology © 2009 American Medical Association. All Rights Reserved.

10

Nervous System

Chapter Outline

Introduction

Twist Drill or Burr Hole

Craniotomy and Craniectomy

Neurostimulator (Intracranial)

Cerebrospinal (CSF) Shunt

Spine and Spinal Cord

Key Terms

anterior approach

anterolateral approach

burr hole

bone flap

carpal tunnel syndrome

central nervous system

costovertebral approach

craniectomy

craniotomy

discectomy

laminectomy

laminotomy

lateral extracavitary
  approach

lumbar puncture

neuroplasty

neurorrhaphy

neurostimulator

peripheral nervous
  system

posterior approach

somatic nerves

shunt

sympathetic nerves

transpedicular approach

Chapter Objectives

At the conclusion of this chapter, the student should be able to:

- Identify anatomical structures of the nervous system.
- Describe common surgical procedures of the nervous system.
- Explain coding guidelines applicable to the nervous system.
- Use references to assist with coding assignment.
- Given a case scenario, accurately assign CPT codes and modifiers (if necessary).

2010 Current Procedural Terminology © 2009 American Medical Association. All Rights Reserved.

Introduction

The nervous system consists of the brain, spinal cord, and nerves (Figure 10-1).

The **central nervous system** consists of the brain and spinal cord. It's considered the body's central control system because it receives and interprets all stimuli and relays nerve impulses to muscles and glands where the action takes place. The **peripheral nervous system** is composed of 12 pairs of cranial nerves and 31 pairs of spinal nerves extending from the spinal cord. It allows the brain and spinal cord to communicate with the rest of the body.

The most common procedures performed in this specialty include neurostimulators, laminectomies, discectomies, and spinal fusions. In addition to these frequently performed procedures, this chapter will also focus on repair of nerves, insertion of shunts, and spinal injections.

This chapter in the CPT book is divided into three anatomical sections.

* Skull, Meninges, and Brain
* Spine and Spinal Cord
* Extracranial Nerves, Peripheral Nerves, and Autonomic Nervous System

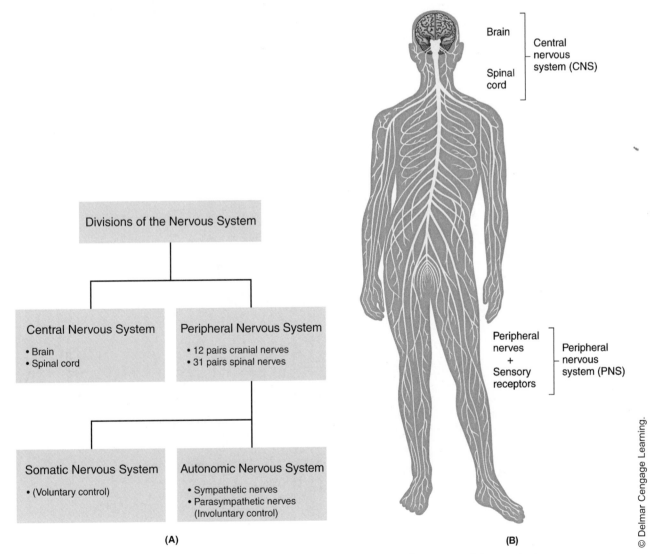

Figure 10-1 Nervous system. (A) Divisions of the nervous system. (B) Structure of the central nervous system and peripheral nervous system

2010 Current Procedural Terminology © 2009 American Medical Association. All Rights Reserved.

In the Skull, Meninges, and Brain section, there are several subsections (Figure 10-2):

- Injection, Drainage, or Aspiration (codes 61000–61070)
- Twist Drill, Burr Hole(s), or Trephine (codes 61105–61253)
- Craniectomy or Craniotomy (codes 61304–61576)
- Surgery of Skull Base (codes 61580–61619)
- Endovascular Therapy (codes 61623–61642)
- Surgery for Aneurysm, Arteriovenous Malformation, or Vascular Disease (codes 61680–61711)
- Stereotaxis (codes 61720–61795)
- Neurostimulators (Intracranial) (codes 61850–61888)
- Repair (codes 62000–62148)
- Neuroendoscopy (codes 62160–62165)
- Cerebrospinal Fluid (CSF) Shunt (codes 62180–62258)

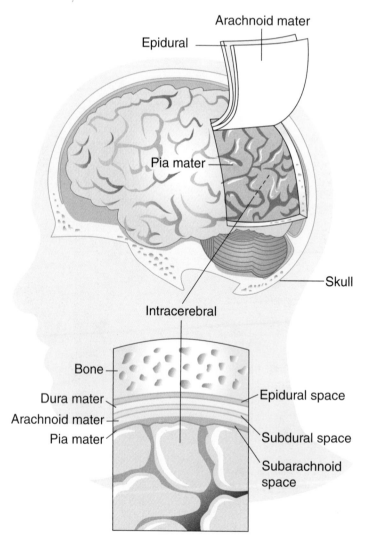

© Delmar Cengage Learning.

Figure 10-2 Scalp, skull, meninges, and brain

2010 Current Procedural Terminology © 2009 American Medical Association. All Rights Reserved.

Twist Drill or Burr Hole

A twist drill or **burr hole** is an opening of the brain created with a surgical drill. It is considered to be a minimally invasive procedure that can be done to relieve pressure (such as with hydrocephalus), to insert monitoring devices, for a needle biopsy, or to inject contrast material. It is often necessary to perform this procedure when intracranial surgery is planned. The hole leaves the skull intact and can be repaired at a later time.

The CPT codes for these procedures (61105–61253) are based on the reason for the hole (e.g., implantation of a pressure device, drainage of a hematoma, or biopsy) and, in some cases, the location of the hole (e.g., supratentorial or infratentorial).

> **Note:**
>
> *When burr holes are created for the purpose of performing drainage procedures (e.g., hematoma, abscess, or cyst) and additional procedures are performed, the burr hole and drainage procedure is not separately coded and reported. An exception to this would be a staged procedure.*

Craniotomy and Craniectomy

A **craniotomy** is any bony opening that is cut into the skull. A **bone flap** is removed to access the brain underneath. If the bone flap is not going to be replaced, then the procedure is considered a **craniectomy**. The CPT codes for these types of procedures are in the range 61304–61576 and are specified by the site of the procedure or the reason for the craniotomy or craniectomy.

> **EXAMPLE 1:** A burr hole was created for drainage of a subdural hematoma.
>
> Correct coding assignment: 61154
>
> **EXAMPLE 2:** Patient had a twist drill hole created for evacuation of a subdural hematoma.
>
> Correct coding assignment: 61108

Exercise 10-1: Burr Hole and Craniotomy Procedures

Assign CPT codes to the following procedures. Append CPT/HCPCS Level II modifiers if applicable. Concentrate on application of coding guidelines, and do not focus on sequencing codes or assignment of modifier 51.

1. The patient presents to the hospital after a fall and was diagnosed with an extradural hematoma. A burr hole was created to evacuate the hematoma.

Code(s) _____

2. A 65-year-old man was sent to the hospital to have a biopsy of an intracranial lesion. The biopsy was done through a burr hole.

Code(s) _____

3. A patient presents to the hospital with a large intracerebellar hematoma after falling from a ladder. The patient was taken to the operating room, where an intracerebellar craniotomy was performed to relieve the pressure.

Code(s) _____

Neurostimulator (Intracranial)

A **neurostimulator** consists of two key components: a pulse generator inserted into a subcutaneous pocket (either in the chest or abdomen) and one or more leads that are connected to a generator, tunneled, and placed in the target area. The pulse generator contains a battery that will eventually need to be replaced. Codes 61850–61888 are used for coding the insertion and replacement of intracranial neurostimulators.

2010 Current Procedural Terminology © 2009 American Medical Association. All Rights Reserved.

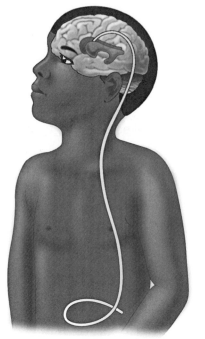

© Delmar Cengage Learning.

Figure 10-3 A cerebrospinal shunt allows drainage of cerebrospinal fluid (CSF) from the brain into the peritoneal cavity

EXAMPLE: A 68-year-old man with a brain stimulator due to advanced Parkinson's disease was seen for replacement of the single array pulse generator, which was failing.

Correct coding assignment: 61885

Cerebrospinal (CSF) Shunt

A **shunt** is a flexible tube placed into the ventricular system of the brain, which diverts flow of cerebrospinal fluid (CSF) to another region of the body, usually the abdominal cavity, where it can be absorbed. The most common reason for insertion of this shunt is hydrocephalus: an abnormal accumulation of fluid within the ventricles of the brain. The shunt consists of three parts (Figure 10-3):

- An inflow catheter that drains CSF from the ventricles to a valve
- A valve mechanism, which controls flow through the shunt tubing
- An outflow catheter, which directs CSF flow from the valve to the drainage site

  The codes in this section are based on the position of the catheters, both inflow and outflow.

  Codes 62180–62194 are used for creation of or replacement of a shunt in the subarachnoid/subdural area.

  Codes 62200–62225 are used for creation of or replacement of a shunt in the ventricles.

EXAMPLE: A 7-year-old boy presented with hydrocephalus. The physician recommended and performed creation of a ventriculo-atrial shunt.

Correct coding assignment: 62220

Spine and Spinal Cord

Under the Spine and Spinal Cord section, there are several subsections.

- Injection, Drainage, or Aspiration (62263–62319)

- Catheter Implantation (62350–62355)

- Reservoir/Pump Implantation (62360–62368)

- Posterior Extradural Laminotomy or Laminectomy for Exploration/Decompression of Neural Elements or Excision of Herniated Intervertebral Discs (63001–63051)

- Transpedicular or Costovertebral Approach for Posterolateral Extradural Exploration/Decompression (63055–63066)

- Anterior or Anterolateral Approach for Extradural Exploration/Decompression (63075–63091)

- Lateral Extracavitary Approach for Extradural Exploration/Decompression (63101–63103)

- Incision (63170–63200)

- Excision by Laminectomy of Lesion Other Than Herniated Disc (63250–63295)

- Excision, Anterior or Anterolateral Approach, Intraspinal Lesion (63300–63308)

- Stereotaxis (63600–63615)

- Neurostimulators (Spinal) (63650–63688)

- Repair (63700–63710)

- Shunt, Spinal CSF (63740–63746)

Injection, Drainage, or Aspiration

In this subsection, there are procedure codes for such procedures as lumbar puncture, blood patch, and spinal injections.

A **lumbar puncture** (also called a spinal tap) is performed by inserting a needle into the lower back (lumbar) and collecting a sample of spinal fluid (CSF) (Figure 10-4).

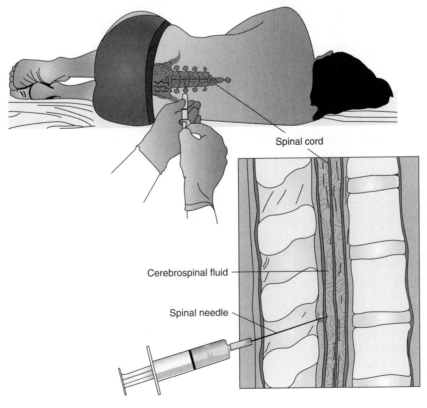

Spinal cord

Cerebrospinal fluid

Spinal needle

© Delmar Cengage Learning.

Figure 10-4 Lumbar puncture

2010 Current Procedural Terminology © 2009 American Medical Association. All Rights Reserved.

This procedure can be done to find a diagnosis for infectious symptoms (such as meningitis), to diagnose certain diseases of the brain and spinal cord (such as multiple sclerosis), or to measure CSF pressure, or it can be done to inject anesthetics or dye into the CSF.

- Code 62270 describes a diagnostic lumbar puncture.

- Code 62272 describes a therapeutic lumbar puncture for drainage of cerebrospinal fluid.

Code 62290 would be used if a discography was being performed at the lumbar level. Code 62291 would be used if the discography was performed at the cervical or thoracic level.

Spinal injections, or infusions, are coded according to the site of the injection and the substance injected. Spinal injections deliver medications through a needle placed into a structure or space in the spine to allow the physician to identify the source of pain and/or reduce it. Typical medications used include local anesthetics and corticosteroids. Local anesthetics numb the nerves, and corticosteroids help reduce inflammation.

> **Note:**
>
> *Injection of contrast during fluoroscopic guidance and localization is an inclusive component of these codes and would not be coded separately.*

> **Note:**
>
> *The administration of local anesthesia before a lumbar puncture is included and would not be coded separately.*

Review of Documentation

During the review of the operative report for a spinal injection, the coder will search for answers to the following questions:

- What is the injection site?

- What substance is being injected?

- Was it a single injection (codes 62310–62311) or a continuous injection (codes 62318–62319)?

  - Cervical epidural injection of Phenol

    Correct coding assignment: 62310

  - Diagnostic Lumbar Puncture

    Correct Coding Assignment: 62270

> **Note:**
>
> *The codes for a transforaminal epidural injection are in a different section (codes 64479–64484).*

Exercise 10-2: Injections

Assign CPT codes to the following procedures. Append CPT/HCPCS Level II modifiers if applicable. Concentrate on application of coding guidelines, and do not focus on sequencing codes or assignment of modifier 51.

1. A patient is seen in the emergency department with low back pain that has been going on for about two months. He was sent to radiology where an epidural steroid injection was performed in the L5-S1 interspace.

   Code(s) _____

2. A 65-year-old man visited his physician due to chronic neck pain. The physician decided to perform a continuous epidural injection in C4-5.

   Code(s) _____

2010 Current Procedural Terminology © 2009 American Medical Association. All Rights Reserved.

Laminotomy, Laminectomy, Discectomy

Here are a few definitions of key terms in this section.

> **Laminotomy**—the removal of part of the lamina from one side of the vertebra
>
> **Laminectomy**—the excision of the entire posterior arch or lamina of the vertebra
>
> **Discectomy**—the removal of an intervertebral disk

The procedures listed above are typically performed to relieve pressure on the spinal cord or nerves that are compressed by abnormal structures surrounding the spinal canal. Examples are bone spurs, herniated discs, tumors, and overgrown ligaments that cause arm or leg pain due to compression of the nerves in the spinal canal.

> **Note:**
>
> *A laminotomy is also known as a hemilaminectomy. When reviewing an operative report, be sure to differentiate between a laminectomy and a hemilaminectomy.*

The CPT codes for surgical procedures involving the spine are based on:

- Surgical approach

- Anatomic location

- Type of procedure performed

The CPT codes in this subsection are organized according to the approach.

Posterior Approach

The **posterior approach** is the most traditional method of performing back surgery where an incision is made in the back.

Codes 63001–63017 describe laminectomies or decompression *without* foraminotomy, facetectomy, or discectomy. The codes are differentiated based upon the number of segments and location of the spine.

Codes 63020–63048 describe laminotomy procedures *including* foraminotomy (facetectomy, excision of herniated disc) and are differentiated by the vertebral level. Note that each code identifies a procedure performed at a single level, and, if another level is operated upon, an add-on code (63035, 63043, 63044, and 63048) should be reported.

> **Note:**
>
> *It is very important to review the operative report and note the approach that is being used. If you have the wrong approach, you will get the wrong code!*

Transpedicular or Costovertebral Approach

Codes 63055–63057 describe procedures using the **transpedicular approach**. This is performed through and inside the pedicle (segment between transverse process and vertebral body) of a thoracic vertebra to access a thoracic disk. This approach may involve removal of the lamina and facet joint.

Codes 63064 and 63066 describe procedures using the **costovertebral approach**. This is performed where the ribs connect with thoracic vertebrae. The physician makes an incision laterally to the spine, cutting through epidermis, dermis, subcutaneous, fascia, and muscle tissue and a section of rib.

> **Note:**
>
> *There is a parenthetical note under this heading that states if these procedures are performed along with a spinal fusion, you would not use these codes but would go to the section where codes 22590–22614 reside.*

Anterior or Anterolateral Approach

The **anterior approach** involves the patient lying on his or her back, and the operation is performed from the front.

> **Note:**
>
> *Note that there are add-on codes for each approach if more than one segment is operated upon.*

2010 Current Procedural Terminology © 2009 American Medical Association. All Rights Reserved.

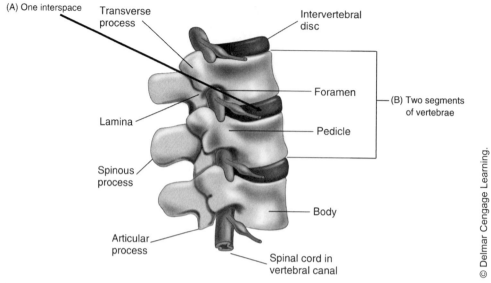

(A) One interspace
Transverse process
Intervertebral disc
Foramen
(B) Two segments of vertebrae
Lamina
Pedicle
Spinous process
Articular process
Body
Spinal cord in vertebral canal

© Delmar Cengage Learning.

Figure 10-5 Interspaces and vertebrae. (A) One interspace. (B) Two segments of vertebrae.

The **anterolateral approach** involves making an incision along the rib that corresponds to the vertebra.

Codes 63075–63078 are used when a discectomy is performed from the anterior approach. Each code denotes a different vertebral level, and there is an add-on code (Figure 10-5).

Codes 63081–63091 describe vertebral corpectomy procedures and are differentiated by the segment (e.g., cervical, lumbar) that is operated upon. In addition, there are add-on codes to use if more than one segment is operated on.

Lateral Extracavitary Approach

The **lateral extracavitary approach** allows access to the vertebral bodies as well as the posterior elements through a single incision. This approach is best used for patients who have complicated medical conditions that make having a staged procedure less desirable. It is most appropriate to use this approach for patients who need anterior and posterior stabilization.

Code 63101 describes a vertebral corpectomy using the lateral extracavitary approach at the thoracic segment. Code 63102 describes the procedure at the lumbar segment. Code 63103 is an add-on code for each additional segment operated on.

Excision of Intraspinal Lesions

Laminectomies and corpectomies can be performed for reasons other than excising herniated disks. The codes in range 63250–63290 describe laminectomies performed for excision of intraspinal lesions and biopsies and excisions of intraspinal neoplasms.

Codes 63300–63307 describe vertebral corpectomies for excision of intraspinal lesions. The codes describe the vertebral segment at which the procedure was performed and whether the lesion was intradural or extradural. There is also an add-on code (63308) for each additional segment that was operated on.

> **Note:**
>
> *Sometimes when a procedure is performed anteriorly, one surgeon will create the incision and another physician will actually perform the procedure, or both surgeons could work on different sections. If this is the case, be sure that the procedures that each surgeon performs are coded and modifier 62 is added to denote that two surgeons were performing the procedures.*

> **Coding Tip:**
>
> *The add-on codes must be used in conjunction with the CPT code for the procedure performed. They cannot be used alone.*
>
> *Procedure codes 63081–63091 include discectomy above and/or below vertebral segment.*
>
> *When spinal fusion follows procedures coded with 63075–63091, report a code from the range 22548–22812 also.*

EXAMPLE:1 Patient underwent decompression of spinal cord at T1, using costovertebral approach.

Correct coding assignment: 63064

EXAMPLE:2 Patient underwent laminectomy with decompression of the spinal cord on one segment of the thoracic vertebra.

Correct coding assignment: 63003

Exercise 10-3: Spine Procedures

Assign CPT codes to the following procedures. Append CPT/HCPCS Level II modifiers if applicable. Concentrate on application of coding guidelines, and do not focus on sequencing codes or assignment of modifier 51.

1. Patient presents with a herniated cervical disk. A hemilaminectomy with partial facetectomy and excision of the herniated disk was performed.

   Code(s) _____

2. The surgeon performs surgery on the spine that includes laminectomy, decompression of the spine, facetectomy of the L4 vertebra, and laminotomy with excision of intervertebral disk at L1.

   Code(s) _____

3. A 47-year-old woman was admitted to the hospital where she had a discectomy performed at C1-2 and C2-3. This was performed using the anterior approach.

   Code(s) _____

4. The patient was scheduled to have a lumbar lesion excised. The surgeon performed a laminectomy with excision of an intradural lumbar lesion.

   Code(s) _____

Neurostimulators (Spinal)

A spinal neurostimulator delivers low-voltage electrical stimulation to the spinal cord to block the sensation of pain. The device consists of a pulse generator and one or two electrodes.

The CPT codes in this section specifically describe either an implantation or a revision/removal.

- **Code 63650**—percutaneous implantation
- **Code 63655**—laminectomy for implantation
- **Codes 63661-63662**—removal spinal neurostimulator
- **Codes 63663-63664**—revision spinal neurostimulator
- **Code 63685**—insertion or replacement of pulse generator
- **Code 63688**—revision or removal of pulse generator

EXAMPLE: Patient underwent revision of an implanted spinal neurostimulator pulse generator.

Correct coding assignment: 63688

Repair

CPT codes 63700–63710 describe procedures for the repair of meningoceles or dural/cerebrospinal fluid leaks.

Note:

For electronic analysis of implanted neurostimulator pulse generator system, see codes 95970–95975.

2010 Current Procedural Terminology © 2009 American Medical Association. All Rights Reserved.

EXAMPLE: Patient underwent repair of a cerebrospinal fluid leak without laminectomy.

Correct coding assignment: 63707

Note:

For cervical laminectomy and section of dentate ligaments, with or without dural graft, see 63180 and 63182.

Extracranial Nerves, Peripheral Nerves, and Autonomic Nervous System

The CPT codes in this section describe procedures performed on the types of nerves listed previously. To report procedure codes properly, review the operative note to identify the following:

- Anatomic site (e.g., somatic nerve or sympathetic nerve)
- Type of procedure performed (e.g., injection or neurostimulator implantation)

Somatic nerves control voluntary movements (performed by skeletal muscles) and conscious sensation (e.g., hearing, sight, and touch), and they include voluntary motor and sensory nerves.

Sympathetic nerves control involuntary actions, such as the beating of your heart and the widening or narrowing of the arteries. They originate in the thoracic and lumbar regions of the spinal cord.

Codes 64400–64530 describe procedures for the introduction or injection of an anesthetic agent (e.g., nerve block). These codes describe injection procedures to somatic and sympathetic nerves for diagnostic and therapeutic reasons (e.g., pain management).

Review of Documentation

During the review of the operative report for the injection, the coder will search for answers to the following questions:

- What type of substance was injected?
- What nerves were involved? Somatic? Sympathetic?
- What type of block was used? (e.g., single, multiple, or regional)
- What was the duration of the infusion? (single, continuous)

Coding Tip:

The codes in this section should not be used in conjunction with codes from the anesthesia section.

When coding injections into an area surrounding the spinal cord are performed, report codes 62310–62319 (e.g., pain management). The codes in this section are reported when injections into nerves are performed.

EXAMPLE 1: The patient underwent a continuous injection of an anesthetic agent in the femoral nerve.

Correct coding assignment: 64448

EXAMPLE 2: Patient with chronic pain receives a nerve block, anesthetic agent into the branch of the sciatic nerve.

Correct coding assignment: 64445

Neurostimulators (Peripheral Nerve)

A peripheral nerve stimulator system includes an electrode and a pulse generator that are implanted along peripheral nerves to alleviate pain or control spasms.

The peripheral neurostimulator is either inserted percutaneously (64553–64565) or an incision can be made for insertion (codes 64573–64581). Codes 64585–64595 describe procedures where the electrodes or pulse generator are removed or replaced. Figure 10-6 shows what the coder must determine when coding the insertion of peripheral neurostimulators.

EXAMPLE 1: Patient underwent implantation of a percutaneous neurostimulator in the autonomic nerve.

Correct coding assignment: 64560

EXAMPLE 2: Patient was seen for removal of the peripheral neurostimulator electrodes.

Correct coding assignment: 64585

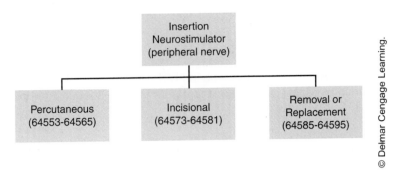

Figure 10-6

Neuroplasty (Exploration, Neurolysis, or Nerve Decompression)

Neuroplasty is the decompression or freeing of intact nerve from scar tissue. It also includes decompression, exploration, external neurolysis, and/or nerve transposition. These procedures are included in the codes in this section and are not coded separately.

Carpal tunnel syndrome is a painful progressive condition caused by compression of the medial nerve at the wrist. It is usually caused by repetitive motion injuries such as those caused by keyboarding or assembly line work. Tendon sheaths become inflamed (tenosynovitis), which causes increased pressure to the median nerve (Figure 10-7).

Carpal tunnel release is the procedure performed to relieve this condition. This procedure releases compression of the median nerve.

> **EXAMPLE:** Patient underwent neuroplasty and transposition of the median nerve.
>
> Correct coding assignment: 64721

> **Note:**
>
> *When internal neurolysis requires use of an operating microscope, use 64727 along with the code for the procedure.*

Neurorrhaphy

Neurorrhaphy is the surgical suturing of a divided nerve. Codes 64831–64876 are reported for procedures including the suture and anastomosis of proximal nerves (e.g., ulnar, lumbar plexus). Codes 64885–64911 describe neurorrhaphy procedures in which a nerve graft was used.

The operative report should be reviewed to determine:

- Anatomic site repaired (head and neck, hand or foot, or arm or leg)
- Number of nerves repaired (there are add-on codes for additional nerves)
- Length of the nerve graft (up to 4 cm or more than 4 cm)

> **EXAMPLE:** Patient underwent suture of the ulnar motor nerve.
>
> Correct coding assignment: 64836

> **Note:**
>
> *Remember that the add-on codes are used in addition to the procedure code.*

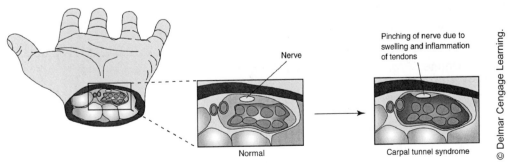

Figure 10-7 Carpal tunnel syndrome

Exercise 10-4: Nerve Procedures

Assign CPT codes to the following procedures. Append CPT/HCPCS Level II modifiers if applicable. Concentrate on application of coding guidelines, and do not focus on sequencing codes or assignment of modifier 51.

1. Using an operating microscope, the physician performs a neuroplasty of the right ring finger.
   Code(s) _____

2. Neurorrhaphy of digital nerves of right thumb and right index finger.
   Code(s): _____

3. The surgeon performed a sciatic neuroplasty on the patient's leg.
   Code(s) _____

4. Patient presents to the hospital with a laceration of his posterior tibial nerve. It was repaired by neurorrhaphy.
   Code(s) _____

5. A 45-year-old man went to his physician and had a vagus nerve block injection performed.
   Code(s) _____

Summary

- The nervous system chapter is divided into three anatomical sections.

- When a burr hole is created for drainage and a more extensive procedure is performed, the burr hole would not be coded separately.

- If a craniotomy is performed and the bone flap is not replaced, code the procedure as a craniectomy.

- The administration of local anesthesia before a lumbar puncture is not coded separately.

- A laminotomy is also known as a hemilaminectomy.

- There are several different approaches that can be used for laminotomy, laminectomy, and discectomy procedures. It's important to be sure you are coding the correct approach.

- There are many add-on codes in the nervous system chapter. Remember that the add-on codes must be used in conjunction with the CPT code for the procedure performed.

- When coding anesthetic nerve blocks, codes from the anesthesia section of CPT are not used.

- There are several areas that neurostimulators can be implanted in: intracranial, spinal, and peripheral nerves.

Internet Links

Human Anatomy Online: *http://www.innerbody.com*
Tutorial designed by body system

Mayfield Clinic: *http://www.mayfieldclinic.com*
Descriptions of procedures and illustrations

Medline Plus: *http://www.nlm.nih.gov/medlineplus/tutorials/myelogram/htm/_no_50_no_0.htm*
Tutorial about myelogram

2010 Current Procedural Terminology © 2009 American Medical Association. All Rights Reserved.

Review

I. Medical Terminology Assessment

Match the following terms with the correct definition:

_____ 1. neuroplasty	A. complete removal of lamina
_____ 2. shunt	B. surgical suturing of nerve
_____ 3. lumbar puncture	C. flexible tube insertion
_____ 4. neurorrhaphy	D. surgical repair of nerve
_____ 5. laminotomy	E. insert needle into lower back
_____ 6. laminectomy	F. partial removal of lamina

II. Case Studies

Directions: Assign CPT surgical codes to the following case studies. The focus is on surgical coding; therefore, do not assign codes for radiological procedures, lab, etc.

Case Study 10-1: Operative Report

Preoperative Diagnosis: Backache unspecified; work-related back and leg pain

Postoperative Diagnosis: Same

Procedures Performed:

IV sedation

Fluoroscopic guidance to the procedure.

Fluoroscopic myelography injection, extradural in the lumbar/sacral area

Lumbar epidural steroid injection L5-S1 interspace

Interpretation of permanent film

Caudal with sedation

Indications for Procedure: The patient is a 41-year-old male with severe work-related back and leg pain, more left than right. The patient understands the reasons for the procedure. The patient is anxious and needed IV sedation and tolerated the pain associated with injection.

Details of Procedure: For the procedure, the patient was sedated with 2 mg of Versed and 1250 mg of Alfenta. The patient was monitored throughout the procedure and afterwards with pulse oximeter and Dinamap. The pulse oximetry ranged in the lower and upper 90 range. The patient tolerated the IV well. For the procedure, the patient was placed prone on the fluoroscopy table with a pillow under the patient's abdomen. We identified the sacral hiatus, prepped the skin with alcohol and DuraPrep, and applied drapes and anesthetized the skin with Xylocaine.

Next, we used fluoroscopy to guide the 17-gauge needle into the spinal canal through the sacral hiatus. This was advanced under AP and lateral fluoroscopic guidance with loss of resistance. We verified proper depth and placement with myelography injection. The lumbar myelography injection was extradural in the lumbosacral area and consisted of 2 cc of Isovue 300. This showed we were in the spinal canal and highlighting the nerve roots at the lumbosacral region.

2010 Current Procedural Terminology © 2009 American Medical Association. All Rights Reserved.

Next, we placed the catheter to the L5-S1 interspace. Through the catheter, we injected steroid solution, which contained 80 mg of Depo-Medrol, 3 cc of 0.75% Marcaine, and 4 cc of Omnipaque 300. This was injected under fluoroscopy, visualizing the nerve roots well throughout the lower lumbar area, more left than right. We cleared the catheter and needle solution and removed them from the back. Permanent films were taken, and the patient was taken to the recovery room in good condition.

Code(s) _____

Case Study 10-2: Operative Report

Preoperative Diagnosis: Neurogenic bladder with an implanted sacral nerve stimulator

Postoperative Diagnosis: Neurogenic bladder with an implanted sacral nerve stimulator

Procedure Performed: Removal of InterStim sacral nerve stimulator

Anesthesia: MAC with local

Complications: None

Indication for Procedure: This 96-year-old female with a history of neurogenic bladder with recurrent urinary tract infections due to poor emptying is here for removal of her sacral nerve stimulator, which had subsequently quit working. After all of the risks, benefits, and expected outcomes were explained, she agreed to proceed.

Details of Procedure: She was brought to the operating suite, given a light intravenous anesthetic, laid in the prone position. The area overlying the InterStim neurostimulator was infiltrated using 1% lidocaine mixed with 0.25% Marcaine. Once this was done, an incision was made over this, and dissection was carried down to the InterStim neurostimulator. This was removed from its pouch. The leads, which were tunneled down to the S3 foramina, were identified, and with careful manipulation we were able to remove them in their entirety. Once this was done, hemostasis was obtained. The wound was copiously irrigated using antibiotic solution. The 3-0 Vicryl pop-offs were used to close the subcutaneous tissue. 4-0 Monocryl was used to close the skin. Benzoin, SteriStrips, and Tegaderm were applied. She tolerated the procedure well and was taken to the recovery room in stable condition.

Code(s) _____

Case Study 10-3: Operative Report

Preoperative Diagnosis:

> Right lower extremity radiculopathy
>
> Spinal stenosis, L4-5 and L5-S1

Postoperative Diagnosis:

> Right lower extremity radiculopathy
>
> Spinal stenosis, L4-L5 and L5-S1

Procedures Performed:

> Lumbar decompression via laminectomy, L5-S1 and L4-L5

2010 Current Procedural Terminology © 2009 American Medical Association. All Rights Reserved.

Anesthesia: General

Estimated Blood Loss: 75 mL

Complications: None

Operative Indications: The patient is a 48-year-old gentleman with a history of severe right lower extremity pain following a work-related accident. He has tried and failed exhaustive nonoperative care. He does have a transitional vertebra on plain films as well as on MRI, which made the exact surgical count slightly more difficult. I considered the rudimentary type disc S1-2, although the radiologist had termed it L5-S1. I therefore made it clear that the lowest two true disks were the levels in which surgery was going to take place. The operative procedure, risks, and benefits—including, but not limited to, bleeding, infection, further surgery, nerve injury, vascular injury, dural tear, failure to relieve pain, need for future surgery, postoperative low back pain and/or instability, anesthesia, paralysis, and death—were all discussed. He understood no guarantees could be provided and wished to proceed.

Details of Procedure: After seeing the patient in the preoperative holding area and confirming the operative site as well as informed consent, he was taken to the operating room where general anesthesia was induced. He was placed prone on a Wilson frame. Pressure points and extremities were padded in the routine fashion. He was given routine preoperative prophylactic antibiotics. The spine was then prepped and draped in the standard sterile fashion. Following that, I had a timeout to confirm the operative site. I made an incision from the L4 to the S1 spinous processes with a 15 blade. Bovie cautery was used to dissect down to the fascia. The fascia was then opened, and I subperiosteally dissected over the L4, L5, and S1 spinous processes and lamina bilaterally, taking care to preserve the facet joints. I had localizing radiographs taken and sent down to be interpreted by Dr. Mark Welling, which I also sent down my preoperative plain radiographs as well as the MRI to confirm with him that I was truly indeed at the lowest true disk level. He concurred with my intraoperative interpretation. I then performed an L5 laminectomy as well as laminectomy of the caudal portion of L5 with the Horsley bone biter. I began my decompression centrally with a rongeur as well as an AMH high-speed burr. After performing my central decompression, I also was able to work out laterally toward the pedicles bilaterally. A facetectomy was performed on the right side of the L4-L5 and L5-S1. Following that, I still felt that the neural foramina were significantly stenotic and foraminotomies were performed at each level. Following my foraminotomy, I also was able to gently retract the dural sac to be sure that there was no free disk fragment. There was not. I cauterized some epidural veins over the L4-L5 disk space and gently probed this area with a Penfield 4 retractor, but again there was no obvious free disk fragment. Similarly at L5-S1, there was no obvious free disk fragments located. I could easily pass a Murphy ball probe at the neural foramen at both L4-L5 and L5-S1. I could easily visualize the traversing L5 as well as S1 nerve roots with no obvious compressive pathology. Following that, I copiously irrigated the entire incision and confirmed excellent hemostasis. I had the anesthesiologist perform Valsalva maneuver. There was no evidence of CSF leak, whatsoever. I then again copiously irrigated and confirmed hemostasis. I then closed the fascia using 0 Vicryl in a figure-of-eight fashion for watertight seal. I again copiously irrigated and closed the subcutaneous tissue with 2-0, followed by 3-0 Vicryl in interrupted fashion, and a 4-0 Monocryl running subcuticular suture for the skin. Dermabond and SteriStrips were applied as well as 0.5% Marcaine for analgesia and a sterile dressing. Sponge and needle counts were correct x 2. The patient was awakened, seemed to be moving all four extremities, and taken to recovery in stable condition.

Code(s) _____

Case Study 10-4: Operative Report

Preoperative Diagnosis: Right sphenoid wing meningioma

Postoperative Diagnosis: Right sphenoid wing meningioma

Operation Performed: Right frontal temporal craniotomy and zygomatic osteotomy and resection of the meningioma

Indications for Surgery: The patient is a 55-year-old gentleman who has been found during a workup to have an instrumentally large tumor spreading from the sphenoid wing laterally and growing into the brain with significant mass effect and midline shift and also some edema around the tumor. The tumor measures approximately 6 cm and growing from the temporal fossa into the frontoparietal area. The patient is legally noncompetent, so permission for surgery has been obtained from his legal guardian.

Description of the Surgery: The patient was intubated and placed in the supine position with the head tilted to the left. Then, a large frontotemporoparietal flap was made and was prepped and draped in a sterile fashion. An incision was made with #10 blade scalpel and Bovie coagulators and then an incision was carried out to the temporalis muscle. The zygomatic arch was sharply cut, the muscle was retracted, and then frontotemporoparietal craniotomy was performed. The middle fossa was exposed extensively, so the tumor was coagulated completely on its base. After the devascularization of the tumor, the attention was directed to the dura, which was opened all around the base of the tumor, which now from a skull-base tumor has become a complexity tumor. The tumor was then resected with the use of ultrasonic aspirators and Bovie loops. At the end of the case, the entire tumor was resected at the base, and the tumor bed was then also controlled for bleeding, and FloSeal was used. At this point, the dura was patched with the Dura-Guard, reinforced with DuraGen and Tisseel. The bone flap was replaced and fixed with miniplates, and the bone flap, which was infiltrated by tumor, was replaced with a titanium mesh. The muscle was closed with #2-0 Vicryl sutures. Subcutaneous tissue was closed with #3-0 Vicryl sutures, and the skin was closed with staples. A Jackson-Pratt was left in subgaleal space. The patient was sent to the recovery room in good condition.

Code(s) _____

Case Study 10-5: Operative Report

Preoperative Diagnosis: C5-6 disc herniation

Postoperative Diagnosis: C5-6 disc herniation

Operation Performed: Anterior cervical discectomy

Indications and Details for Procedure: This 45-year-old gentleman presents with a six-month history of neck pain, right shoulder pain, right intra-scapular pain, and pain radiating on the outer aspect of the right arm. He was found to have wasting of the supra and infra-spinatus muscles and the EMG confirmed a C-6 radiculopathy. MRI scan showed a lateral disc herniation at the level of C5-C6. The patient tried initial conservative measures, which did not help; hence, recommendation of surgery was made. The risks and benefits were explained. The patient fully understands and agrees to go ahead with the procedure.

The patient was anesthetized and positioned supine with shoulder support, and the neck was prepared and draped in the usual manner. Mid-cervical crease incision was marked, both 4 cm incisions were placed transversely, and the skin was sharply cut, and then the platysma was cut in the line of incision. The cervical fascia was dissected. Then we entered the plane between the trachea and the carotid sheath by blunt dissection reaching the prevertebral space. The prevertebral fascia was incised longitudinally. The disc bulge at 5-6 was easily identified, and the spinal needle place was confirmed. The anterior osteophytes were prominent. They were removed, and then we entered the disc space. The disc space itself had collapsed, and there was only desiccated disc material. We curetted out the disc and the cartilage plate, and the vertebral spreader was put in. More disc was removed from the lateral parts of the disc extending toward the uncas on both sides. As we moved posteriorly toward the ligament,

2010 Current Procedural Terminology © 2009 American Medical Association. All Rights Reserved.

there was subligamentous disc herniation to the right side, and it was removed, and the ligament was reached. The ligament was lifted with a blunt hook and opened with micro-punches. Using a Midas Rex drill, the posterior parts of the bone in this region were drilled doing a right foraminotomy, and the nerve root was decompressed. No free fragment was identified inside the canal, and the entire ligamentum disc was removed over the nerve root. The bone was punched in those corners to give adequate space. The ligament was cut across the width of the space, and on the left side also foraminotomy was done, removing the osteophytes in the corner and decompressing the nerve root. After we were satisfied with the decompression, the space was irrigated with antibiotic solution, and hemostasis was achieved with some Gelfoam powder, and the wound was thoroughly irrigated. Hemostasis was achieved in the muscle plane, and closure was done with 3-0 Vicryl for the platysma and subcutaneous layer, and the skin was closed with 4-0 subcuticular Vicryl. Dressings were applied in the usual manner with SteriStrips, Telfa gauze, and Tegaderm. The patient was reversed from anesthesia, and he had an uneventful recovery.

Code(s) _____

Eye and Ocular Adnexa

Chapter Outline

Introduction
Removal of Foreign Body
Anterior Segment
Anterior Sclera

Posterior Segment
Ocular Adnexa
Conjunctiva

Key Terms

anterior segment

aqueous
  shunt

blepharoplasty

blepharoptosis

cataract

conjunctiva

cornea

fistulization

glaucoma

keratoplasty

lens

macula

ocular adnexa

optic nerve

pupil

radial
  keratotomy

retina

sclera

slit lamp

strabismus

vitrectomy

Chapter Objectives

At the conclusion of this chapter, the student should be able to:

- Identify anatomical structures of the eye and ocular adnexa.
- Describe common surgical procedures of the eye and ocular adnexa.
- Explain coding guidelines applicable to the eye and ocular adnexa.
- Use references to assist with code assignment.
- Given case scenarios, accurately assign CPT codes and modifiers (if necessary).

2010 Current Procedural Terminology © 2009 American Medical Association. All Rights Reserved.

Introduction

The eye is the organ of sight and is comprised of many parts, which include the cornea, iris, lens, pupil, sclera, retina, macula, optic nerve, and vitreous (Figure 11-1.)

The **cornea** is the bulge on the front of the eye and is the place where light enters the eye. The **lens** is the colored part of the eye, and the **pupil** is the dark center of the eye. Both of these regulate the amount of light that enters the eye. The **sclera** is the white of the eye and protects the inner parts of the eye. The **retina** is a nerve layer that lines the back of the eye and transmits impulses to the **optic nerve**, which then transmits them to the brain. The **macula** is within the retina and allows us to see fine details. Vitreous humor is a jelly-like substance that fills most of the space in the eyeball.

This chapter will focus on the most common procedures performed on the eye, which include removal of foreign bodies, glaucoma treatments, cataract treatments, vitrectomy, and repair of retinal detachments. In addition to the frequently performed procedures, the chapter will also include strabismus surgery, repair of blepharoptosis, and conjunctivoplasty.

This chapter in the CPT book is divided into five anatomical sections:

- Eyeball
- Anterior Segment
- Posterior Segment
- Ocular Adnexa
- Conjunctiva

In the Eyeball section, there are several subsections.

- Removal of Eye (65091–65114)
- Secondary Implant(s) Procedures (65125–65175)
- Removal of Foreign Body (65205–65265)
- Repair of Laceration (65270–65290)

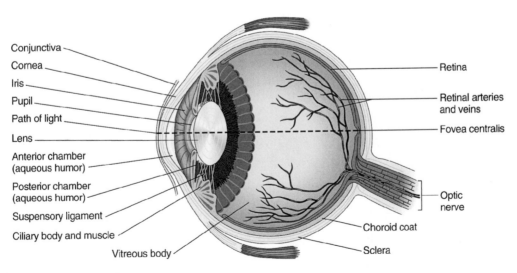

Figure 11-1 Eye and ocular adnexa

© Delmar Cengage Learning.

Removal of Foreign Body

The CPT codes in this subsection are used specifically for the removal of foreign bodies around the eyeball. Codes 65205 and 65210 are used for the removal of a foreign body of the conjunctiva, either superficial or embedded. Codes 65220 and 65222 describe removal of a foreign body from the cornea, either with or without a slit lamp. The **slit lamp** uses flourescein staining to visualize a corneal foreign body or abrasion.

Codes 65235–65265 are used to describe an intraocular foreign body removal from either the anterior or posterior segment.

- The location (conjunctiva, cornea, or intraocular)
- Whether the foreign body is superficial or embedded
- Whether or not a slit lamp was used

   EXAMPLE: Patient underwent the removal of a foreign body, intraocular, from posterior segment, nonmagnetic extraction.

      Correct coding assignment: 65265

> **Coding Tip:**
>
> *Look for the following information when coding removal of a foreign body from the external eye or eyeball.*

> **Note:**
>
> *The repair of laceration codes in this section are used for laceration repairs to the conjunctiva or cornea. If the repair is being performed on the eyelid, be sure to use codes from the integumentary system (12011–12018).*

Anterior Segment

The **anterior segment** section contains codes for procedures on the cornea, anterior chamber, anterior sclera, iris, ciliary body, and the lens.

The Anterior Segment section contains several subsections.

- Cornea (65400–65782)
- Anterior Chamber (65800–66030)
- Anterior Sclera (66130–66250)
- Iris, Ciliary Body (66500–66770)
- Lens (66820–66940)
- Intraocular Lens Procedures (66982–66986)
- Other Procedures (66990–66999)

Keratoplasty (corneal transplant) is a common procedure performed by replacing the cornea with a graft, either fresh or preserved. Preparation of the donor material is included. Below are listed some common reasons that patients have a corneal transplant performed.

- Scarring from infections such as herpes
- Hereditary factors
- Thinning of the cornea or irregular shape
- Complications from LASIK

Code assignment is based on the thickness of the corneal grafting. The options are:

- Lamellar (65710)—partial thickness
- Penetrating (65730–65755)—full thickness
- Endothelial (65756)—replacement of corneal endothelium through a limbal scleral tunnel incision

2010 Current Procedural Terminology © 2009 American Medical Association. All Rights Reserved.

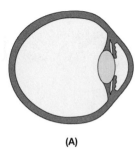  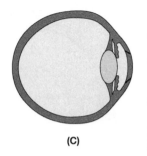

(A)   (B)   (C)

© Delmar Cengage Learning.

Figure 11-2 Radial keratotomy. (A) Cross-section of eye prior to surgery. (B) Small incisions are made in the cornea from the middle outward. (C) Radial keratotomy causes the cornea to become flatter, improving vision.

Radial keratotomy (65771) is performed to correct nearsightedness. The physician cuts slits into the cornea using a scalpel, which changes the shape of the cornea. This procedure is quickly being replaced with a laser procedure, which is quicker and causes less complication. See Figure 11-2.

> **Note:**
>
> *This procedure was discovered accidently by Dr. Svyatoslav Fyodorov, who was removing glass from a patient's eye when he noticed that the slits in the cornea from the glass allowed the patient to see better.*

EXAMPLE: Penetrating keratoplasty was performed to correct aphakia.

`Correct coding assignment: 65750`

Anterior Sclera

Glaucoma is a group of eye disorders that cause progressive damage to the optic nerve, which results in a loss of vision. The two most common types of glaucoma are open angle glaucoma and angle-closure glaucoma.

Codes 66150–66172 describe treatments for glaucoma that involve fistulization of the sclera by different means. **Fistulization** is the creation of a track to another location to allow the aqueous fluid to drain. The operative report should be reviewed to determine the method of fistulization.

- Trephination with iridectomy
- Thermocauterization with iridectomy
- Sclerectomy with punch or scissors, with iridectomy
- Iridencleisis or iridotasis
- Trabeculectomy ab externo

Another way to treat glaucoma is the implantation of an **aqueous shunt**. The shunt reduces and controls intraocular pressure by draining aqueous fluid from the anterior chamber. Code 66180 is used for the placement of the aqueous shunt, and code 66185 is used for revision of the aqueous shunt.

> **Coding Tip:**
>
> *When coding trabeculectomy ab externo, use code 66170 if the patient has not had previous surgery and code 66172 if the patient has scarring from a previous surgery.*

A **cataract** is a clouding of the lens of the eye. Some of the common causes of cataracts are diabetes, trauma, and aging. The best treatment for cataracts is a replacement of the lens. The two following surgical methods are typically used to remove the lens and the cataract (Figure 11-3).

- Extracapsular cataract removal includes removal of the lens and anterior portion of capsule
- Intracapsular cataract removal includes removal of lens and surrounding capsule

> **Note:**
>
> *Aqueous shunts are typically implanted in patients where trabeculectomy has failed.*

2010 Current Procedural Terminology © 2009 American Medical Association. All Rights Reserved.

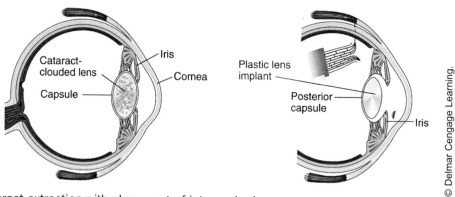

Figure 11-3 Cataract extraction with placement of intraocular lens

The cataract removal codes include the following procedures, meaning that they are not separately coded and reported:

- Lateral canthotomy
- Iridectomy
- Iridotomy
- Anterior capsulotomy
- Use of viscoelastic agents
- Enzymatic Zonulysis
- Use of other pharmacologic agents
- Subconjunctival or sub-tenon injections
- Insertion of intraocular lens prosthesis (IOL) when performed during the same operative session

CPT code 66984 is the most commonly performed procedure for cataract surgery. This code describes an extracapsular cataract extraction with insertion of IOL during the same operative session. The newest technology for this procedure is called phacoemulsification, which is when a specially designed instrument is used to break up the cataract with ultrasound waves.

> **Note:**
>
> *According to CPT* Assistant *from February 2001, code 66982 was created for complex cataract surgeries performed on children or complex adult patients. This code would not be reported for traditional cataract extraction.*

Posterior Segment

The Posterior Segment section contains several subsections.

- Vitreous (67005–67043)
- Retina or Choroid (67101–67229)
- Posterior Sclera (67250–67255)

A **vitrectomy** is the removal of the vitreous or gel of the eyeball. The most common reasons this procedure is done are retinal detachment, macular hole or cyst, floaters, or diabetic retinopathy.

CPT codes 67005–67043 describe procedures performed on the vitreous. These include vitrectomies, *except* if it's done for a retinal detachment. For the use of vitrectomy in retinal detachment, either code 67108 or 67113 would be reported. Codes 67101–67229 describe procedures performed on the retina or choroid.

CPT codes 67208–67229 describe procedures used for destruction of lesion of the retina, choroid, or retinopathies. These code descriptions state that the treatment occurred for one or more sessions, so the code would only be reported one time for the defined treatment period.

Ocular Adnexa

The Ocular Adnexa section has several subsections.

- Extraocular muscles (67311–67399)
- Orbit (67400–67599)
- Eyelids (67700–67999)

The **ocular adnexa** include the extraocular muscles, eyelids, eyelashes, orbit, conjunctiva, and the lacrimal apparatus. The extraocular muscles work together to allow binocular vision. The eyelids protect the eyes and keep them moist. The eyelids and eyebrows keep debris out of the eye. The orbit is the bony structure that the eyeball sits in. The conjunctiva is a mucous membrane that protects the eyeball. The lacrimal apparatus is responsible for producing, storing, and removing tears.

Strabismus is a condition where the eyes are misaligned such as cross-eyes, where one eye points inward, also referred to as lazy eye. To correct this, strabismus surgery is performed to realign the eyes. A recession (lengthening of the muscle) or a resection (shortening of the muscle) is done to reposition, strengthen, or weaken the eye muscles so that the eyes align correctly.

Codes 67311–67399 are used for these procedures. Each code represents performing the procedure on one eye so modifier 50 would be used for a bilateral procedure.

Blepharoptosis is a condition where the eyelid droops. This can cause loss of vision or headaches due to straining to keep the eyelid open.

The May 2004 *CPT Assistant* pages 12–13 describe the revision of CPT codes to differentiate between true blepharoplasty and repair of blepharoptosis. **Blepharoplasty** is defined as the removal of excess eyelid skin, some orbicularis muscle, and orbital fat. These procedures are coded in the musculoskeletal chapter using codes 15820–15823. Repair of blepharoptosis is captured using codes 67900–67924.

Conjunctiva

The **conjunctiva** is a thin membrane that lines the surface of the inner eyelid and the white part of the eyeball. It secretes oil and mucous that keeps the eye moistened.

The codes in this section (68020–68399) describe procedures such as incision and drainage, excision and/or destruction, injection, conjunctivoplasty, and other procedures performed on the conjunctiva.

EXAMPLE 1: The doctor performed an incision for drainage of a conjunctival cyst.

Correct coding assignment: 68020

> **Note:**
>
> Code 67108 is used to report the repair of a retinal detachment. This code includes the following procedures: vitrectomy, air or gas tamponade, focal endolaser photocoagulation, cryotherapy, drainage of subretinal fluid, scleral buckling, and/or removal of lens by the same technique. These procedures cannot be separately reported.

> **Note:**
>
> The most common procedure performed to correct blepharoptosis involves a shortening of the elevator muscle of the eyelid. The goal is to strengthen the muscle, which elevates the eyelid.

> **Coding Tip:**
>
> If a blepharoplasty is performed at the same time as a repair of ectropion (ptosis), codes 15820 and 67917 could both be used with a modifier 59 on the secondary procedure.

> **Note:**
>
> Per the note at the beginning of the "Eye and Ocular Adnexa" subsection, the use of an operating microscope is included in codes 65091–68850. Code 69990 does not need to be reported.

2010 Current Procedural Terminology © 2009 American Medical Association. All Rights Reserved.

EXAMPLE 2: The lacrimal system or apparatus is responsible for producing and storing tears, which keep the conjunctiva moist. Codes 68400–68899 describe procedures such as incision, excision, repair, and probing and/or related procedures. Physician performed a biopsy of the lacrimal sac.

Correct coding assignment: 68525

Exercise 11-1: Eye Surgery

Assign CPT codes to the following procedures. Append CPT/HCPCS Level II modifiers if applicable. Concentrate on application of coding guidelines, and do not focus on sequencing codes or assignment of modifier 51.

1. Removal of an embedded piece of metal from the conjunctiva.
   Code(s) _____

2. Patient underwent repair of laceration of conjunctiva using direct closure.
   Code(s) _____

3. During Stage 1, the physician removed the lens material using phacofragmentation technique.
   Code(s) _____

4. Patient underwent vitrectomy with endolaser panretinal photocoagulation.
   Code(s) _____

5. A 65-year-old man was seen for destruction of his diabetic retinopathy using cryotherapy.
   Code(s) _____

6. Physician performs strabismus surgery on the medial and lateral rectus muscles.
   Code(s) _____

7. A 73-year-old woman had a biopsy of her extraocular muscle performed.
   Code(s) _____

8. Physician performs optic nerve decompression.
   Code(s) _____

9. A 10-year-old boy was seen for removal of an embedded wood splinter of the eyelid.
   Code(s) _____

10. The surgeon performed an incision and drainage of a conjunctival cyst.
    Code(s) _____

Summary

- The Eye and Ocular Adnexa chapter is divided into five anatomical sections.
- A slit lamp is used to help when searching for a foreign body or abrasion in the eye.
- Procedures to repair lacerations of the skin of the eye are not coded in this section.
- Corneal grafting procedures are based on the thickness of the graft.
- The procedure of radial keratotomy was discovered by accident.
- There are many smaller procedures that are included in the removal of cataracts and are not coded separately.
- Blepharoplasty and repair of blepharoptosis are two totally different procedures that are coded in different sections of the CPT book.

2010 Current Procedural Terminology © 2009 American Medical Association. All Rights Reserved.

Internet Links

Glaucoma Research Foundation: *http://www.glaucoma.org*
Anatomy of eye, glaucoma definitions, and diagnostic test information

National Eye Institute: *http://www.nei.nih.gov/health*
Extensive list of eye diseases and disorders; basic eye anatomy

Medline Plus: *http://www.nlm.nih.gov/medlineplus/tutorial.html*
Interactive tutorials

Medicine Net: *http://www.medicinenet.com*
Comprehensive list of diseases and conditions

Review

I. Image Labeling

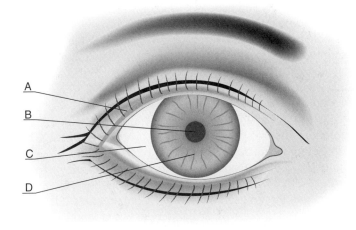

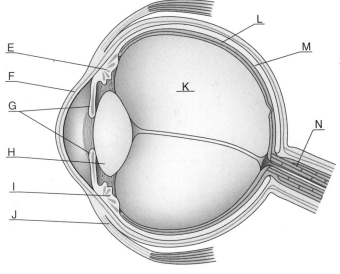

© Delmar Cengage Learning.

Figure 11-4

2010 Current Procedural Terminology © 2009 American Medical Association. All Rights Reserved.

II. Case Studies

Case Study 11-1: Operative Report

Preoperative Diagnosis: Retinal detachment, left eye

Postoperative Diagnosis: Retinal detachment, left eye

Procedures Performed:

1. Pars plana vitrectomy

2. Air-fluid exchange

3. Cryoretinopexy, left eye

Indications for Procedure: The patient is a 59-year-old gentleman who noted a gradual progressive decline in vision in the left eye over the past two or three days. On evaluation, he was found to have a visual acuity of counting fingers in the left eye. A superior retinal detachment was present involving the macula. The findings were discussed with the patient. It was recommended that he undergo retinal detachment repair.

Details of Procedure: The patient was identified and brought to the operating room, where he was placed in the supine position on the operating table, and the appropriate monitoring devices were attached. Akinesia and anesthesia were obtained using a 50/50 mixture of 2% lidocaine with 0.75% Marcaine and one ampule of Wydase 5 mL given in retrobulbar fashion, followed by a 5 mL lid block with good results. The patient was then prepped and draped in the usual sterile fashion, and a lid speculum was placed in the left eye. A standard three-port pars plana vitrectomy using the 23-gauge system was prepared measuring 4 mm posterior to the limbus. The infusion cannula was visualized prior to commencing infusion. With the aid of the wide-angle viewing system, a pars plana vitrectomy was performed. The vitreous was removed 360 degrees out to the periphery and trimmed overlying the area of the retinal detachment, which extended from the 11 o'clock to the 4 o'clock position. There were two fairly large retinal breaks along a peripheral superotemporal arcade and some area of lattice degeneration. The vitreous was trimmed overlying the area of the detachment surrounding the retinal breaks relieving vitreous traction. There was a bridging vessel through the retinal break. The breaks were diathermized for visualization, and the vessel was cauterized with the diathermy. An air-fluid exchange was then performed with the vitrectomy handpiece aspirating via the retinal break with complete flattening of the retina. Cryo was then placed around the retinal breaks with good uptake. Fluid was drained off of the optic nerve. The retina was flat and attached. The trocars and instruments were removed from the eye. The intraocular pressure was normal to palpation. No wound leak was detected. The eye was irrigated with Neosporin Ophthalmic Solution. Subconjunctival injections of 2 mg of dexamethasone, 20 gm of tobramycin, and 100 mg of Kefzol were given. Topical 1% atropine was placed on the eye, and the eye patched in the usual fashion. The patient tolerated the procedure well and returned to the same-day surgery in satisfactory condition.

Code(s) _____

Case Study 11-2: Operative Report

Preoperative Diagnosis:

1. Corneal edema right eye due to aqueous shunt tube migration and tube-corneal touch

2. Status post aqueous shunt implant, right eye, for treatment of uncontrolled glaucoma

2010 Current Procedural Terminology © 2009 American Medical Association. All Rights Reserved.

3. Past ocular history, right eye of keratouveitis, cataract extraction with intraocular lens, retinal detachment, status post scleral buckle with pars plana vitrectomy and silicone oil, status post silicone oil removal, and status post penetrating keratoplasty

Postoperative Diagnosis:

1. Corneal edema right eye due to aqueous shunt tube migration and tube-corneal touch

2. Status post aqueous shunt implant, right eye, for treatment of uncontrolled glaucoma

3. Past ocular history, right eye of keratouveitis, cataract extraction with intraocular lens, retinal detachment, status postscleral buckle with pars plana vitrectomy and silicone oil, status postsilicone oil removal, and status postpenetrating keratoplasty

Procedures Performed:

1. Revision and reposition of aqueous shunt implant, right eye

2. Scleral reinforcement patch graft, right eye

Indications for Procedure:

1. Same as preoperative diagnosis #1 above; corneal edema in the patient's right eye requires revision and reposition of the aqueous shunt implant tube deeper into the anterior chamber in an attempt to prevent further corneal decompensation and hopefully allow clearing of the corneal edema in the patient's right eye over time.

2. Need a scleral reinforcement patch graft placed over the repositioned aqueous shunt tube in order to prevent conjunctival erosion, wound leakage, recurrent profound hypotony, the complications of profound hypotony, and possible endophthalmitis in the right eye

Details of Procedure: Preoperatively, in same-day surgery, the right eye received three drops of Ciloxan, each separated by 15 minutes for antibiotic prophylaxis. The patient was brought to the operating room in stable condition. Under IV sedation, both Van Lint and retrobulbar anesthesia was performed around the right globe with an equal mixture of 0.75% Marcaine and 1% Xylocaine with epinephrine. The right eye was prepped and draped in the usual routine sterile fashion. A lid speculum was inserted into the right eye. Paracentesis tracks were created in the peripheral cornea using methylene blue on a Grieshaber knife to identify the tracks. A 30-gauge canula was inserted through the paracentesis track into the anterior chamber, and a balanced salt solution was injected into the anterior chamber to repressurize the patient's eye. Two 8-0 nylon sutures were inserted through the corneal scleral limbus on either side of the scleral reinforcement patch graft, which covers the aqueous shunt tube. The patient's eye was rotated into extreme gaze to position the high fomiceal area containing the implant plate into the primary surgical position. The landmarks for the prior aqueous shunt implant surgery were identified, including the scleral reinforcement patch graft, the aqueous shunt implant plate, and the two 5-0 Dacron sutures securing the implant plate to the globe. A location 6 mm behind the lumbus in line with the aqueous shunt tube was identified with s surgical marking pen. A 4 mm circumferential superficial conjunctival incision was created in this location. A careful and meticulous dissection through the conjunctiva and multiple underlying Tenons capsule layers were performed. Extreme care was taken not to cut the underlying aqueous shunt tube. Once the aqueous shunt tube was identified, its margins were carefully cleaned from the overlying and surrounded Tenon's capsule and fibrous tissue layers. The aqueous shunt tube was removed from the anterior chamber of the eye, and the sclerotomy tract was closed with a 2 mm x 2 mm plug of sclera. TranZgraft sclera, tissue ID# CL085051070, was removed from its sterile packaging. A 2 mm x 2 mm scleral plug was created with four separate cuts. The scleral plug was inserted into the anterior sclerotomy and secured with two interrupted 10-0 nylon sutures. A 23-gauge needle attached to a tube of Healon was used to create a new sclerotomy position 2.5 mm posterior to the 1:30 o'clock limbus into the posterior chamber in front of the posterior chamber intraocular lens but well behind the iris. Using tube-inserting forceps, the aqueous tube was threaded through the new sclerotomy tract and positioned in the posterior chamber.

TranZgraft sclera tissue ID# CL0805051070 was removed from a sterile rinsing solution. A 3 mm x 4 mm scleral reinforcement patch graft was created with four separate cuts and positioned over the occluding tube ligatures. The new scleral reinforcement patch graft was approximated to the older scleral reinforcement patch graft and secured with two interrupted 9-0 nylon sutures. The posterior margin of the new scleral reinforcement patch graft was secured to the adjacent sclera with two 9-0 nylon sutures.

The conjunctiva was closed with a running 8-0 Vicryl suture on a tapered needle, ensuring a meticulous watertight closure. A 2% fluorescein solution was applied to all wounds, and there was no evidence of leakage. Next, 2 mg of dexamethasone and 100 mg of cefazolin were injected subconjunctivally into the inferior cul-de-sac. One-half inch of TobraDex ointment was placed on the right eye beneath a pressure patch and Fox shield. The patient tolerated the procedure well and without complications.

Code(s) _____

Case Study 11-3: Operative Report

Preoperative Diagnosis: Macular hole, right eye

Postoperative Diagnosis: Macular hole, right eye

Procedures Performed: Pars plana vitrectomy, removal of posterior hyaloids, internal limiting membrane peel, air-fluid exchange and C3F8 gas injection, right eye

Anesthesia: Local standby

Complications: None

Indications for Procedure: This is an 81-year-old lady who noted a decline in vision in the right eye over the past several weeks to couple of months. Upon evaluation, she was found to have a visual acuity of 20/70 in the right eye. A macular hole was present. The findings were discussed with the patient, and it was recommended that she undergo surgical closure of the hole.

Details of Procedure: The patient was identified and brought to the operating room, where she was placed in the supine position on the operating table. And the appropriate monitoring devices were attached. Akinesia and anesthesia were obtained using a 50/50 mixture of 2% lidocaine with 0.75% Marcaine and one ampule of Wydase 5 mL given in a retrobulbar fashion, followed by 5 mL lid block with good results. The patient was then prepped and draped in the usual sterile fashion, and a lid speculum was placed in the right eye. A standard three-port pars plana vitrectomy using the 25-gauge system was prepared, measuring 5 mm posterior to the limbus. The infusion cannula was visualized prior to commencing infusion. With the aid of the wide-angle viewing system, a pars plana vitrectomy was performed. The vitreous was removed 360 degrees out to the periphery. During removal of the vitreous, the posterior hyaloids face was noted to be separated, and this was trimmed out to the periphery. The high-magnification contact lens was placed on the eye. With the aid of the intraocular forceps, the internal limiting membrane was peeled circumferentially around the macula. There were some pinpoint hemorrhages created with removal of the membrane. The periphery was then examined. No abnormalities were detected. An air-fluid exchange was performed with the vitrectomy handpiece aspirating over the optic nerve. The eye was allowed to rest for approximately three to four minutes, after which additional fluid was removed from the optic nerve. It should be noted that there was some air migration into the anterior chamber with the air-flood exchange. Then, 60 mL of C3F8 gas was exchanged for the intraocular air venting via the trocar. The trocar was removed. The intraocular pressure was normal to palpation. A TB syringe with a 30-gauge needle was used to aspirate a portion of the bubble from the anterior chamber. No wound leak was detected. The pressure was normal. The eye was irrigated with Neosporin Ophthalmic Solution injections of 2 mg of dexamethasone, 20 mg of tobramycin, and 100 mg of Kefzol. Topical 1% atropine was placed on the eye, and the eye was patched in the usual fashion. The patient tolerated the procedure well and was returned to same-day surgery in satisfactory condition in the face-down position.

Code(s) _____

Auditory System

Chapter Outline

Introduction

External Ear

Middle Ear

Inner Ear

Temporal Bone, Middle Fossa
Approach

Key Terms

auditory system

auricle

cochlear implant

external auditory canal

external ear

inner ear

mastoidectomy

middle ear

nerve decompression

tympanic membrane

tympanoplasty

tympanostomy

Chapter Objectives

At the conclusion of this chapter, the student should be able to:

- Identify anatomical structures of the auditory system.
- Describe common surgical procedures of the auditory system.
- Explain coding guidelines applicable to the auditory system.
- Use references to assist with code assignment.
- Given case scenarios, accurately assign CPT codes and modifiers (if applicable).

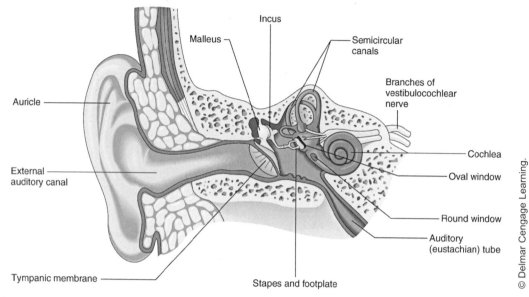

Figure 12-1 The auditory system

© Delmar Cengage Learning.

Introduction

The auditory system consists of the outer ear, middle ear, and inner ear. It is responsible for the functions of hearing and equilibrium (Figure 12-1).

The **auditory system** section in CPT is organized anatomically according to the following subsections:

- External Ear
- Middle Ear
- Inner Ear
- Temporal Bone, Middle Fossa Approach

External Ear

The **external ear** consists of the **auricle** (pinna) and the **external auditory canal** (ear canal). The codes in this subsection (69000–69399) describe incision, excision, removal, and repair procedures on the external ear.

Codes 69100–69155 identify procedures such as biopsy of the external ear and excision of a soft tissue lesion of the ear canal. If a skin grafting is performed to cover this excision, a code from the integumentary system (15004–15261) would be used in addition to the excision code.

A commonly performed procedure is 69210, which identifies "removal of impacted cerumen (separate procedure), one or both ears."

> **Note:**
>
> *Many payers issue limitations for use of removal of impacted cerumen. For example, a simple cerumen (earwax) removal that is not medically necessary will not be paid (e.g., patient is asymptomatic). In addition, CMS developed an HCPCS Level II code G0268—removal of impacted cerumen (one or both ears) by physicians on same date of service as audiologic function testing. CMS further defines criteria for reporting the code that includes documentation that significant time and effort was spent in performing this service.*

2010 Current Procedural Terminology © 2009 American Medical Association. All Rights Reserved.

Middle Ear

The **middle ear** consists of the eardrum (**tympanic membrane**), tympanic cavity (which contains the auditory ossicles: malleus, incus, and stapes), and the Eustachian tube. There are also three openings in the middle ear. The first one is the Eustachian tube, and the others are the round window and the oval window.

A commonly performed procedure is "**tympanostomy** (requiring insertion of ventilation tube), general anesthesia," which is reported with code 69436. This is typically performed on children who have chronic ear infections.

A **tympanoplasty** is the repair or reconstruction of the eardrum or middle ear structures. A **mastoidectomy** is the removal of the mastoid bone and is typically performed to remove benign lesions such as cholesteatomas. Oftentimes a mastoidectomy is performed along with a tympanoplasty. Codes 69601–69676 describe these types of procedures.

When reviewing an operative report, the coder should identify the following:

- Was the procedure a revision?
- Was a mastoidectomy performed along with the tympanoplasty?
- Was ossicular chain reconstruction performed?

> **Note:**
>
> *Codes 69601–69604 and 69635–69646 are considered unilateral procedures, so if the procedure is performed bilaterally, modifier 50 must be used.*

> **Note:**
>
> *If this procedure is performed on both ears, use 69436 with the modifier 50.*

> **Coding Tip:**
>
> *Tympanoplasty codes include canalplasty, atticotomy, middle ear surgery, and/or tympanic membrane repair.*

Inner Ear

The **inner ear** consists of the cochlea, saccule, acoustic nerve, semicircular canals, urticle, and superior and inferior vestibule nerves. A labyrinthotomy or labyrinthectomy can be performed by using a transcanal approach (69801 or 69905), or with a mastoidectomy (69802 or 69910).

A **cochlear implant** is an implanted electronic device for treatment of sensory deafness. This device consists of an external part that sits behind the ear and an internal part that is surgically inserted under the skin. This differs from a hearing aid because the cochlear implant bypasses the damaged part of the ear and directly stimulates the auditory nerve. CPT code 69930 is used when this procedure is performed.

Temporal Bone, Middle Fossa Approach

The codes in this subsection (69950–69979) identify **nerve decompression** or repair procedures. Code 69955, a total nerve decompression, would be used to treat Bell's palsy, which is a unilateral paralysis of facial muscles resulting from dysfunction of the seventh cranial nerve.

Exercise 12-1: Ear Surgery

Assign CPT codes to the following procedures. Append CPT/HCPCS Level II modifiers if applicable. Concentrate on application of coding guidelines, and do not focus on sequencing codes or assignment of modifier 51.

1. The physician performed a simple incision and drainage of an abscess of the external ear.

   Code(s) _____

2. A 5-year-old child had a small pebble removed from the external auditory canal without anesthesia.

   Code(s) _____

3. The plastic surgeon performs otoplasty to improve the appearance of large, protruding ears.

   Code(s) _____

4. Physician performed a modified radical mastoidectomy.

   Code(s) _____

5. Patient underwent an excision of an aural polyp.

   Code(s) _____

6. An 85-year-old woman had a cochlear device implanted due to hearing loss.

   Code(s) _____

7. A revision mastoidectomy was performed that resulted in a radical mastoidectomy.

   Code(s) _____

8. Physician performed a tympanoplasty with a mastoidectomy, which included ossicular chain reconstruction.

   Code(s) _____

9. The physician performed a repair of an oval window fistula.

   Code(s) _____

10. Patient had a lipoma of the temporal bone removed at the hospital.

   Code(s) _____

Summary

- The auditory system is divided into four anatomical sections.
- If a skin graft is performed along with an excision of a lesion of the external ear, a code from the integumentary system section is used.
- The code for removal of impacted cerumen is used whether the procedure is performed on one ear or two.
- Tympanostomies are most common in children due to chronic ear infections.
- Tympanoplasties and mastoidectomies are often performed together.

Internet Links

American Academy of Otolaryngology—Head and Neck Surgery: *http://www.entnet.org*
Click "Health Information" for fact sheets and surgical descriptions

2010 Current Procedural Terminology © 2009 American Medical Association. All Rights Reserved.

Review

I. Medical Terminology Assessment

Match the following terms with the correct definition.

——————	1. stapedotomy	A.	tiny incision made in eardrum to relieve pressure
——————	2. tympanoplasty	B.	surgical procedure to remove infected bone behind the ear
——————	3. myringotomy	C.	reconstructive surgery for eardrum
——————	4. mastoidectomy	D.	cosmetic procedure for protruding ears
——————	5. otoplasty	E.	hole made in foot plate of stirrup-shaped small bone

II. Case Studies

Case Study 12-1: Operative Report

Preoperative Diagnosis: Chronic right serous otitis media with effusion and chronic right Eustachian tube dysfunction

Postoperative Diagnosis: Chronic right serous otitis media with effusion and chronic right Eustachian tube dysfunction

Procedure Performed: Right tympanostomy requiring general anesthesia with the use of the operating microscope with ventilation tube insertion

Indications for Procedure: The patient is a 69-year-old female presenting with a two-month history of popping and cracking and diminished hearing in the right ear. She had a history of pneumonia at the onset of her symptoms. Her pneumonia has cleared; however, her right ear continues to bother her. Preop evaluation reveals an obvious middle ear effusion. Negative pressure is seen on tympanometry. The recommendation for a right myringotomy with tympanostomy tube insertion was given to the patient. All benefits, risks, and alternative therapies and expected outcomes were discussed. Consent forms were signed. The patient presents at this time for the procedure.

Report of Procedure: The patient was taken to the operative suite and placed in the supine position. General inhalant anesthesia was administered by the Department of Anesthesia. Following adequate anesthesia, the patient's head was positioned to the left, thus exposing the right ear. The operating microscope was focused on the tympanic membrane. A myringotomy incision was made, serous fluid suctioned, and a Feuerstein tympanostomy tube placed. TobraDex drops were then instilled and a sterile cotton ball placed. The patient tolerated the procedure well. She was turned over to anesthesia and taken to recovery in satisfactory condition.

Code(s) _____

Case Study 12-2: Operative Report

Preoperative Diagnosis: Left tympanic membrane perforation

Postoperative Diagnosis: Left tympanic membrane perforation

Procedure: Tympanoplasty

After administration of general anesthesia, the patient was prepped and draped in the usual fashion. The left ear canal was injected with 1% Xylocaine with 1:100,000 epinephrine, and the area for graft removal in the scalp superior to the auricle was also injected. The ear was examined, and Rosen's needle was used to remove the rim of the perforation. A knife was used to elevate the tympanomeatal flap down to the annulus. The annulus was then elevated, and Rosen's needle was used to enter the middle ear space and elevate the annulus and tympanomeatal flap anteriorly. The ossicular chain was examined and noted to be intact and mobile. Following this, incision was made in the scalp superior to the auricle through the subcutaneous tissues. Incision was made until the temporalis fascia was identified. A No. 15 knife blade was used to make the incision through the temporalis fascia in 1-cm diameter. A Freer elevator was then used to elevate the temporalis fascia graft, and this was placed into a press and set aside for later use. Hemostasis was then obtained with electrocautery. The incision was then closed with 3-0 nylon suture in a running interlocking stitch. The ear was then reinspected and the middle ear space entered and clotted blood suctioned. The middle ear space was then filled with Gelfoam pledgets. The temporalis fascia graft was then removed form the press with Alligator forceps and placed into the middle ear spaced medial to the tympanomeatal flap and on top of the Gelfoam pledgets. The tympanomeatal flap was then placed down in position. Then using Rosen's needle, care was taken to ensure that the graft was medial to all aspects of the perforation. Reexamination showed that the graft was in good position and touching all the rim of the areas of the perforation. All pledgets were placed on top of the tympanomeatal flap and grasped. The ear canal was then filled with Neosporin ointment, and cotton was placed into the ear canal. The incision site in the scalp was then cleaned with saline, dried, and at this point ointment applied to the head. The patient was awakened and extubated without difficulty and returned to the recovery room in satisfactory condition.

Code(s) _____

Case Study 12-3: Operative Report

Preoperative Diagnosis: Persistent bilateral otitis media

Postoperative Diagnosis: Persistent bilateral otitis media

Procedure: Removal of bilateral permanent ventilation tubes

Anesthesia: Inhalant

Procedure: After the patient was prepped and draped, the right ear was examined. Purulent material in the ear canal was suctioned out. The T tube was grasped with cup forceps and removed. The purulent secretions from the middle ear space were suctioned out. The right ear was then examined, once again cleaned of copious amounts of drainage, and the T-tube removed. Findings were the same as the opposite ear. The patient was awakened and returned to recovery in good condition.

Code(s) _____

Appendix: Answer Key

This appendix provides answers to selected *odd* numbered exercises from the textbook beginning with Exercise 1-3. Faculty resources contain answers to all of the exercises including the Chapter Review questions. In addition to CPT codes, the answer key provides guidance as to the key elements of documentation that supports the coding selection.

Chapter 1: Introduction to Surgical Coding

Exercise 1-1 Abstracting Documentation

1. **Why was the patient being treated surgically?**
   In this case, the patient had an elevated prostate-specific antigen (PSA), which is a screening test for prostate cancer.

2. **What is the main surgical procedure?**
   Biopsy of prostate

3. **Review the coding options in the CPT Index (and subsequently the Tabular section). What documentation is needed to accurately select a code?**
   Searching under the key term "Biopsy, Prostate," the range of possible coding choices includes 55700–55705. The code selection differentiates between needle (or punch) and incisional.

4. **Refer to the operative report to abstract the detailed information to accurately assign a code.**
   A probe was inserted (no incision was made), and needle biopsies were taken; therefore, the code assigned would be 55700. The description for code 55700 indicates that the code is correct for single or multiple biopsies. Further review of the operative report reveals no additional procedures that would be assigned an additional CPT code.

NOTE: In this case study, the pathology report is not needed for the CPT code assignment. In other situations, the pathology report may be vital for an accurate code assignment.

Exercise 1-2 Abstracting Documentation

1. **What technique was used to remove the lesion?**
   Excision

2. **What key elements are needed to assign a code?**
   Review of coding guidelines for removal of lesions will reveal that several pieces of documentation are vital for accurate coding:

   - *Technique (e.g., excision, destruction)*
   - *Where was the lesion?*
   - *Size (excised diameter)*
   - *Morphology (benign, malignant, premalignant)*
   - *Wound closure (was it routine or did it require layered or complex closure?)*

3. **Was the lesion benign or malignant?**
   From the pathology report, the lesion was determined to be benign.

4. **What was the excised diameter?**
   2.0 cm

5. **Why is the specimen size in the pathology report different from the operative report?**
   The specimen may shrink in size due to the use of formalin solution. Best coding practices advise the use of the surgeon's measurement. However, some facilities have coding policies that permit use of the pathology report measurement if the surgeon does not give the excised diameter.

6. **What coding guidelines are applicable to this procedure?**
   Refer to question #2 above. There are many guidelines pertaining to the removal of lesions.

There is a lengthy note that precedes the coding selection (Excision—Benign Lesions), which addresses coding for this section. Note that use of modifier –LT (left) is not appropriate for several reasons:

- *The nose is not a paired organ.*

- *Note that the description for excision of lesions has multiple sites, making use of the modifier inappropriate.*

- *In most instances, removal of skin lesions do not require an anatomic (LT, RT) modifier.*

7. **What is the correct code assignment?**
    11442 Excision, other benign lesion (excised diameter 2.0 cm)

Exercise 1-3 Use of Modifiers

1.

   a. What is the correct coding assignment for physician services?
       45330-52

   b. What is the correct coding assignment for hospital outpatient services?
       45330-74

3. 45384
    45389-59 Use of modifier 59 explains that the biopsy was performed as a distinct service unrelated to removal of the polyp.

5. 20610-LT

Chapter 1 Review Questions

I. Medical Terminology Assessment

1.	C	7.	C
3.	D	9.	A
5.	B		

II. Coding Assessment

1. 12052 (chin), 12002 (all simple wound repairs)

3. 11640

5. 27535-RT (cast is included)

7. 33220

9. 52235

Chapter 2: Integumentary System

Exercise 2-1

1.	B	7.	B
3.	B	9.	B
5.	B		

Exercise 2-2 Coding Lesions

1. 11642 Excision, malignant lesion, nose, 2.0 cm

3. 17000 Destruction, first lesion (liquid nitrogen is a cryogenic agent)

5. 23076-RT Excision tumor shoulder

Exercise 2-3 Wound Repairs

1. 12001 Simple repair, extremities. An anatomical modifier would not be appropriate. Note that the CPT description includes multiple sites.

3. 12032 Intermediate wound repairs (add 2.5 + 3.5 = 6.0) of extremities

    12001 Simple wound repair

5. 12055 Intermediate repair—face (15 cm)

    12015 Simple repair—face (10 cm)

    12002 Simple repair—face (3 cm)

Exercise 2-4 Skin Grafts

1. 15150 Tissue cultured epidermal autograft, legs first 25 sq cm

    15151 additional cm

3. 15260 Full thickness graft, free, nose

    11642 Excision, malignant lesion, nose

    11440 Excision, benign lesion, cheek

Exercise 2-5 Breast Procedures

1. 19120-LT Excision breast mass

3. 10021 Fine needle aspiration

2010 Current Procedural Terminology © 2009 American Medical Association. All Rights Reserved.

Chapter 2 Review Questions

II. Case Studies

Case Study 2-1

Answer:

12032 Intermediate wound repair, knee, 5.5 cm ("repaired with layered closure . . . involving deep subcutaneous tissue and fascia")

12004 Simple wound repair (add repairs for right knee and left hand = 9.5 cm)

Case Study 2-3

Key Documentation: "An incision was made in a longitudinal fashion along the upper arm over the lipoma, which was deep in the subfascia."

Answer:

24076 Excision, tumor, arm; deep

Case Study 2-5

Key Documentation: "Full thickness of the necrotic skin was excised down to the fascial level."

Answer:

11042 Debridement, skin and subcutaneous tissue

Case Study 2-7

Answer:

15120 Split thickness autograft, foot, 1 sq cm
15100 Split thickness autograft, leg, 45 sq cm

Case Study 2-9

Answer:

14001 Adjacent skin graft, trunk (12 sq cm) (includes excision of lesion)

11422 Excision, malignant lesion of heel, 1.8 cm

12041 Intermediate wound repair

Chapter 3: Musculoskeletal System

Exercise 3-1 Treatment of Fractures and Wounds

1. 27235-RT Percutaneous skeletal fixation of femur, proximal end, neck

3. 24635 Open treatment of Monteggia type of fracture (both internal fixation is included and first cast)

5. 20103 Exploration of penetrating wound, extremity

Exercise 3-2 Spinal Surgery

1. 22612 Arthrodesis, lumbar

   20937 Autograft for spine surgery only; morselized

   22851 Application of inter-vertebral biomechanical device (cage)

Exercise 3-3 Bunion Surgery and Arthroscopy Procedures

1. 28296 Mitchell procedure (chevron)

3. 29887 Medial meniscectomy

   G0289 HCPCS Level II (arthroscopy, different compartment of same knee)

Chapter 3 Review Questions

Answers to matching exercise in Faculty Resources

II. Case Studies

Case Study 3-1

Key Documentation:
"An X-ray was taken and revealed a *fracture of the fourth and fifth proximal phalanx*. The patient's right fourth and fifth toes were digitally blocked with 2.5 cc of 2% lidocaine each. *Fractures were reduced* in the fourth and fifth digits and buddy taped."

Answer:

28515-T8 Closed treatment, phalanges (modifiers for fourth and fifth toes, right foot)

28515-T9

Case Study 3-3

Key Documentation:
"The *incisions were both extended* with a knife. The wounds were easily opened merely by spreading the tissue bluntly. There was a return of a large amount of purulence. Cultures were taken. Dissection was carried out in all directions to release the purulence,

2010 Current Procedural Terminology © 2009 American Medical Association. All Rights Reserved.

including extensions in the dorsal direction. *Wounds were irrigated* with a total of 3 liters of irrigation using a Pulsavac system of irrigation. The wounds were then cleaned, and there were no remaining signs of purulence. There was, however, tissue and questionable viability as well as some dead skin. *Grossly dead skin and tissue was debrided.* The *flexor tendon sheath of the fourth finger was located.*"

Answer:

26011 Drainage of finger abscess; complicated (complicated was selected due to the documentation of depth—down to tendon sheath—and debridement and irrigation performed)

Case Study 3-5

Key Documentation: "Open reduction and internal fixation using Kirschner wires of fracture, proximal phalanx"

Answer:

26735-F4 Open treatment of phalangeal shaft fracture, proximal (includes internal fixation)

Case Study 3-7

Key Documentation: "McBride type bunionectomy, left foot"

Answer:

28292-LT McBride procedure

Case Study 3-9

Key Documentation:
"X-ray of the tibia and fibula shows a *displaced fracture of the distal fibula.* The *closed treatment of the fracture was reduced,* and the patient was put in a short leg splint with extensive padding placed over the fracture site."

Answer:

27788-RT Closed treatment of distal fibular fracture with manipulation

Chapter 4: Respiratory System

Exercise 4-1 Nasal Endoscopy Procedures

1. 31231 Nasal endoscopy, diagnostic (no need for modifier since the code specifies "unilateral or bilateral")

3. 31288-LT Nasal/sinus endoscopy, with sphenoidotomy; with removal of tissue

Exercise 4-2 Laryngoscopy Procedures

1. 31510 Laryngoscopy, indirect; with biopsy
3. 31575 Laryngoscopy, flexible fiberoptic, diagnostic

Chapter 4 Review Questions

I. Medical Terminology Assessment

1. C   3. B   5. B

II. Case Studies

Case Study 4-1

Key Documentation:
"The patient denied any signs of pressure, headaches, vision changes, or facial pain. A CT scan was performed by his primary care physician, which *showed complete opacification of the left maxillary sinus with bony remodeling and erosion of the medial maxillary sinus wall and soft tissue extension to the left nasal passage and into the left inferior left sphenoid and ethmoid sinus.*

"*Procedures Performed:*

1. *Left maxillary sinusotomy*

2. *Left anterior ethmoidectomy*

3. *Removal of left nasal polyposis*

"Details of Procedure: The patient was brought to the operating room, and general anesthesia was induced. Bilateral nasal passages were injected with 1% lidocaine with 1:100,000 epinephrine, and injection included nasal septum, inferior turbinates, and superior turbinates as well as left uncinate process. After adequate decongestion, the left naris was suctioned and examined. Medial maxillary wall bulging into the nasal passage could be seen. Polyposis could be seen emanating from beneath the middle turbinate; using the shaver, *polyposis was removed from the middle meatus.* The shaver was then used to perform an uncinectomy. Upon performing the uncinectomy, thick yellow pus began to emanate from the maxillary sinus ostia. This was suctioned and sent for culture.

2010 Current Procedural Terminology © 2009 American Medical Association. All Rights Reserved.

Next, the maxillary sinus ostia were opened using the shaver. Maxillary sinus was then suctioned out, and all pus was removed. After an adequate *maxillary antrostomy* had *been performed, anterior ethmoidectomy was performed.* The shaver was used to enter into the anterior ethmoids. *Some polypoid tissue could be seen emanating from the ethmoid, and this was removed.* Next, the maxillary sinus was copiously irrigated with normal saline."

Answer:

31256-LT Maxillary antrostomy

31254-LT Endoscopy with ethmoidectomy (anterior)

(Note: the uncinate process is a thin, sickle-shaped structure that covers the entrance to the maxillary sinus; the ethmoidectomy procedure begins with removal of uncinate process.)

The space between each turbinate is called a meatus, and each meatus is named for the meatus above it. The anterior (or front) ethmoid cells open into the middle meatus. Removal of the nasal polyps from this area would be bundled with the ethmoidectomy code.

Case Study 4-3

Key Documentation:

- "Direct laryngoscopy was performed in standard fashion . . ."
- "Tooke forceps were used to make an excisional biopsy" (later excised using cold technique)
- "A microscope was brought into position . . ."
- Flexible bronchoscopy was performed

Answer:

31541 Larngoscopy, with excision of tumor with operating microscope

31622 Bronchoscopy, diagnostic

Biopsy of the lesion with subsequent excision would be bundled with the excision code. The biopsy was performed for a definitive pathological diagnosis before the tissue was excised in entirety.

Case Study 4-4

Key Documentation:

- "Procedure Performed: Septorhinoplasty"
- "Dissection was carried back to the bony septum. The bony cartilaginous junction was separated, and the mucoperichondrium and mucoperiosteum on the right side of

the septum was elevated." (*supports coding septoplasty*)

- ". . .resected cartilage was then fashioned into a graft" (*grafting included in septoplasty code*)
- ". . .more symmetric-appearing dorsum of the nose"

Answer:

30520 Septoplasty

To complicate the coding process, the surgeon sometimes uses the terms rhinoplasty, septoplasty, and septorhinoplasty interchangeably, but they have distinct meanings.

The documentation in this operative report supports coding septoplasty (30520) with a simple graft to improve the appearance of the dorsum of the nose. For coding a rhinoplasty (see range 30400–30420), the documentation should include reshaping of external nose (30140)—lateral and alar cartilages. The additional rhinoplasty codes (30140–30420) require fracturing of the lateral nasal bones with chisels (*Coders' Desk Reference*).

Case Study 4-5

Key Documentation:

- "Laryngoscopy"
- ". . . complete visualization with operating microscope"
- "Laser cordotomy"

Answer:

31526 Laryngoscopy, direct, diagnostic with operating microscope

31599 Unlisted procedure

Comments: The laser cordotomy is a fairly new procedure that is an alternative to the traditional surgical techniques. The procedure permits breathing without a tracheotomy and without removal of cartilage. An unlisted procedure code would be selected for this procedure.

Chapter 5: Cardiovascular System

Exercise 5-1 Pacemaker Procedures

1. 33208 Insertion of permanent pacemaker (atrial and ventricular)

3. 33214 Upgrade of implanted pacemaker system (single to dual)

Exercise 5-2 Valve Procedures

1. 33465 Replacement, tricuspid valve, with cardiopulmonary bypass

3. 33417 Aortoplasty for supravalvular stenosis

Exercise 5-3 Coronary Artery Bypass Grafting

1. 33513 CABG; 4 coronary venous grafts

3. 33534 CABG; 2 coronary artery grafts

   33518 CABG; 2 venous grafts

Exercise 5-4 Aneurysm Procedures

1. 34900-RT Endovascular graft replacement

   34820-RT Open iliac artery exposure for delivery of endovascular prosthesis by abdominal incision

3. 33880 Endovascular repair of descending thoracic aorta

   33883 Placement of proximal extension prosthesis

Exercise 5-5 Thrombectomy Procedures

1. 34471 Thrombectomy, direct; subclavian vein

3. 35302 Thromboendarterectomy, superficial femoral artery

Exercise 5-6 Central Venous Access Procedures

1. 36563 Insertion of tunneled centrally inserted central venous access device with subcutaneous pump

3. 36576 Repair of CV access catheter

Exercise 5-7 AV Fistulas and Grafts

1. 36833 Revision, open AV fistula; with thrombectomy

3. 36820 Direct AV fistula by forearm vein transposition

Exercise 5-8 Varicose Vein Procedures

1. 37718 Ligation and stripping, short saphenous vein

3. 37780 Ligation and division, short saphenous vein at saphenopopliteal junction

Chapter 5 Review Questions

Answers to Crossword Puzzle in Faculty Resources

II. Case Studies

Case Study 5-1

Key Documentation:
"The previously implanted Biotronik dual-chamber ICD was interrogated. The atrial lead was confirmed to be dislodged. The device was reprogrammed to disable tachycardia therapies for the duration of the case. After the area was draped and prepped and local anesthesia was administered, an incision was made and carried down to the device. The device was removed from the pocket. The atrial lead was freed and the screw retracted, New J stylet was advanced into the lead to reposition it to a secured position in the right atrium, where the lead screw was again deployed and the lead fluoroscopically viewed to be firmly fixed in place. The lead was then sutured to the surrounding tissue and tested, and it was found to be functioning properly. At this point, the *lead was then attached to the previously implanted ICD, which was then placed back into the pocket.*

"Summary: *Successful atrial lead revision.*"

Answer:

33215 Repositioning of previously implanted electrode

Case Study 5-3

Key Documentation:
"Procedure Performed: *Insertion of right internal jugular Perm-a-Cath*

"Indications for Procedure: This patient is a 52-year-old female with chronic renal failure, presented for a nonworking left subclavian tunneled dialysis

2010 Current Procedural Terminology © 2009 American Medical Association. All Rights Reserved.

catheter. She also has a right internal jugular triple lumen for antibiotics. The subclavian line was removed to preserve the subclavian vein for access, and the right jugular Perm-a-Cath was placed under fluoroscopy guidance.

"Details of the Procedure: The patient's neck was prepped and shaved in the usual manner. The triple lumen was accessed with a guidewire. Under fluoroscopy, this was removed over sheath, and, through this sheath and dilator, a guidewire was introduced. A cut down was made, sheath and introducer were placed, and the superior vena cava was accessed with this introducer. *An Arrow-Cannon II was placed in the superior vena cava—right atrial junction. This was tunneled to the anterior chest wall, transected, attachments were placed*, and flushed for inflow and outflow; it performed well."

Answer:

36558 Insertion of centrally located tunneled central venous line

Comments: See note before code 36555. If an existing central venous access device is removed and a new one placed via a separate venous site, appropriate codes for both procedures. In this case, it was the same venous site; therefore, an additional code is not warranted.

The documentation in the "Indications for Procedure" states that she presented for a nonworking left subclavian tunneled dialysis catheter. This was not addressed in the details of the operative report; therefore, it is not coded. The case might be clarified by documentation in other sections of the health record; otherwise, a physician query may be necessary.

Case Study 5-5

Key Documentation:

"Procedure: Cimino right *radiocephalic fistula* with ligation of venous side of branches

"Indications: Patient is a 69-year-old male with a history of hypertension and has developed end-stage renal disease and is in *need of access for dialysis*.

"Patient's right upper extremity was prepped with DuraPrep and Betadine and draped in a standard sterile fashion. With the consent of anesthesia, we proceeded with the operation. A small incision was made on the lateral aspect of the distal forearm in between the cephalic and radial artery. This was preceded by the infusion of 1% lidocaine without epinephrine. The incision was made. Electrocautery was used to dissect down. A combination of

electrocautery and blunt dissection was used *to dissect out both the cephalic vein and radial artery*. Once these were both sufficiently isolated, a vessel loop was passed around the radial artery distally. We then took the cephalic vein, padded off distally, and dissected it. Pott's scissors were then used to open the os of the vessel sufficiently. It was then brought to the radial artery, which was clamped off proximally the distally with bulldogs. A small arteriotomy was made with a #11 blade. The Pott's scissors were then used to open up the same approximately. The *arteriovenous anastomosis was accomplished* with a running #7-0 Gore-Tex suture on both the posterior and anterior surfaces. Once these were tied down, the clamps were withdrawn, and the vein was felt appropriately."

Answer:

36821 AV anastomosis, direct (joining neighboring artery (radial) and vein (cephalic)

Chapter 6: Digestive System

Exercise 6-1 Upper Gastrointestinal Endoscopy Procedures

1. 43200 Esophagoscopy

    43453 Dilation of esophagus, over guidewire (not through scope)

3. 43248 EGD with dilation, all performed through the scope

Exercise 6-2 Colonoscopy Procedures

1. 45385 Colonoscopy with removal of polyp by snare
    45384 Removal by hot biopsy forceps

    Note: Control of bleeding would be an integral part of the procedure.

3. 45385 Colonoscopy with snare removal of polyp

    Note: The only code needed is for the snare removal. Electrocautery of remnants is consider an integral part of the procedure.

Exercise 6-3 Hernia Repairs

1. 49657 Laparoscopic repair, incisional and incar-cerate. Insertion of mesh is included in the code.

2010 Current Procedural Terminology © 2009 American Medical Association. All Rights Reserved.

Chapter 6 Review Questions

Answers to matching exercise in Faculty Resources

II. Case Studies

Case Study 6-1

Key Documentation:

"Procedures Performed: Esophagogastroduodenoscopy with esophageal dilation

"*The scope was removed. Because of the patient's dysphagia to solids, I did pass a 50 French Maloney dilator . . .*"

Answer:

43235 EGD

43450 Dilation of esophagus

Case Study 6-3

Key Documentation:

"Procedure: Endoscopic Retrograde Cholangiopancreatography (ERCP)"

Answer:

43260 -ERCP, diagnostic, with or without brushings or washings

Case Study 6-5

Key Documentation:

"Operation: Repair of right inguinal hernia

"History: This 46-year-old male has a large symptomatic right inguinal hernia. No previous history of hernia repair."

Answer:

49505 Repair of initial inguinal hernia (age >5 years)

Case Study 6-7

Key Documentation:

"The Olympus video *gastroscope was introduced* into the posterior pharynx and passed easily to the esophagus with swallowing. The *scope was advanced* under direct vision to the esophagus into the stomach and through the pylorus into the duodenal bulb in the second portion. The duodenal bulb appeared normal. The endoscope was withdrawn into the stomach. The stomach was normal in appearance. The esophagus was judged normal in appearance. The satisfactory *site for a placement of a gastrostomy tube* was identified in the lower body of the stomach. The *skin was anesthetized* with infiltration of local lidocaine, a needle catheter was introduced transcutaneously into the gastric lumen, and suture material was introduced through this catheter. The suture material was grasped with the endoscopic snare and pulled through the esophagus and out the mouth. This suture material was affixed to the leading edge of the *gastrostomy tube, which was pulled down through the esophagus and into the stomach and out the cutaneous tract leaving only the internal bolster of the gastrostomy tube present in the stomach.*

Answer:

43246 EGD with placement of PEG

Case Study 6-9

Key Documentation:

"Procedure: The patient was placed in the left lateral decubitus position and IV sedation was administered. The *scope was passed into the anal canal* and the rectal mucosa was visualized and appeared normal. The scope was then passed to the rectosigmoid junction, where there were exudative changes with erythematous mucosa extending approximately 10 cm proximally into the sigmoid colon. Beyond this region, the mucosa appeared normal with abnormal mucosal vascular pattern. *I was able to advance the colonoscope up to the splenic flexure, but the procedure had to be terminated due to a poor prep.*"

Answer:

Facility Coding: 45378-74 Colonoscopy (modifier indicates procedure discontinued after anesthesia administered)

Physician Services:

Payers often dictate how physicians should report this procedure. CPT guidelines state that modifier 52 (Reduced services) should be appended to CPT code 45378. CMS directs coders to submit 45378-53 (modifier for discontinued procedure), and payment will be adjusted.

2010 Current Procedural Terminology © 2009 American Medical Association. All Rights Reserved.

Case Study 6-11

Key Documentation:

"Procedure: Hemorrhoidectomy

"Indications: The patient is a 55-year-old male who presented to the surgery center with a chief complaint of prolapsing, itching, bleeding hemorrhoid tissue. Physical examination disclosed the presence of a grade 4 *mixed internal and external right posterior hemorrhoid associated with a sizable left internal hemorrhoid as well. He was scheduled for elective hemorrhoidectomy.*

"Operative Procedure: . . . Based on these findings, it was elected to perform an *excisional hemorrhoidectomy* on the right posterior column, as this appeared to be the most symptomatic of his lesions. . . . The *left group was examined and felt to be amenable to treatment with placement of hemorrhoidal bands.* The left hemorrhoidal group was elevated into a McGilvery hemorrhoidal-banding gun. The hemorrhoid was seen to engorge over the top of these bands."

Answer:

46255 Hemorrhoidectomy, internal and external single

46221-59 Hemorrhoid banding (Because this was a distinct procedure, separate from treatment of the other hemorrhoids, modifier 59 would override the edits—it is possible that the third-party payer will want to see documentation.)

Chapter 7: Urinary System

Exercise 7-1 Cystoscopy Procedures

1. 52353 Cystourethroscopy with ureteroscopy with lithotripsy

3. 52341 Cystourethroscopy with treatment of ureteral stricture

   52351 Cystourethroscopy, with ureteroscopy (Note: According to *CPT Assistant*, October 2001, CPT code 52351 would be reported with modifier 59. The procedures were performed on opposite sides of the body.)

Chapter 7 Review Questions

Answers to labeling exercise in Faculty Resources

II. Case Studies

Case Study 7-1

Key Documentation:

"It should be noted that prior to this, he was noted to have meatal anastomosis and had to *be dilated* with Van Buren sounds starting at #12 French going to #20 French without difficulty. The scope was able to be reinserted. . . . Once inside the bladder, the right ureteral stent was easily visualized, and a grasper was used to *remove the stent* under direct vision."

Answer:

52310 Cystourethroscopy, with removal of ureteral stent

52281 Cystourethroscopy with dilation of urethral stricture or stenosis

(Note: Documentation supports that a meatal anastomosis had to be dilated; therefore, the cystourethroscopy was used for treatment not just as an approach. It is likely that modifier −59 should be appended to indicate that the scope was distinct and not part of the main procedure—referencing editing software.)

Case Study 7-3

Key Documentation:

"The position of the *indwelling ureteral stent* was confirmed."

Answer:

52332 Cystoscopy with insertion of indwelling ureteral stent

Case Study 7-5

Key Documentation:

"Impression: Successful left nephrostomy tube replacement"

Answer:

50398 Change of nephrostomy tube

(Note: Removal of a nephrostomy tube—without replacement—that does not require fluoroscopic

2010 Current Procedural Terminology © 2009 American Medical Association. All Rights Reserved.

guidance is considered inherent to evaluation and management [E/M] services; therefore, it would not be assigned a surgical CPT code.)

Case Study 7-7

Key Documentation:

- "Right nephrectomy"
- "He has consented for a laparoscopic versus open . . . "
- "The kidney was completely free."

Answer:

50546-RT Laparoscopic nephrectomy

Chapter 8: Male Genital System

Answers are in the Faculty Resources

Chapter 8 Review Questions

II. Case Studies

Case Study 8-1

Key Documentation: " . . . and approximately 12 prostate needle biopsy cores were taken . . . "

Answer:

55700 Biopsy, prostate; needle—multiple

Case Study 8-3

Key Documentation:

"Procedure: Repair of recurrent indirect right inguinal hernia and right orchiopexy"

"The previous incision, which was about 3 cm long, was opened up in the right inguinal region." (approach to code Orchiopexy)

Answer:

49520 Repair recurrent inguinal hernia

54640 Orchiopexy, inguinal approach, with or without hernia repair

(Note: The coding guidance located beneath code 54640 can be misleading. Orchiopexy by inguinal approach is coded separately in addition to the

inguinal hernia repair. For inguinal hernia repair performed in conjunction with inguinal orchiopexy, see 49495–49525. Source: *CPT Assistant*, January 2004.)

Case Study 8-5

Key Documentation:

- 6-month-old
- 1% lidocaine (local anesthesia)
- use of clamp
- blanching was obtained

Answer:

54150-52 Circumcision, using clamp. Important to note that a regional block was not used; therefore, CPT guidelines instruct the coder to report modifier 52 with the code.

(Note: Coding for lysis of adhesions is controversial. Typically, payers require documentation to support "extensive" adhesions and evidence that the procedure took significantly longer than normal. For this particular case, the documentation does not support an additional code.)

Case Study 8-7

Key Documentation: "Cystoscopy with transurethral resection of prostate"

Answer:

52601 Transurethral resection of prostate

(Note: Cystoscopy is included in code description.)

Chapter 9: Female Genital System

Exercise 9-1 Hysterectomy and Hysteroscopy Procedures

1. 58571 Laparoscopy, surgical, with total hysterectomy, for uterus 250 g or less; with removal of tube(s) and/or ovary(s)

3. 58543 Laparoscopy, supracervical (uterus over 250 g)

Challenge Question: (answer in the Faculty Resources)

Chapter 9 Review Questions

Answers to Crossword Puzzle in Faculty Resources

II. Case Studies

Case Study 9-1

Answer:

58671 Laparoscopic occlusion of oviducts (banding)

Case Study 9-3

Key Documentation:

"This was first done to the left labial lesion and then done at the perirectal lesion. The *excised diameter of the labial lesion was 2.5 cm ×
1.0 cm × 0.2 cm. The excised diameter of the perineum lesion was 4.2 cm × 2.1 cm × 0.5 cm.* The perineum lesion could not be appropriately performed without getting into the anal wart. So, this *lesion being quite large, was removed at its base by incising the skin and then using cautery to go through its stalk.* Hemostasis was achieved using electrocautery. The right labial lesion was closed using a #4-0 Vicryl suture in a subcuticular fashion. The perirectal lesion was closed using a single #4-0 stitch to reapproximate the skin. The posterior perineum lesion was closed similar to that of an episiotomy. The *deep tissue* was reapproximated using #2-0 chromic sutures of a crown stitch."

Pathology Report

Specimen A: Clinically, left labia minora lesion excision: *Squamous cell carcinoma* in situ with mild dysplasia present at the margin.

Specimen B: Clinically, posterior perineum: *Squamous cell carcinoma* in situ

Specimen C: Clinically, perianally *condyloma*

Answer:

11623 Excision, malignant lesion, genital (2.5 cm)

11626 Excision, malignant lesion, perineum (4.2 cm)

46922 Destruction of lesion of anus—surgical excision

12042 Layer closure of perineum. Largest size of lesion was 4.2 cm, used as a guide for repair size.

Comment: This operative report is a good example of multiple procedures pertaining to female genital system, but codes are found in the Integumentary and Digestion System sections.

Case Study 9-5

Key Documentation:
The os was dilated without difficulty. A 3 mm *hysteroscope was inserted* using a distention medium of Ringer's lactate. We were able to visualize the entire uterine cavity. There appeared to be no irregularities, fibroids, polyps, etc. The uterine surface looked pretty much within normal limits as well. *A sampling of endometrial tissue was obtained.* Instrumentation was withdrawn. The patient tolerated the procedure without complications and left the operating room in good condition.

Answer:

58558 Hysteroscopy with sampling

Chapter 10: Nervous System

Exercise 10-1 Burr Hole and Craniotomy Procedures

1.   61154 Burr hole for drainage of hematoma

3.   61315 Craniotomy for intracerebellar hematoma

Exercise 10-2 Injections

1.   62311 Injection, lumbar (steroid), single

Exercise 10-3 Spine Procedures

1.   63040 Hemilaminectomy

3.   63075, 63076 Discectomy

Exercise 10-4 Nerve Procedures

1.   64702-F8 Neuroplasty, digital

64727 Add-on code for use of operating microscope

3.   64712 Neuroplasty, sciatic nerve, leg

5.   64408 Injection, anesthetic agent (nerve block) vagus nerve

2010 Current Procedural Terminology © 2009 American Medical Association. All Rights Reserved.

Chapter 10 Review Questions

Answers to Matching Exercise in Faculty Resources

II. Case Studies

Case Study 10-1

Key Documentation:

> IV sedation
>
> Fluoroscopic guidance to the procedure.
>
> Fluoroscopic myelography injection, extradural in the lumbar/sacral area
>
> *Lumbar epidural steroid injection L5-S1 interspace*
>
> Interpretation of permanent film
>
> Caudal with sedation

"*Next, we placed the catheter to the L5-S1 interspace. Through the catheter, we injected steroid solution, which contained 80 mg of Depo-Medrol, 3 cc of 0.75% Marcaine, and 4 cc of Omnipaque 300.*"

Answer:

62311 Injection, single, steroid, lumbar/sacral

Case Study 10-3

Key Documentation:

"Procedures Performed: Lumbar decompression via *laminectomy, L5-S1 and L4-L5*"

"I then *performed an L5 laminectomy* as well as laminectomy of the caudal portion of L5 with the Horsley bone biter. I began my *decompression* centrally with a rongeur as well as an AMH high-speed burr. After performing my central decompression, I also was able to work out laterally toward the pedicles bilaterally. *A facetectomy was performed on the right side of the L4-L5 and L5-S1.* Following that, I still felt that the neural foramina were significantly stenotic and *foraminotomies were performed at each level.*"

Answer:

63047 Laminectomy, facetectomy and foraminotomies, lumbar

63048 Each additional segment

Case Study 10-5

Key Documentation:
"Preoperative Diagnosis: C5-6 disc herniation"

"Postoperative Diagnosis: C5-6 disc herniation"

"Operation Performed: *Anterior cervical discectomy*"

"*The disc bulge at 5-6 was easily identified, and the spinal needle placed confirmed the position to be 5-6. The anterior osteophytes were prominent. They were removed, and then we entered the disc space. The disc space itself had collapsed, and there was only desiccated disc material. We curetted out the disc and the cartilage plate, and the vertebral spreader was put in.*"

Answer:

63075 Discectomy, anterior, cervical, single interspace

Chapter 11: Eye and Ocular Adnexa

Exercise 11-1 Eye Surgery

1. 65210 Removal of foreign body, conjunctival
3. 66850 Removal of lens material, phacofragmentation technique
5. 67227 Destruction of extensive or progressive retinopathy, cryotherapy
7. 67346 Biopsy of extraocular muscle
9. 67938 Removal of embedded foreign body, eyelid

Chapter 11 Review Questions

Answers to Labeling Exercise in Faculty Resources

II. Case Studies

Case Study 11-1

Key Documentation:
"Retinal detachment, left eye"

" . . . a pars plana vitrectomy was performed."

2010 Current Procedural Terminology © 2009 American Medical Association. All Rights Reserved.

Answer:

67110-LT Repair of retinal detachment; by injection of air (cryoretinopexy)

Case Study 11-3

Key Documentation:

"Postoperative Diagnosis: Macular hole, right eye"

"Procedures Performed: Pars plana vitrectomy, removal of posterior hyaloids, internal limiting membrane peel, air-fluid exchange and C3F8 gas injection, right eye"

Answer:

67042-RT Vitrectomy, pars plana approach with removal of internal limiting membrane of retina (includes air exchange)

Chapter 12: Auditory System

Answers to Matching Exercise in Faculty Resources

Exercise 12-1 Ear Surgery

1. 69000 Drainage, external ear
3. 69300-50 Otoplasty
5. 69540 ExcisiSon aural polyp

7. 69603 Revision mastoidectomy resulting in radical mastoidectomy
9. 69666 Repair of oval window fistula

Chapter 12 Review Questions

II. Case Studies

Case Study 12-1

Key Documentation: "Right tympanostomy requiring general anesthesia with the use of the operating microscope with ventilation tube insertion"

Answer:

69436-RT Tympanostomy

69990 Operating microscope

Case Study 12-3

Key Documentation:

"Procedure: Removal of bilateral permanent ventilation tubes"

"Anesthesia: Inhalant"

Answer:

69424-50 Ventilating tube removal requiring general anesthesia

2010 Current Procedural Terminology © 2009 American Medical Association. All Rights Reserved.

Glossary

A

ablation   surgical removal or destruction of tissue

acellular dermal replacement   synthetic skin replacement

actinic keratosis   precancerous condition of thick, scaly patches of skin

adenocarcinoma   cancer that develops in the lining or inner surface of some organs

adenoma   benign growth

adjacent tissue transfer   transplantation of healthy, flat sections of skin to cover an adjacent wound

advancement flap   a flap of tissue is stretched and sutured in place to cover a defect

allograft   tissue transplanted from one individual to another

aneurysm   balloon-like bulge of a blood vessel

aqueous humor   watery fluid

arteries   vessels that carry blood away from the heart

arteriovenous fistula   abnormal connection (or passageway) between an artery and a vein

arthrocentesis   puncture of joint to remove fluid or inject medication

arthrodesis   bone or joint fusion

atherosclerosis   disease in which plaque builds up on the inside of arteries

autograft   tissue transplanted from one site to another on the same individual

automatic implantable cardioverter defibrillator (AICD)   device implanted in the chest to monitor a patient's heart rate

B

basal cell carcinoma   most common form of skin cancer

benign   cell growth that is not cancerous

benign prostatic hyperplasia (BPH)   enlargement of the prostate by disease or inflammation

biopsy   removal of a piece of tissue

bipolar cautery   destroying tissue with use of high-frequency electrical current

bladder   triangle-shaped, hollow organ located in the lower abdomen that holds urine

bronchial biopsy   small pieces of tissue are removed from the lung

bronchioles   fine, thin-walled, tubular extensions of a bronchus

bronchus   air tubes leading from the trachea to the lungs that convey air to and from the lungs

bundled   the grouping of CPT codes related to a procedure when submitting a claim

bunions   condition that causes the big toe to point toward the second toe, causing a bump on the edge of the foot

burr hole   small opening in the skull made with a surgical drill

C

calculi   abnormal stone formed in body tissues by an accumulation of mineral salts

capillaries   thin, fragile blood vessels that form a network throughout the body. Blood flows from the heart to arteries, which branch into arterioles and then capillaries.

carcinoma   cancer found in the epithelial tissue (tissue that covers the surfaces of organs, glands, or body structures)

cardiac bypass   commonly called CABG (cabbage) for coronary artery bypass graft. The surgeon reroutes or bypasses blood around clogged arteries.

carpal tunnel syndrome   compression of median nerve at the wrist, which may result in numbness, tingling, weakness, or muscle atrophy in the hand and fingers

Centers for Medicare & Medicaid Services (CMS)   the division of the Department of Health and Human Services that is responsible for developing health care policy in the United States and for administering the Medicare program and the federal portion of the Medicaid program; called the Health Care Financing Administration (HCFA) prior to 2001

central venous access device (CVAD)   small, flexible tubes inserted into large veins for patients who require frequent access to the blood stream

cervix   lower, narrow part of the uterus located between the bladder and the rectum

closed reduction   applying external manipulation to fractures to restore alignment

CMS-1450   a Medicare form used for standardized uniform billing (also known as the Uniform Bill-04 (UB-04). The claim form is used by hospitals, nursing homes, hospices, home health agencies, and other institutional providers.

CMS-1500   standard claim form used by a non-institutional provider or supplier to bill Medicare carriers and durable medical equipment regional carriers (DMERCs)

code editor   software that evaluates the clinical consistency and completeness of health record information and identifies potential errors that could affect accurate prospective payment group assignment

coded data   data that are translated into a standard nomenclature of classification so that they may be aggregated, analyzed, and compared

coding   the process of assigning numeric representations to clinical documentation

cold knife biopsy   procedure in which a laser or surgical scalpel is used to remove a piece of tissue

colon polyps   small, fleshy, mushroom-shaped growths in the colon

colonoscopy   surgical visualize of the entire colon with the use of a scope

colposcopy   instrument (scope) examines the cervix

complex wound repair type of wound that requires more than layer closure (e.g., scar revision, debridement, extensive undermining)

conization surgery to remove a cone-shaped piece of tissue from the cervix and cervical canal

conjunctiva white-colored outer covering of the eye that contains blood vessels (covers sclera)

cornea outer transparent dome-like structure that covers the iris and pupil. Light rays enter the eye through the cornea.

Correct Coding Initiative (CCI) a national initiative designed to improve the accuracy of Part B claims processed by Medicare carriers

CPT Assistant the official publication of the American Medical Association that addresses CPT coding issues

Current Procedural Terminology, **Fourth Edition (CPT)** a comprehensive, descriptive list of terms and numeric codes used for reporting diagnostic and therapeutic procedures and other medical services performed by physicians; published and updated annually by the American Medical Association

cystoscopy (also called cystourethroscopy) examination in which a scope is inserted through the urethra to examine the bladder and urinary tract

D

debridement removal of dead, damaged, or infected tissue

deep fascia strong connective tissue layer beneath dermis and subcutaneous fascia

Department of Health and Human Services (HHS or DHHS) the cabinet-level federal agency that oversees all of the health and human services–related activities of the federal government and administers federal regulations

dermal autograft epidermis and subcutaneous fat is removed and used in place of fascia

dermis layer of skin composed of connective tissue, nerves, blood vessels and hair follicles

diagnosis a word or phrase used by a physician to identify a disease from which an individual patient suffers or a condition for which the patient needs, seeks, or receives medical care

dilation and curettage (D&C) cervix is dilated so that the cervical canal and uterine lining can be scraped with a curette (spoon-shaped instrument)

direct laryngoscopy visualization of larynx with the use of a scope

documentation the recording of pertinent health care findings, interventions, and responses to treatment, which serves as a business record and form of communication among caregivers

dysplasia abnormal development of tissue

E

E/M coding *see* **evaluation and management codes**

embolus obstruction of vessel due to blood clot

endometrial biopsy sample of tissue is obtained through a tube that is inserted into the uterus

endometrium inner membrane of the uterus

endoscope lighted tube used to examine the interior of a body cavity or organ

endoscopic retrograde cholangiopancreatography (ERCP) procedure combines X-ray and use of endoscope to visualize the stomach and duodenum and inject dyes into the ducts in the biliary and pancreas

epidermal autograft tissue graft consisting primarily of epidermal tissue

epidermis outermost layer of skin

epididymis structure within scrotum attached to backside of testis, used to store, mature, and transport spermatozoa between the testis and the vas deferens

epigastric upper central region of the abdomen

esophagus organ that connects the mouth to the stomach

esophagogastroduodenoscopy (EGD) examination of esophagus, stomach, and duodenum with the use of a scope

ethmoid bone that separates the nasal cavity from the brain

evaluation and management (E/M) codes CPT codes that describe patient encounters with health care professionals for assessment, counseling, and other routine health care services

excisional biopsy removal of a piece of tissue to be submitted for pathological diagnosis (not to be confused with removal of entire lesion)

exostosis formation of a new bone on the surface of a bone (bone spurs)

external fixation device to keep fractured bones stabilized and in alignment

F

fascia connective tissue that performs a number of functions, including enveloping and isolating the muscles of the body, providing structural support and protection

femoral hernia protrusion of a loop of the intestine through a weakening in the abdominal wall, located in the groin near the thigh

fine needle aspiration obtain cells or bits of tissue by a process of suctioning through a fine needle attached to a syringe

flexible laryngoscopy use of flexible scope to visualize the larynx

frontal sinuses airspaces within the bones of the face and skull

full-thickness skin graft harvesting epidermis and dermis for grafting

G

gastrectomy operation in which part or all of the stomach is removed

gastrointestinal relating to the stomach and the intestines

glaucoma elevated intraocular pressure

global surgery package a CPT code denoting a normal surgical procedure with no complications that includes all the elements needed to perform the procedure

glomerulus blood capillaries in the kidney

H

hallux valgus *see* **bunion**

HCFA-1500 previous name for **CMS-1500**; *see* **CMS-1500**

HCFA-1450 previous name for **CMS-1450**; *see* **CMS-1450**

HCFA Common Procedure Coding System (HCPCS) previous name for the **Healthcare Common Procedure Coding System**

Health Care Financing Administration (HCFA) previous name for the **Centers for Medicare & Medicaid Services**

health record   a paper- or computer-based tool for collecting and storing information about the health care services provided to a patient in a single health care facility; also called a patient record, medical record, resident record, or client record, depending on the health care setting

Healthcare Common Procedure Coding System (HCPCS) a classification system that identifies health care procedures, equipment, and supplies for claim submission purposes. The three levels are as follows: I, *Current Procedural Terminology* codes, developed by the AMA; II, codes for equipment, supplies, and services not covered by *Current Procedural Terminology* codes, as well as modifiers that can be used with all levels of codes, developed by CMS; and III (eliminated December 31, 2003, to comply with HIPAA), local codes developed by regional Medicare Part B carriers and used to report physicians' services and supplies to Medicare for reimbursement.

hemorrhoids   swollen veins in the lower portion of the rectum or anus

hernia   organ protrudes through a weak area of muscle

hot biopsy forceps   surgical technique using small tweezers (forceps) to remove a piece of tissue for biopsy. In some cases, the entire polyp is removed using this method.

hyperplasia   abnormal or unusual increase in the number of cells present

hysterectomy   surgery to remove the uterus

hysteroscopy   endoscopic examination of the cervix and interior of the uterus

I

ileum   final section of the small intestines

incisional biopsy   removal of a piece of tissue for examination

incisional hernia   bulging occurring in the area of any prior surgical incision

indirect laryngoscopy   view of larynx using a hand mirror at the back of the throat

inguinal hernia   protrusion of abdominal cavity contents through the inguinal canal

integumentary system   organ system that includes the hair, nails, and sweat and oil glands

intermediate wound repair   layered closure of one or more deeper layers of subcutaneous tissue and superficial (non-muscle) fascia, in addition to the skin closure

internal fixation   use of mechanical devices (pins, rods, wires) to stabilize and join the ends of fractures

iris   pigmented portion of the eye that regulates the amount of light entering the eye by adjusting the size of the pupil

J

jejunum   second portion of the small intestines

K

keratoplasty   plastic surgery on the cornea

kidney   bean-shaped organs located near the middle of the back on each side of the spine. Kidneys are responsible for removing waste products from the blood to produce urine, which flows to the bladder through tubes called ureters.

L

laminectomy   operation to remove a portion of the vertebral bone called lamina

laparoscopy   scope is inserted through a small incision in the abdomen

large intestines   part of the intestines that go from the cecum to the rectum

laryngoscopy   examination of voice box

lesion   abnormal tissue growth (e.g., keloid, mole); often called neoplasm

lipoma   benign tumor consisting of fat tissue

lobectomy   surgical excision of a lobe; such as the lung

lumpectomy   surgery to remove the cancerous lump and a portion of normal tissue around the breast cancer lump (mass)

M

macula   central area of the retina

maxillary sinuses   largest of paranasal sinuses that are shaped like a pyramid; located beneath the cheeks, above the teeth on either sides of the nose

Medical record   see **health record**

Medicare Carriers Manual **(MCM)**   provides direction about services and procedures to be reimbursed by the Medicare administrative contractor

meniscectomy   surgical removal of all or part of a torn meniscus (cartilage of knee)

mesh   textured material used in surgical repairs

mitral valve   valve that lies between the left atrium and left ventricle of the heart

modified simple mastectomy   removal of all breast tissue, but skin and nipple are left intact

Mohs micrographic surgery   technique for removing certain carcinomas that allows precise microscopic marginal control by using horizontal frozen sections

N

national codes (HCPCS Level II codes)   five-digit alphanumeric codes for procedures, services, and supplies that are not classified in CPT

National Correct Coding Initiative (NCCI)   a series of code edits on Medicare Part B claims

needle biopsy   use of needle to extract tissue, cells, or fluid for microscopic examination

nephrons   filtering units of the kidney

neuroma   tumor that starts in the nerve cells

neuroplasty   plastic surgery of the nerves

nodule   growth that may be either benign or malignant

O

oophorectomy   surgery to remove one or both ovaries

open fracture treatment   surgically cutting open the skin of the area over the fracture so bone fragments can be put back into place

operation   see **surgical operation**

operative report   a formal document that describes the events surrounding a surgical procedure or operation and identifies the principal participants in the surgery

orchiectomy   surgical removal of the testicles

Outpatient Code Editor (OCE)   a software program linked to the Correct Coding Initiative, which applies a set of logical rules to determine whether various combinations of codes are correct and appropriately represent the services provided

P

pacemaker small, battery-operated device that helps the heart beat regularly

partial mastectomy removal of lesion (or mass) of breast with adequate surgical margins

partial thickness skin graft (split thickness) grafts of portions of the skin (epidermis and part of the dermis)

patient health record see **health record**

pedicle skin graft technique that allows a piece of skin from a nearby area to remain attached while the main part of the piece is reattached over the defect

percutaneous endoscopic gastrostomy (PEG tube) tube inserted through the abdominal wall that rests on the stomach and is used to give nutrients to patients who cannot swallow

percutaneous skeletal fixation surgeon inserts fixation device (screws, Kirschner wires) into the bones across the fracture site under radiological imaging

percutaneously inserted central catheter (PICC) small flexible tube that is inserted for intravenous access and can be used for a prolonged period of time (e.g., chemotherapy)

perineum area between the anus and sex organs

pharynx commonly called the throat. It moves food toward the esophagus and moves air to the larynx.

pleura cavity that contains the lungs

pneumocentesis lung is punctured to drain fluid

pneumonectomy surgical removal of the lung

polyp growth that projects from the lining of a mucous membrane

prepuce fold of skin that covers the head of the penis; also called foreskin

primary defect original defect to close (associated with skin grafts)

procedural codes the numeric or alphanumeric characters used to classify and report the medical procedures and services performed for patients

procedures and services (outpatient) all medical procedures and services of any type (including history, physical examination, laboratory, X-ray or radiograph, and others) that are performed pertinent to the patient's reasons for the encounter, all therapeutic services performed at the time of the encounter, and all preventive services and procedures performed at the time of the encounter

proctoscopy examination of rectum and anus

proctosigmoidoscopy examination of rectum and sigmoid colon

prostate sex gland in males; surrounds the neck of the bladder and urethra.

pulmonary valve valve between the right ventricle and pulmonary artery

puncture aspiration needle is inserted and fluid is withdrawn

R

radical mastectomy surgical procedure in which the breast, underlying chest muscle (including pectoralis major and pectoralis minor), and lymph nodes of the axilla are removed

radical prostatectomy surgery to remove the prostate along with the two seminal vesicle glands attached to the prostate

radical retropubic prostatectomy operation to remove the entire prostate gland and seminal vesicles through the lower abdomen

rectum lower end of the large intestine, leading to the anus

retina innermost layer of the eye that lines the back of the eye; contains the nerve cells that capture and transmit visual images through the optic nerve to the brain

S

salpingectomy surgical removal of one or both fallopian tubes

salpingo-oophorectomy surgery to remove the fallopian tubes and ovaries

sarcoma malignant tumor growing from connective tissues, such as cartilage, fat, muscle, or bone

sclera white outer surface of the eye

scrotum the bag of skin that holds the testicles

secondary defect created by movement of tissue necessary to close the primary defect (skin graft)

segment resection removal of a larger portion of lung lobe than a wedge resection (does not remove entire lobe)

shunt hole or passage allowing fluid to move from one part of the body to another

significant procedure a procedure that is surgical in nature or carries a procedural or an anesthetic risk or requires specialized training

sigmoidoscopy endoscopic examination of sigmoid colon and rectum

simple complete mastectomy removal of all breast tissue along with portion of skin and nipple

simple wound repair single-layer wound closure

skin biopsy a sample of breast tissue is removed and examined under a microscope

skin replacement tissue or graft that permanently replaces lost skin with healthy skin

skin substitute biomaterial, engineered tissue or combinations of materials and cells/tissue that can be substituted for skin autograft or allograft

small intestines section of digestive tract between the stomach and the large intestine

snare wire loop instrument used to remove colon polyps

sphenoid sinuses sinuses found behind ethmoid sinuses. The left and right sphenoid sit next to each other and are separated by a thin plate of bone (septum).

spigelian hernia (ventral hernia) abdominal hernia through the semilunar line

spinal instrumentation method of keeping the spine rigid after spinal fusion surgery by surgically attaching hooks, rods, and wires to the spine for proper alignment

split thickness removal of epidermis and very thin portion of dermis (skin)

squamous cell carcinoma form of skin cancer that affects about 20% of patients with skin cancer

strabismus condition in which both eyes do not look at the same place at the same time

stricture a narrowed area

subcutaneous fascia located below the dermis; stores fat and water

subcutaneous layer layer beneath the skin that helps to anchor the skin to underlying structures

subcutaneous mastectomy similar to simple complete mastectomy except breast is dissected from the pectoral fascia and from the skin. The skin, nipple, and areola are usually preserved.

surgery an umbrella term referring to the procedures of incision, excision, amputation, introduction, endoscopy, suture, and manipulation

surgical operation one or more surgical procedures performed at one time for one patient via a common approach or for a common purpose

surgical procedure any single, separate, systematic process upon or within the body that can be complete in itself; is normally performed by a physician, dentist, or other licensed practitioner; can be performed either with or without instruments; and is performed to restore disunited or deficient parts, remove diseased or injured tissues, extract foreign matter, assist in obstetrical delivery, or aid in diagnosis

T

testis one of the pair of male gonads that produce semen; situated in the scrotum

thoracentesis procedure to remove fluid from the space between the lining of the outside of the lungs (pleura) and the wall of the chest

thorax area of the body between the neck and diaphragm, partially encased by the ribs and containing the heart and lungs (chest)

thrombectomy surgical excision of blood clot

thrombus blood clot that can lodge in a blood vessel and block the normal flow of blood

tissue cultured autograft tissue-engineered graft; tissue is grown from one's own skin cells

trabeculectomy surgeon creates a passage in the sclera (white part of the eye) for draining excess eye fluid

trachea thin-walled, cartilaginous tube descending from the larynx to the bronchi and carrying air to the lungs

transbronchial biopsy scope is inserted to collect several pieces of lung tissue with the use of tiny forceps

transbronchial needle biopsy aspiration of tissue for histological examination

transurethral resection of the prostate (TURP) surgical procedure by which portions of the prostate gland are removed through the penis

transurethral surgery surgery in which no external incision is needed. For prostate transurethral surgery, surgeon reaches the prostate by inserting an instrument through the urethra.

tricuspid valve valve located between the right atrium and right ventricle

tumor abnormal lump or mass of tissue. Tumors can be benign (not cancerous) or malignant (cancerous).

turbinates (nasal concha) long, narrow and curled bone shelf which protrudes into the breathing passage of the nose.

U

umbilical hernia outward bulging of the abdominal lining or part of the abdominal organ(s) through the area around the belly button

unbundling the practice of using multiple codes to bill for the various individual steps in a single procedure rather than using a single code that includes all the steps of the comprehensive procedure

undercoding a form of incomplete documentation that results when diagnoses or procedures that should be coded are missing

Uniform Bill-04 (UB-04) see **CMS-1450**

unlisted procedure a CPT procedure code assigned when the provider performs a procedure or service for which there is no CPT code

upcoding the practice of assigning diagnostic or procedural codes that represent higher payment rates than the codes that actually reflect the services provided to patients

upper gastrointestinal (GI) system consists of mouth, pharynx, esophagus, stomach, and duodenum

ureters two narrow tubes that carry urine from the kidneys to the bladder

ureteral stent thin, flexible tube threaded into the ureter to help urine drain from the kidney to the bladder

urethra narrow channel through which urine passes from the bladder out of the body

urolithiasis process of forming stones in any part of the urinary system

uterus hollow, pear-shaped organ located in a woman's lower abdomen, between the bladder and the rectum

V

vagina passageway through which fluid passes out of the body. The vagina connects the cervix (opening of the uterus) and the vulva (external genitalia).

vaginal hysterectomy uterus is removed through the vaginal opening

varicose veins enlarged veins that have been filled with an abnormal collection of blood

vein vessel that carries blood from the capillaries to the heart

ventral hernia an abdominal incisional hernia

vitrectomy surgical removal of vitreous gel from the middle of the eye

vulva external female genitalia

W

wedge resection (lung) surgeon removes a small wedge-shaped piece of lung

W-plasty surgical trimming of both edges of a wound or defect into the shape of a W or multiple Ws.

X

xenograft tissue transplanted from one species to another (e.g., pig to human)

Z

Z-plasty making a surgical incision along with two additional incisions, one above and another below, creating a Z formation

Index